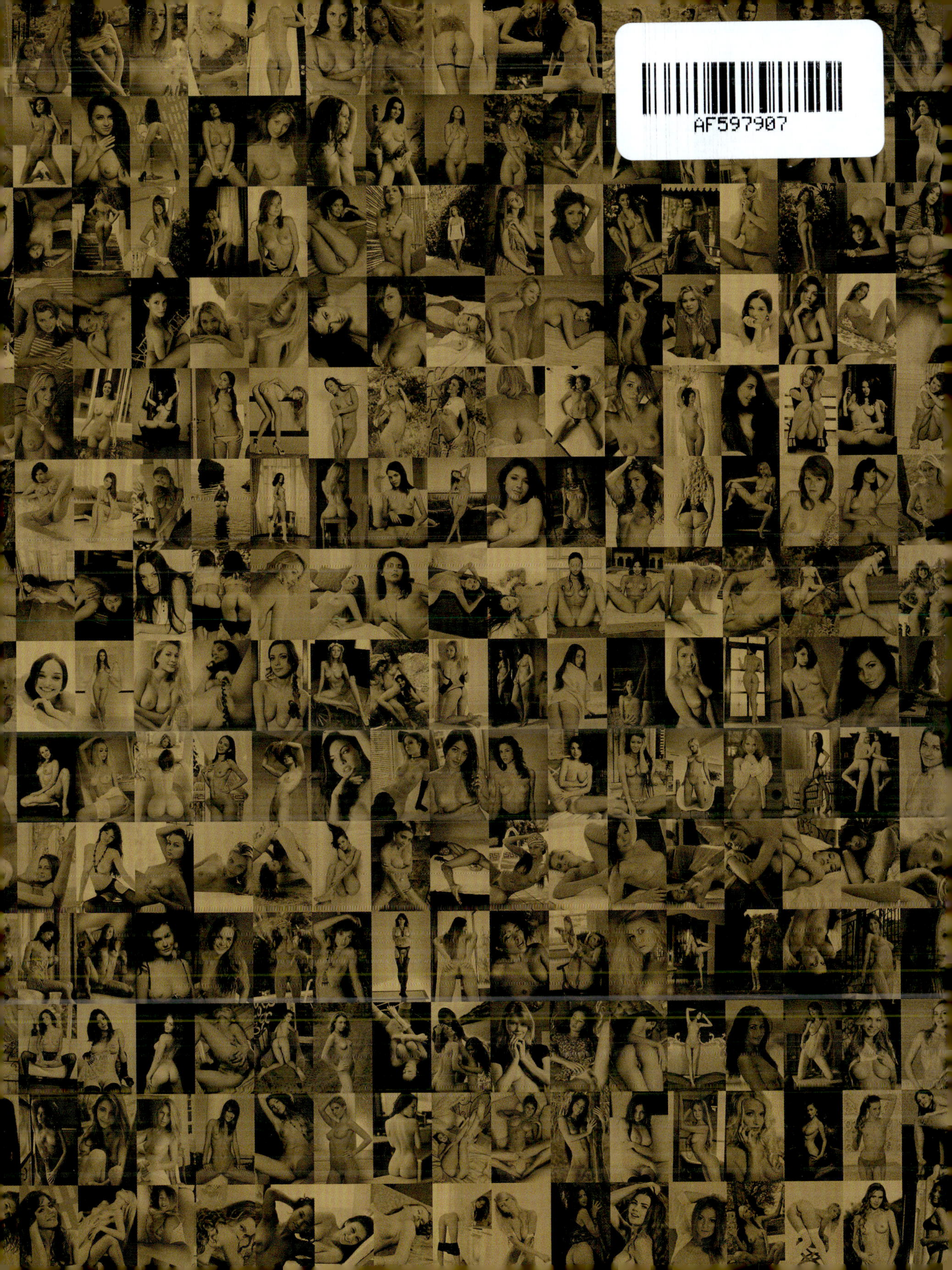

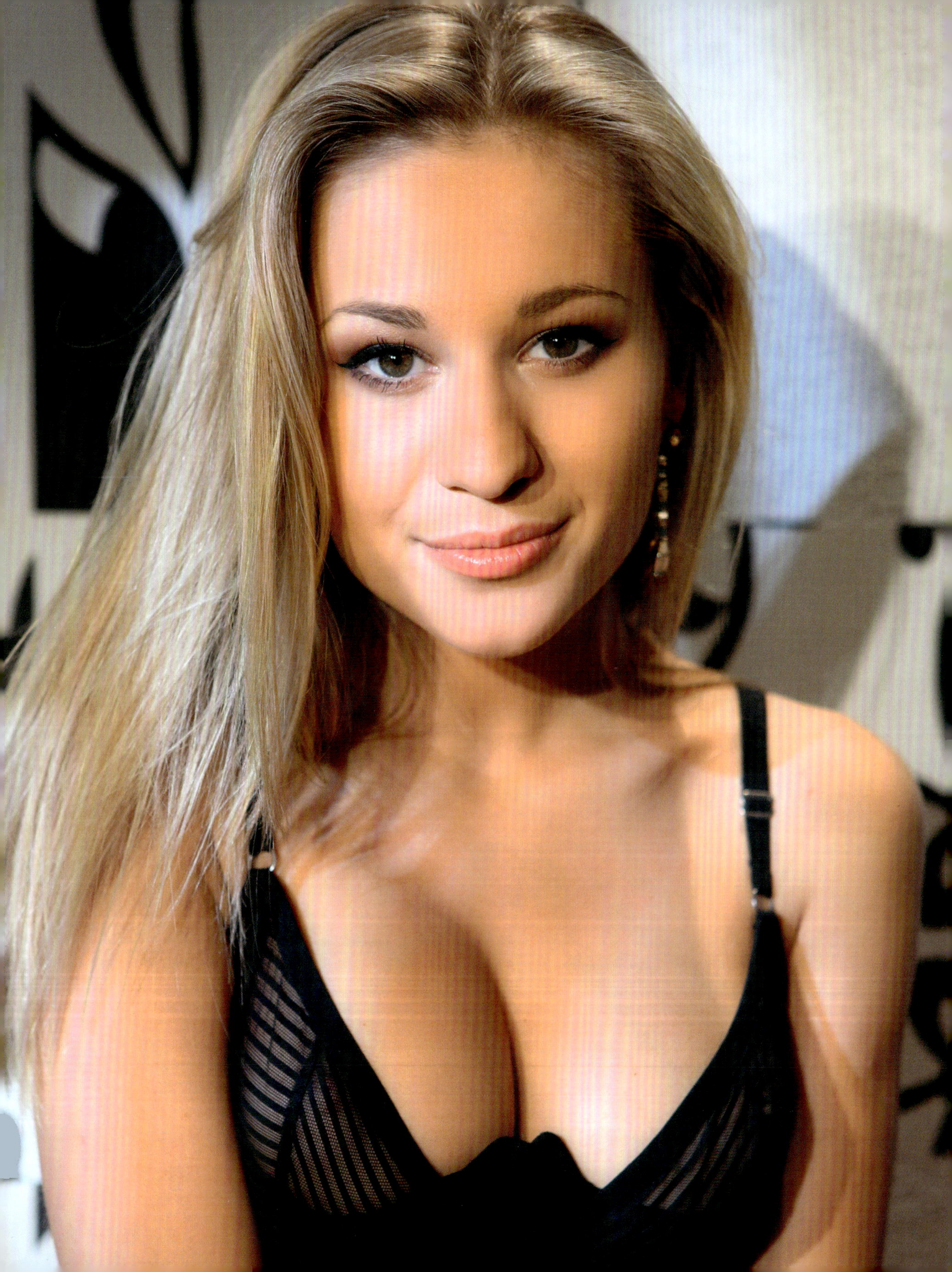

TOP MODELS OF

METART.COM

WHERE FLAWLESS BEAUTY MEETS ART

CANDICE B

COLLECTED AND EDITED BY ISABELLA CATALINA

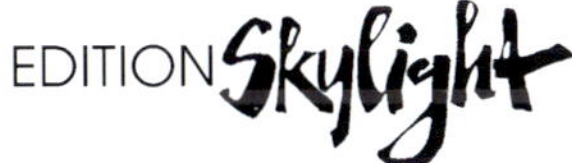

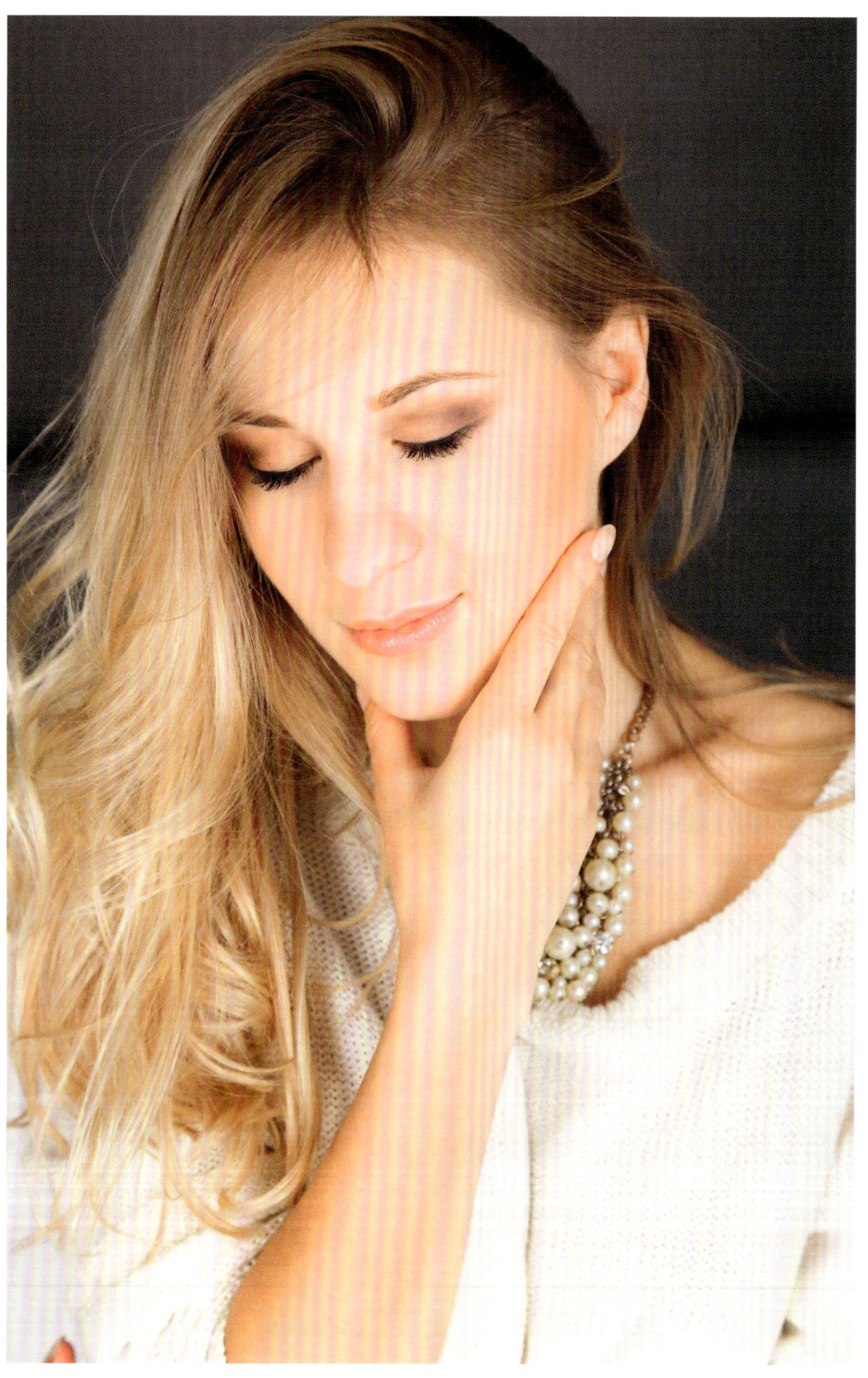

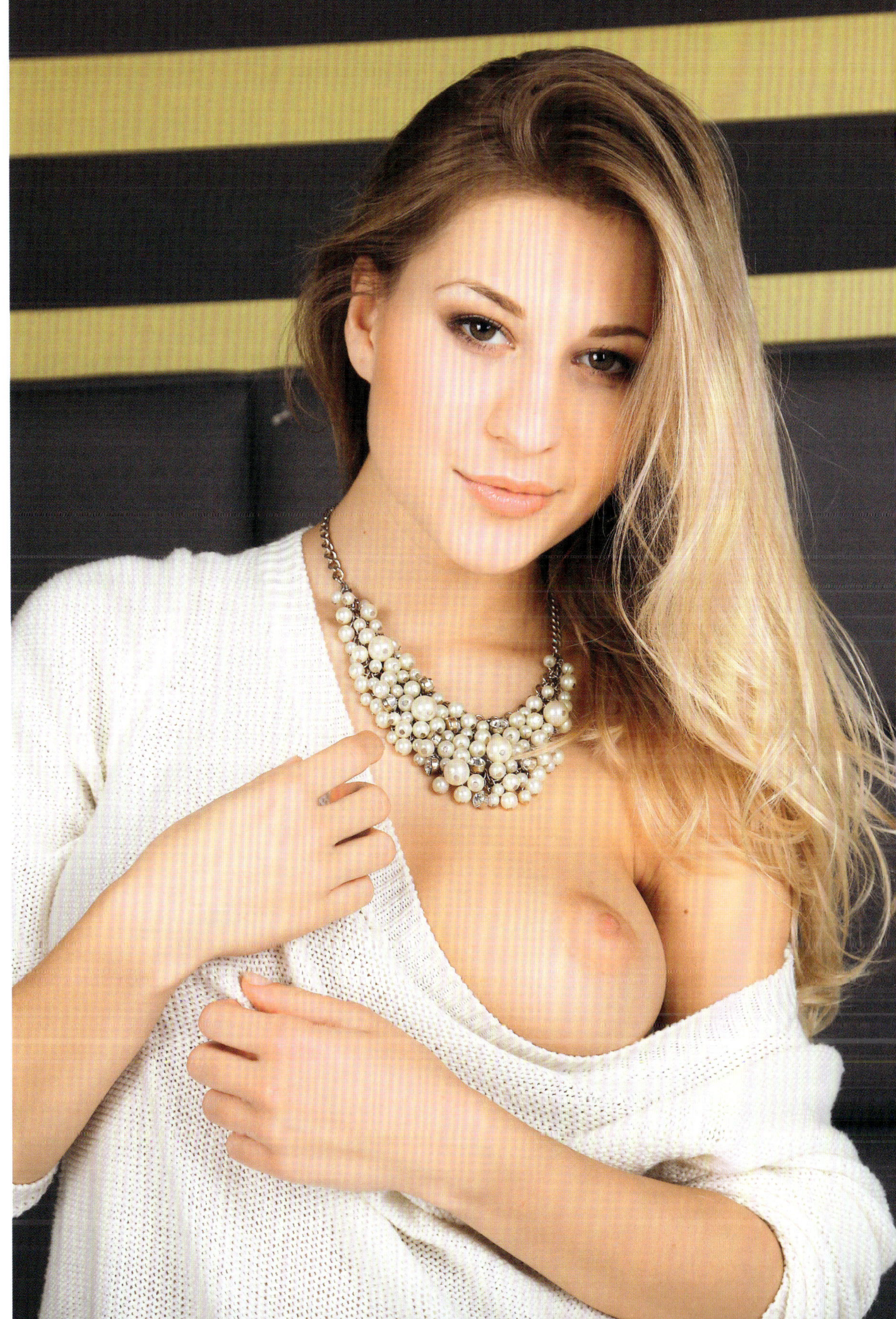

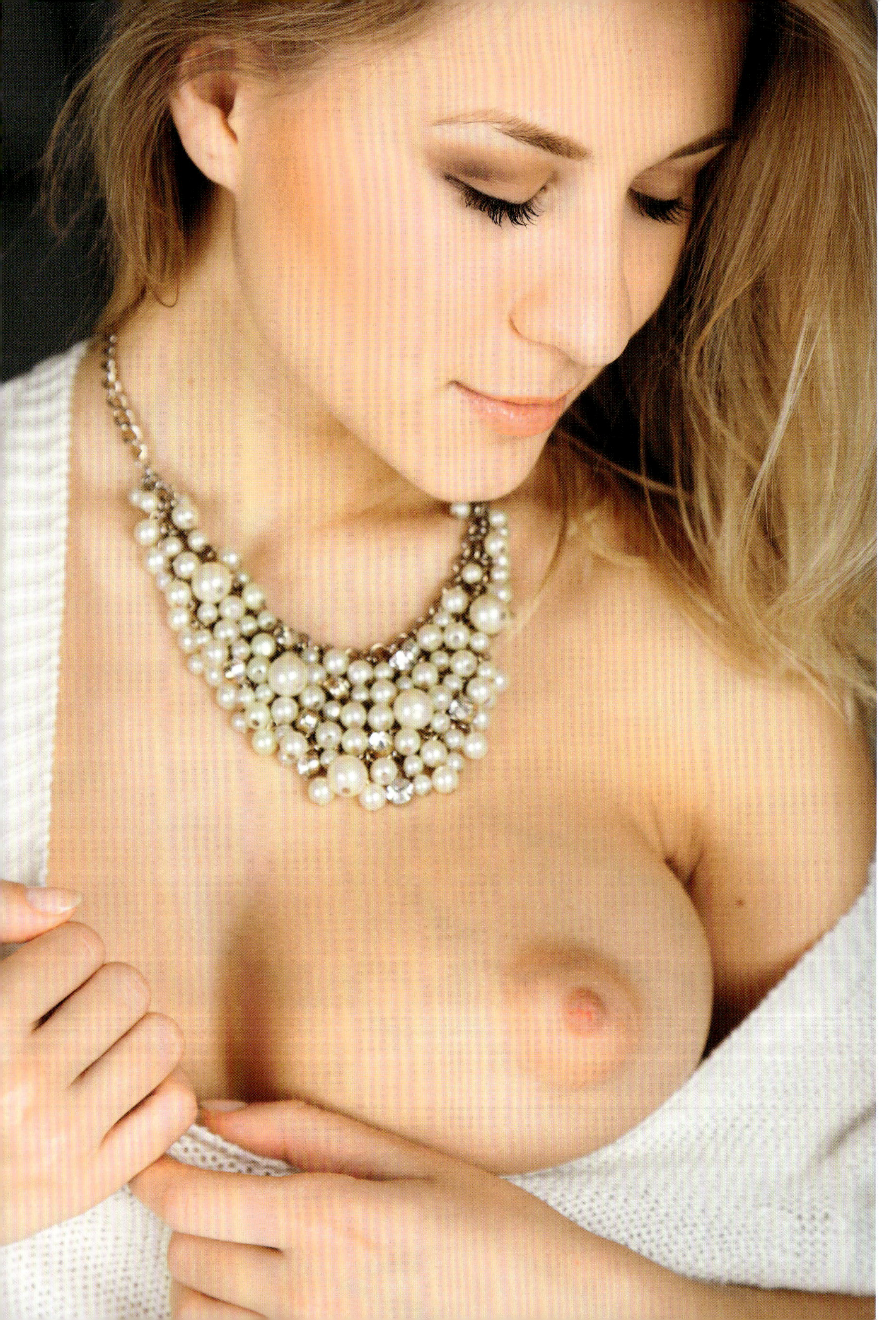

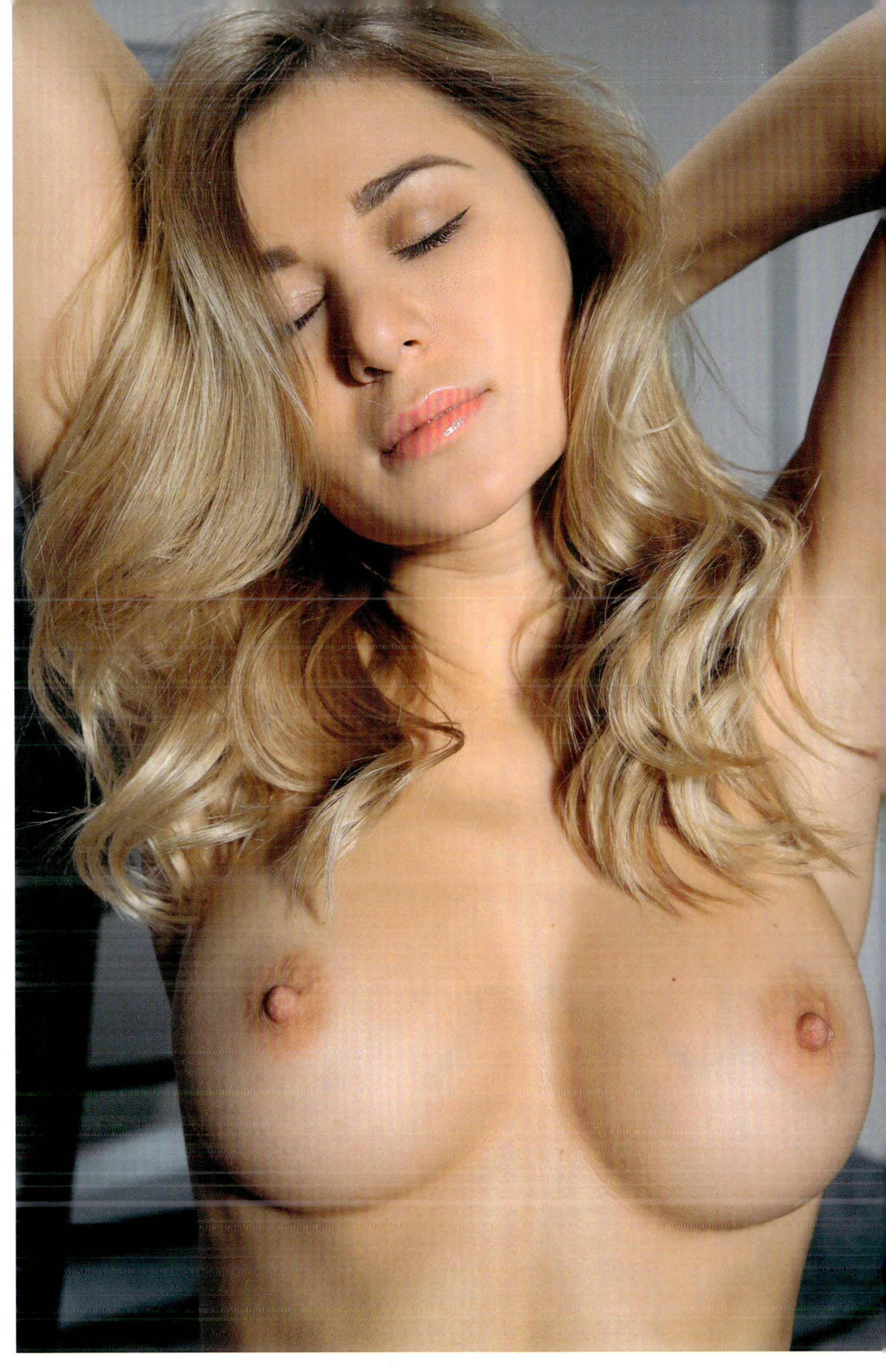

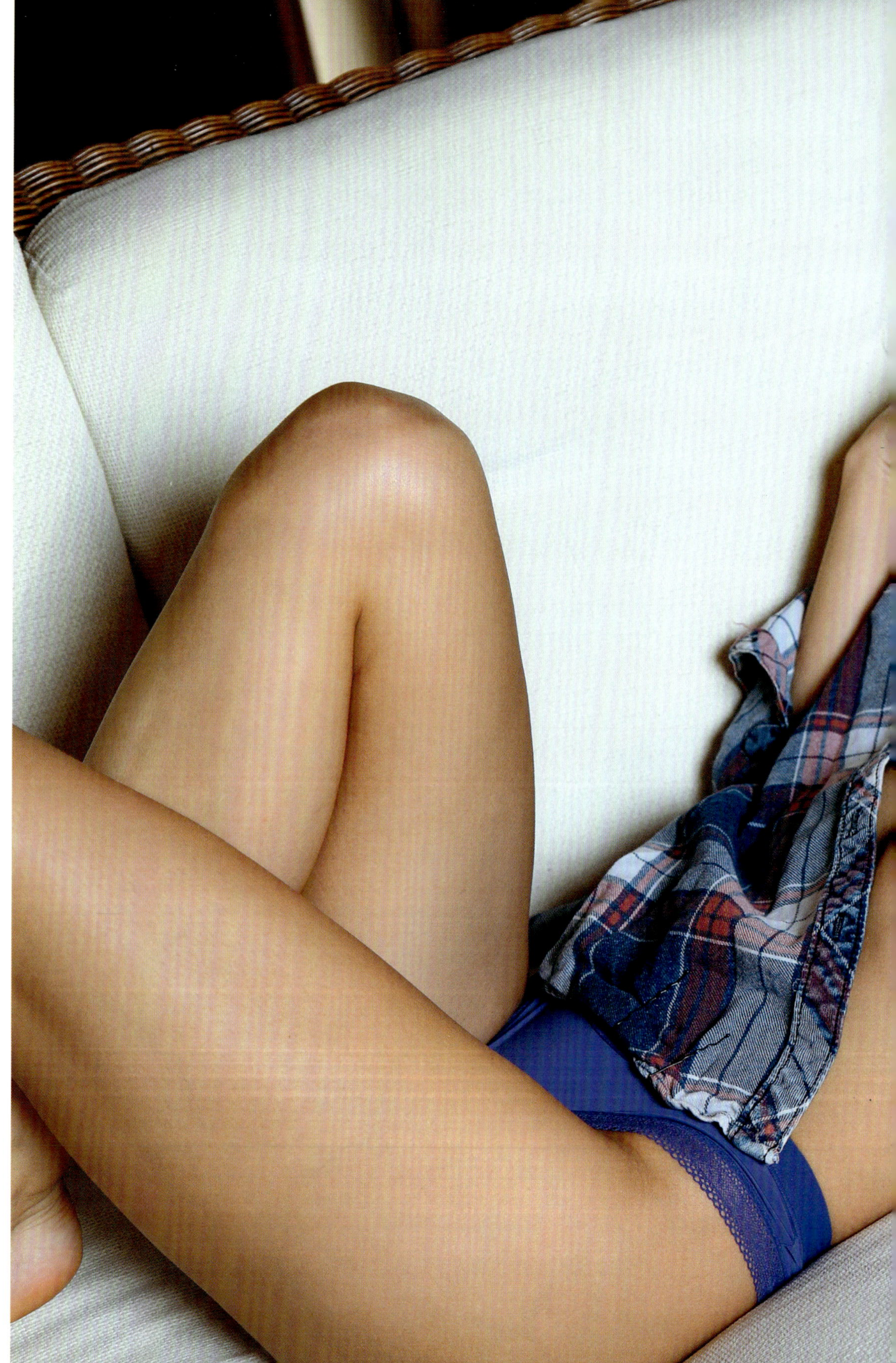

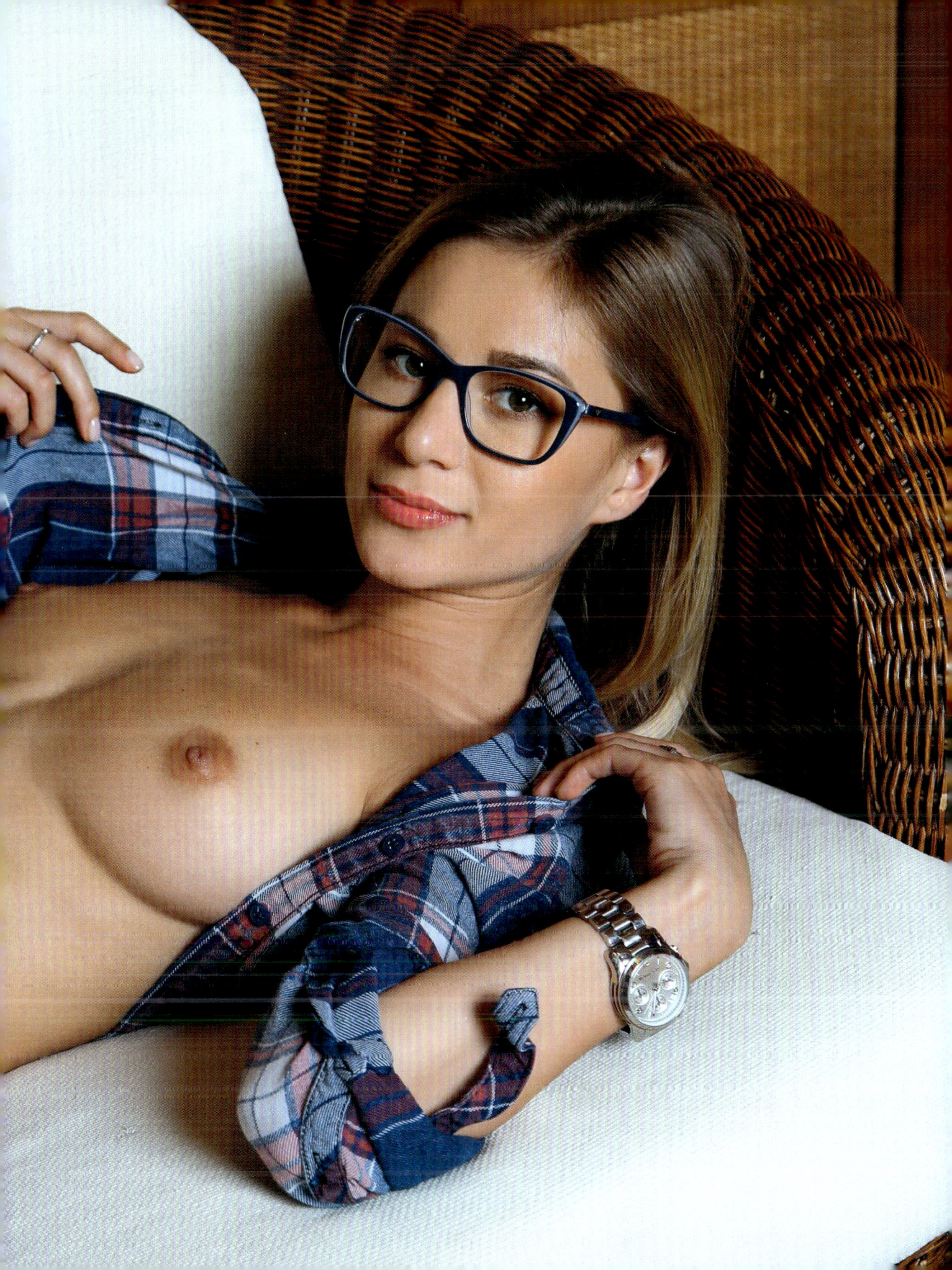

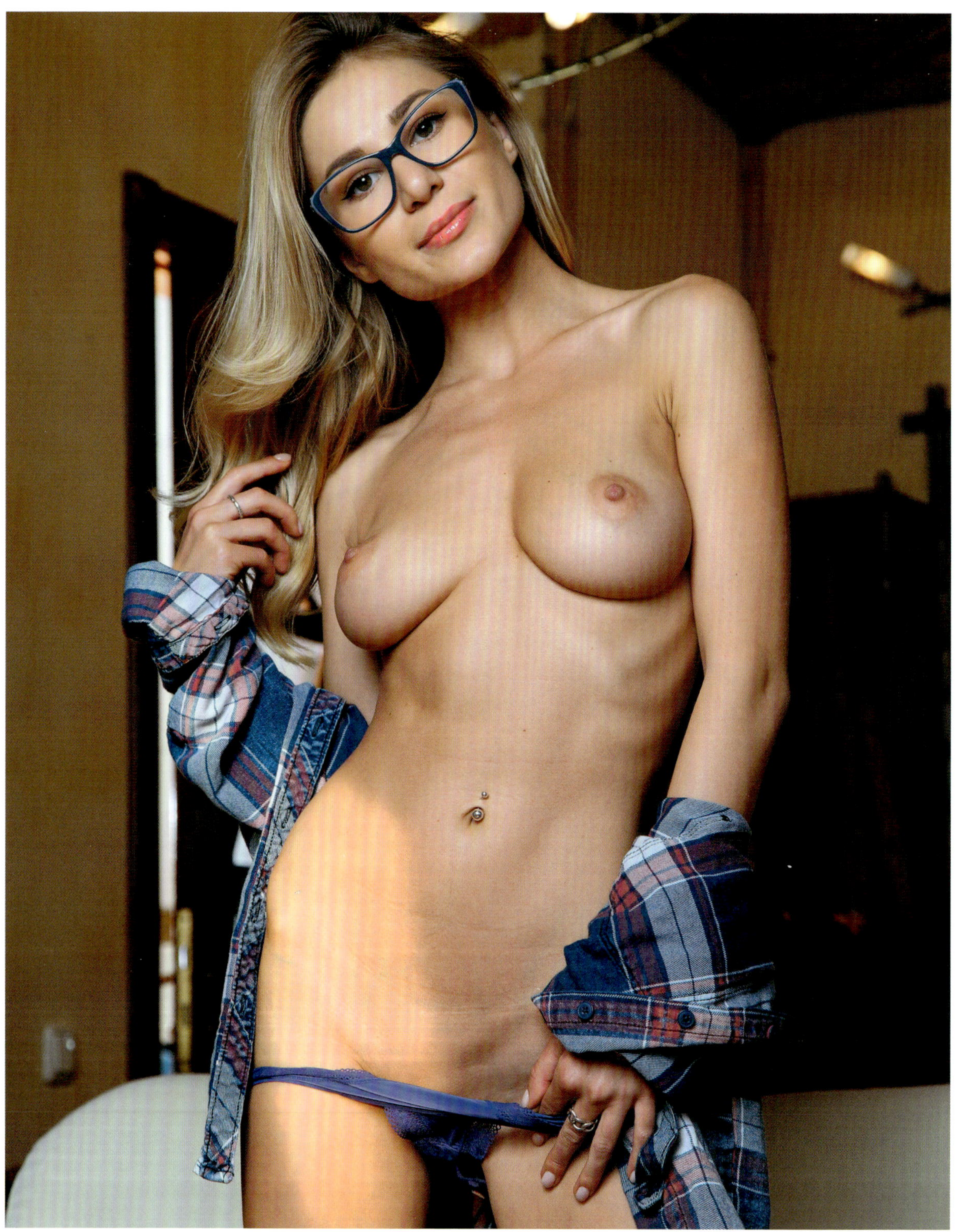

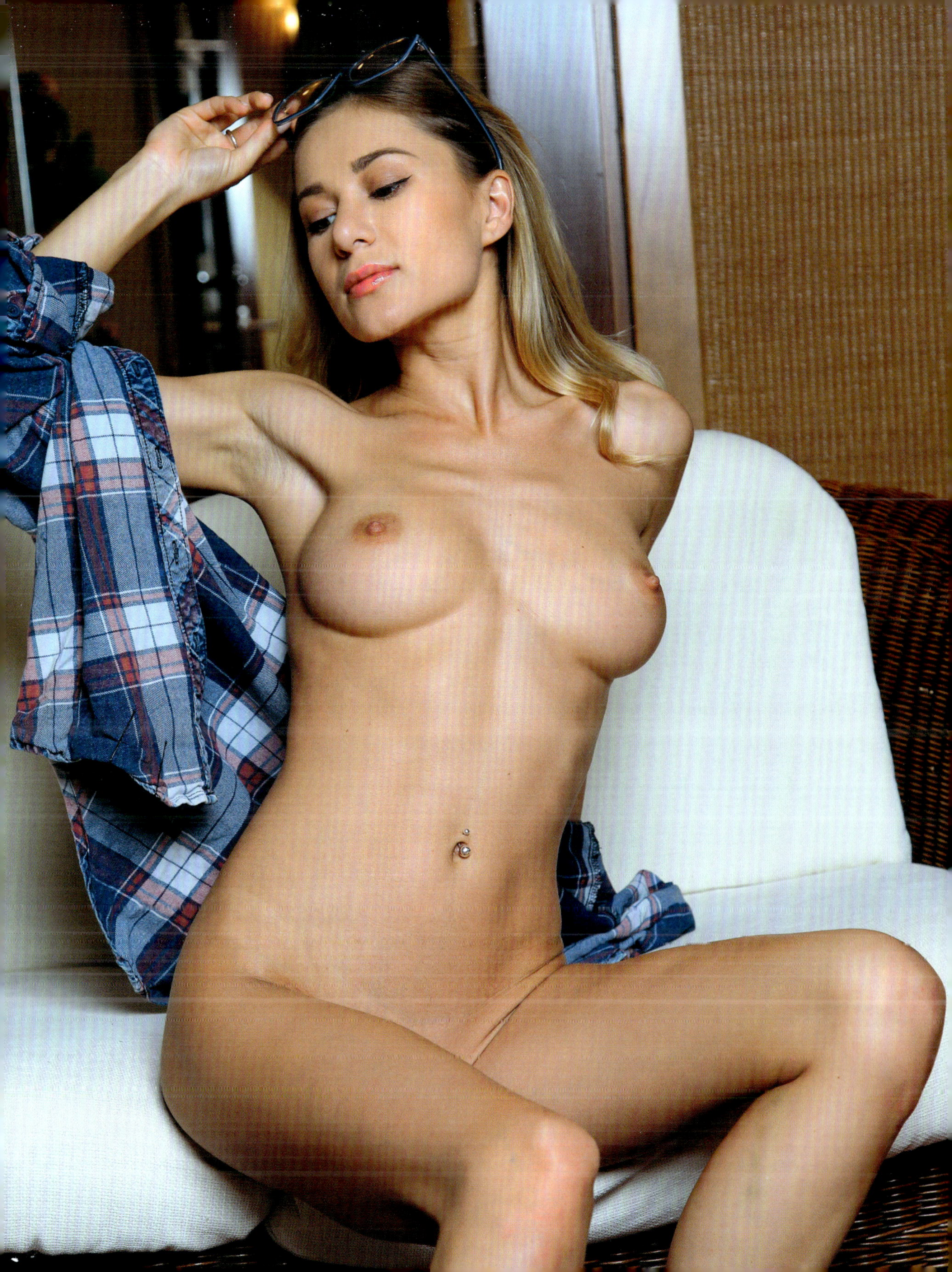

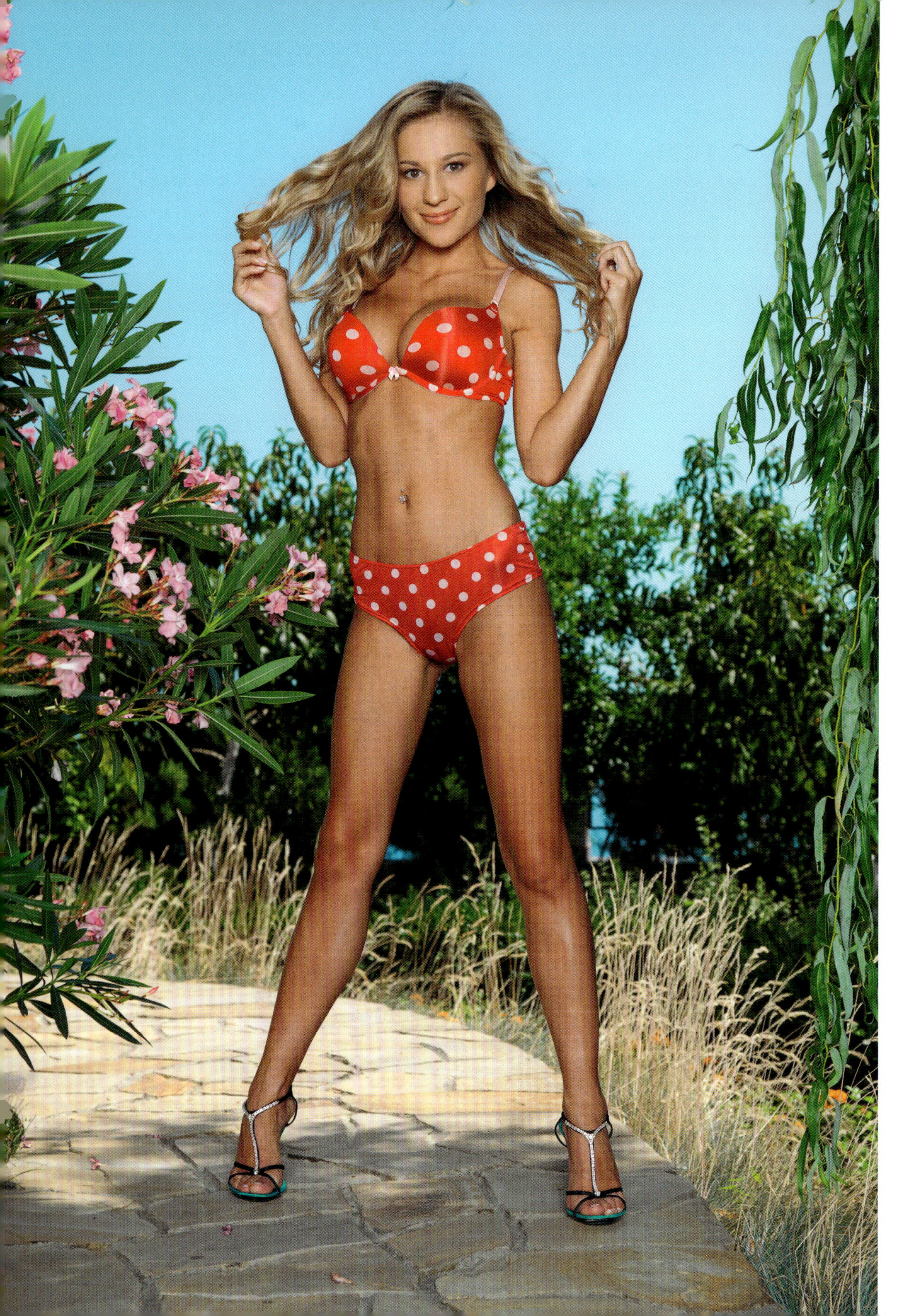

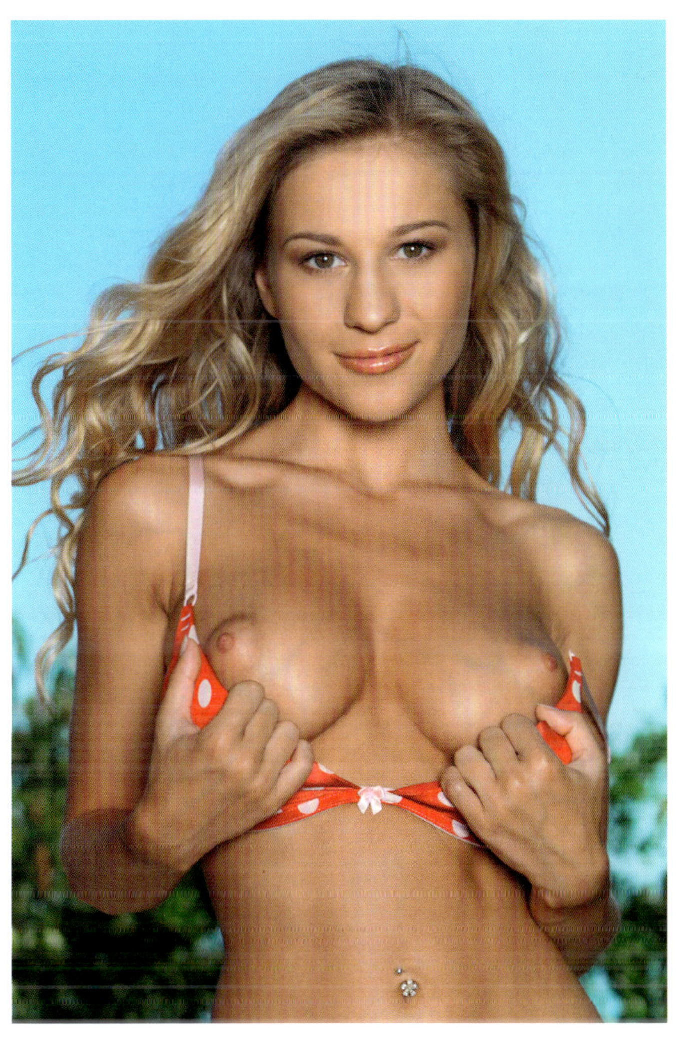

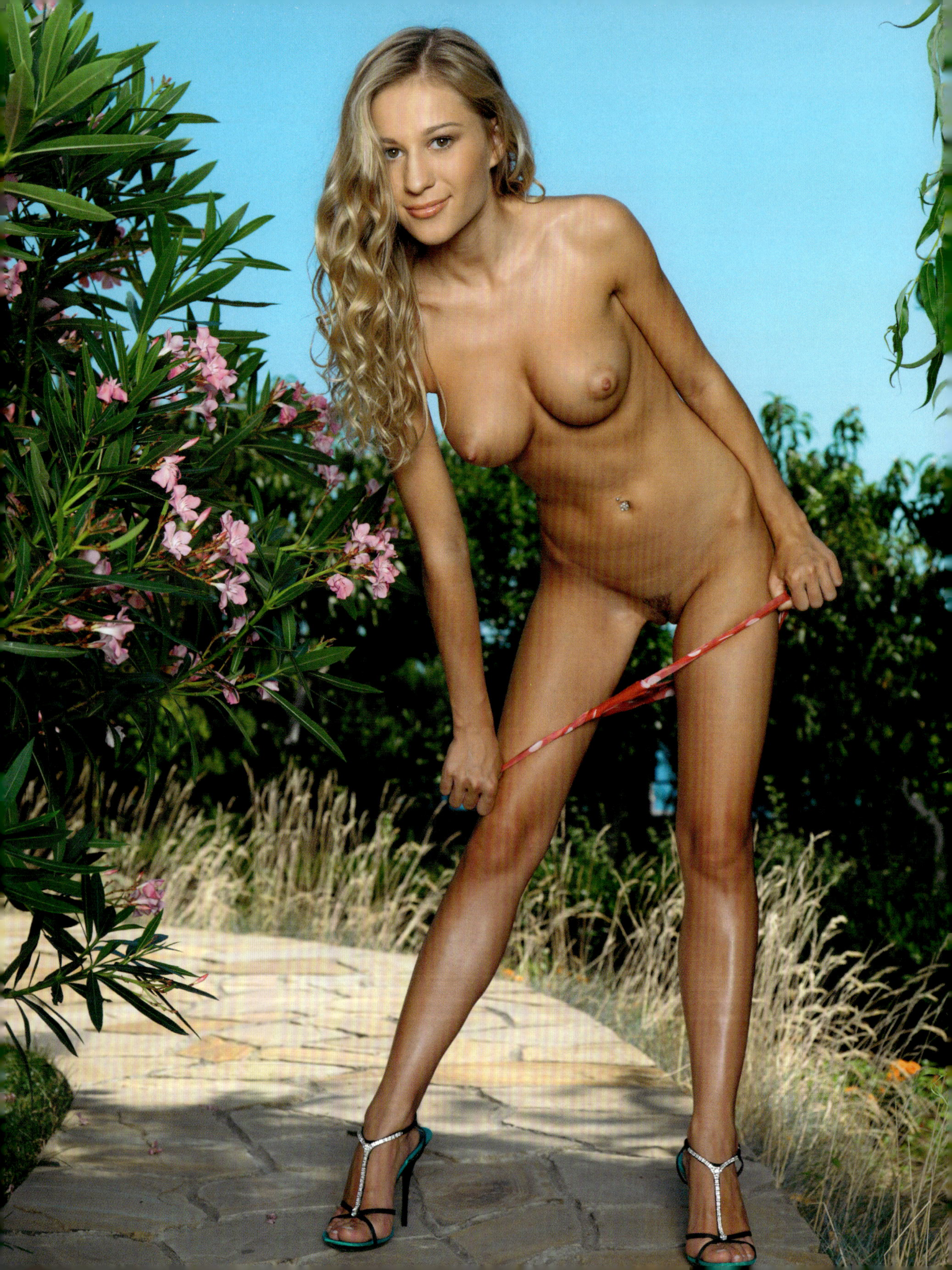

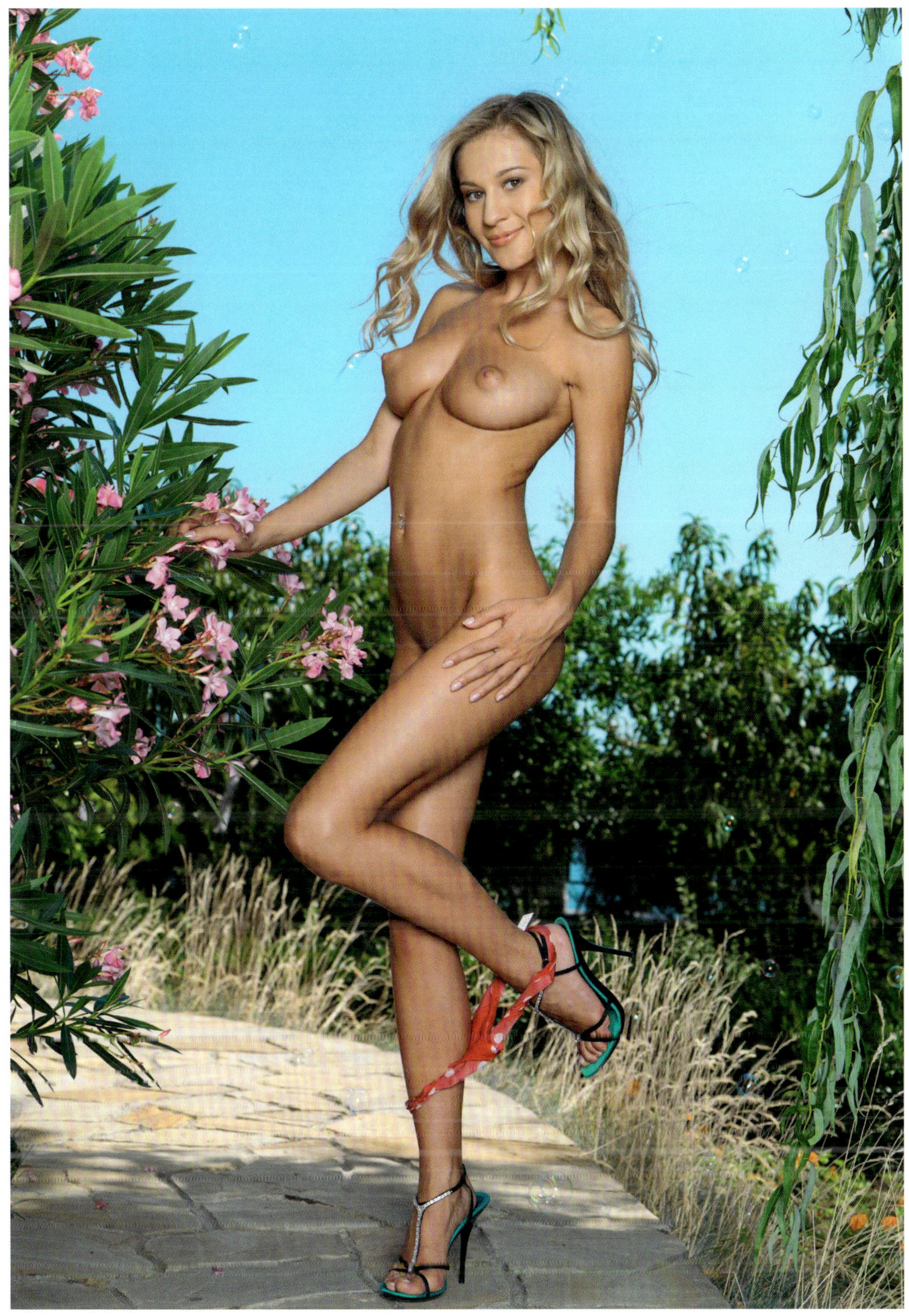

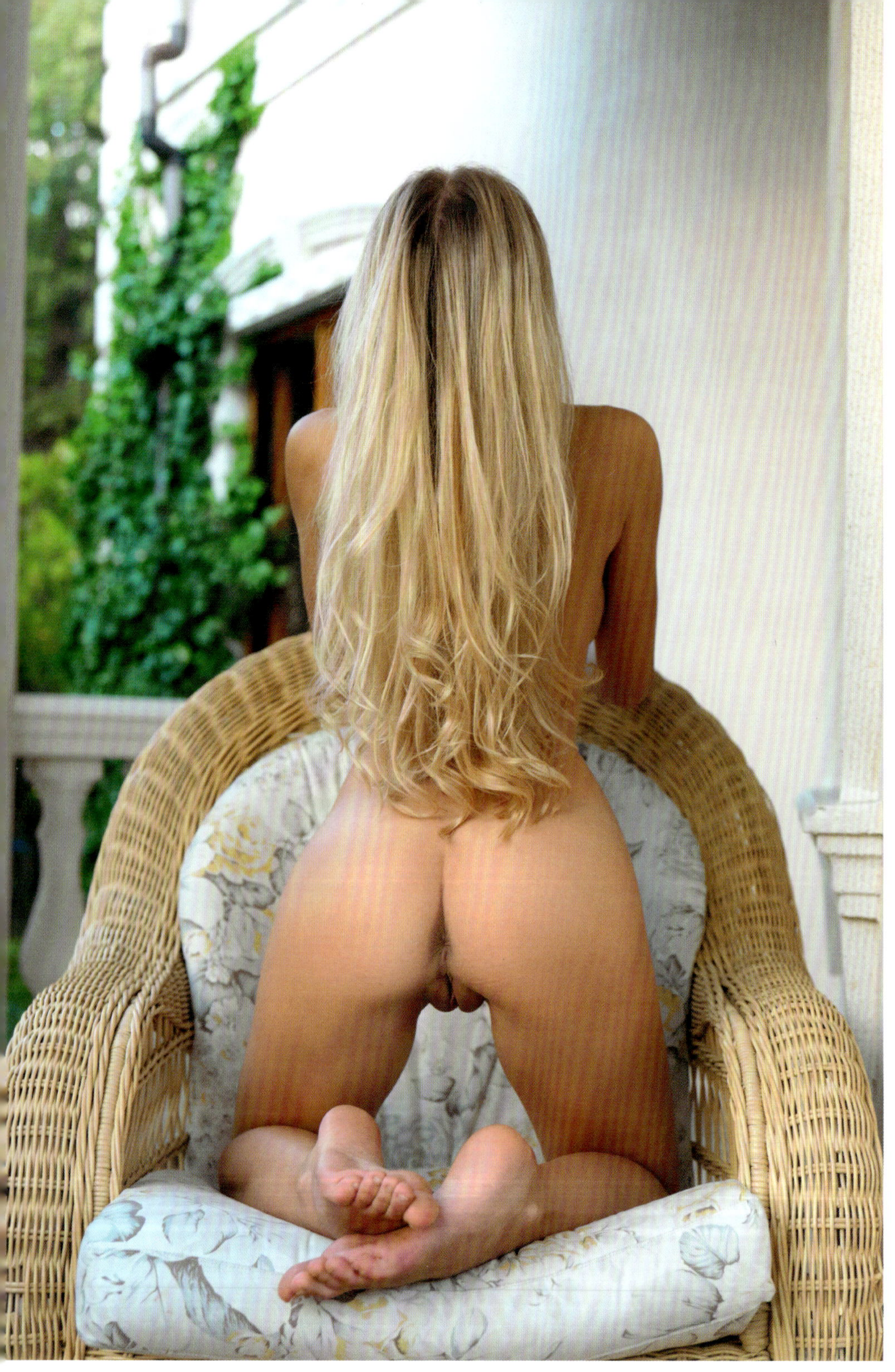

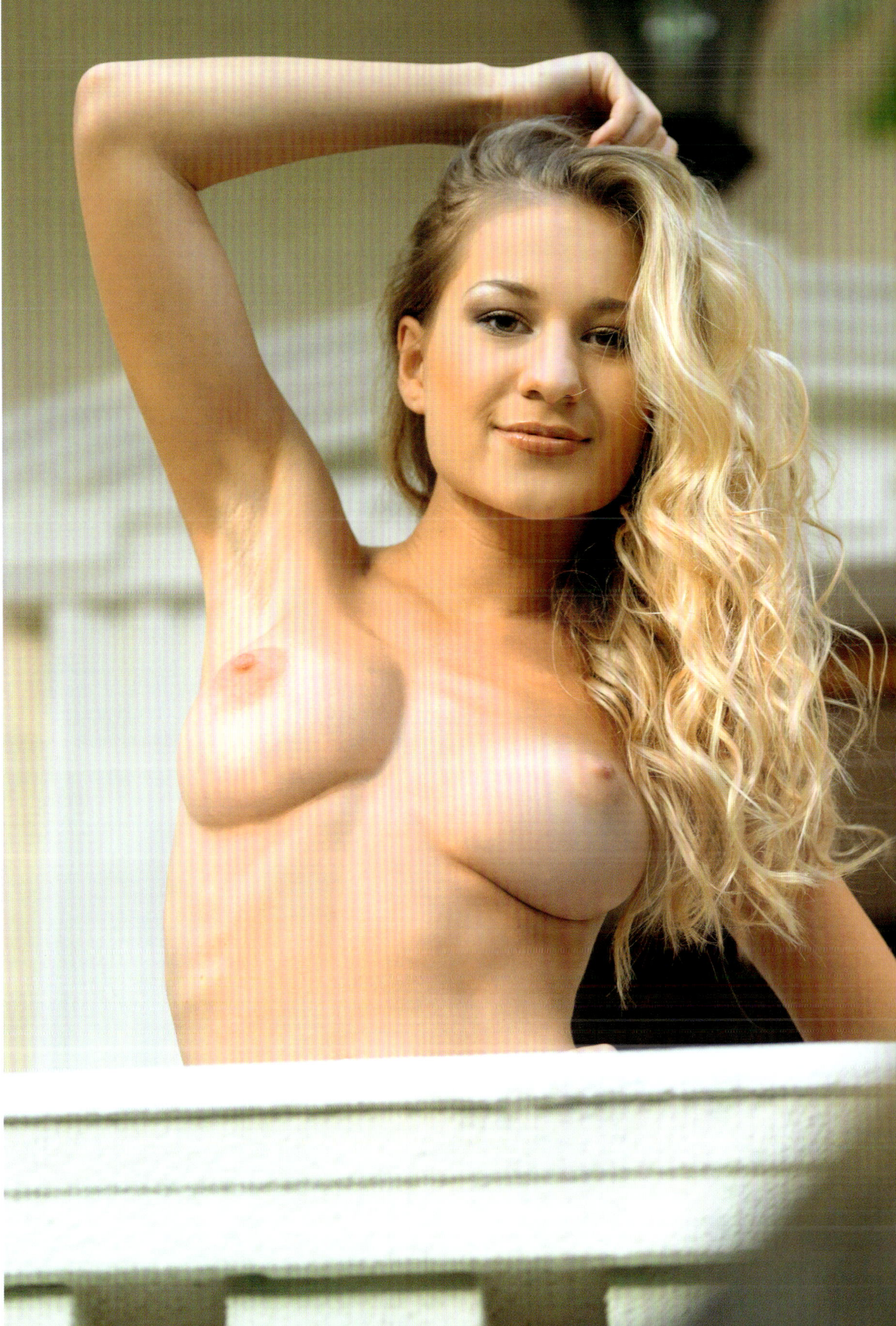

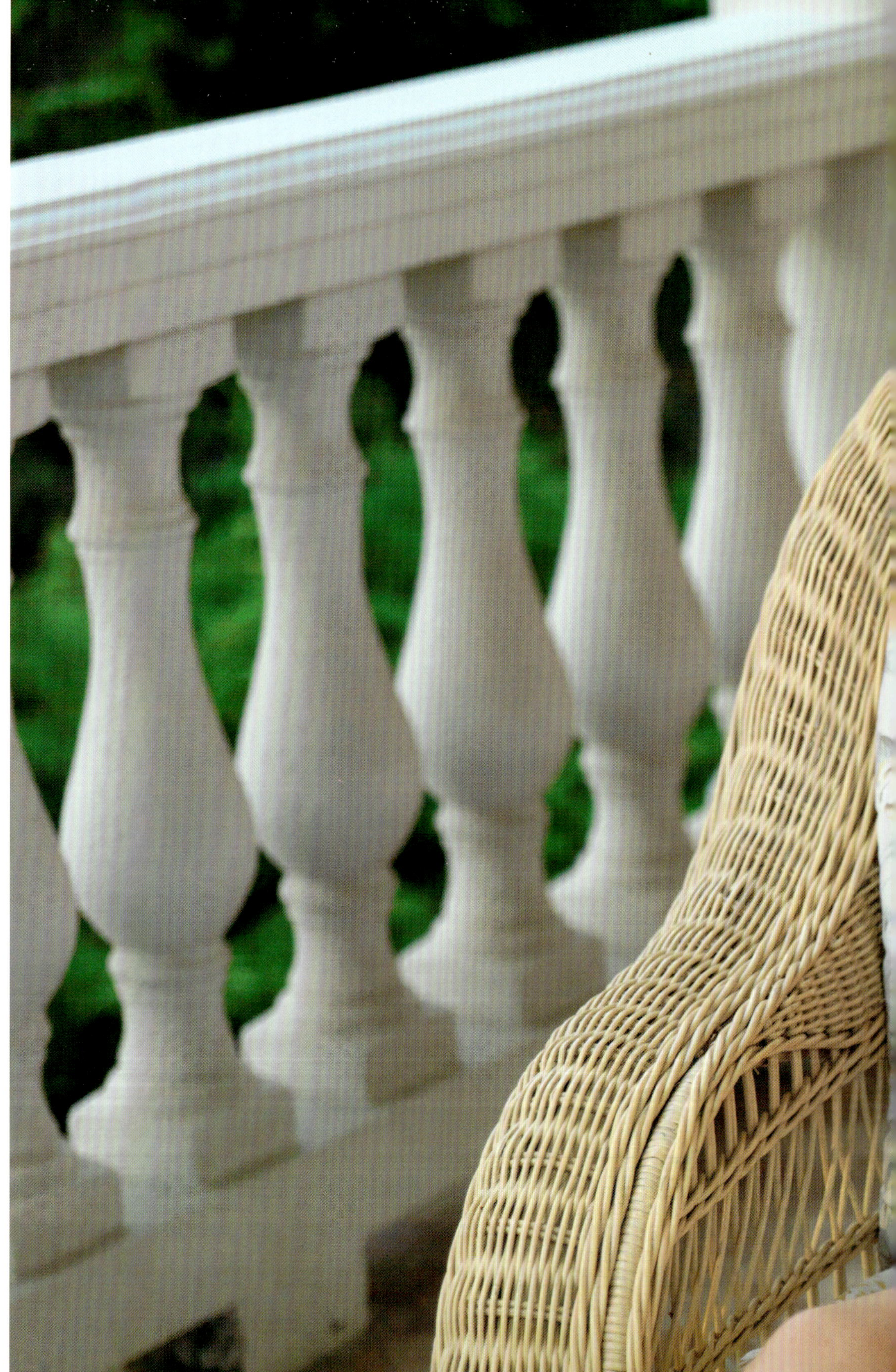

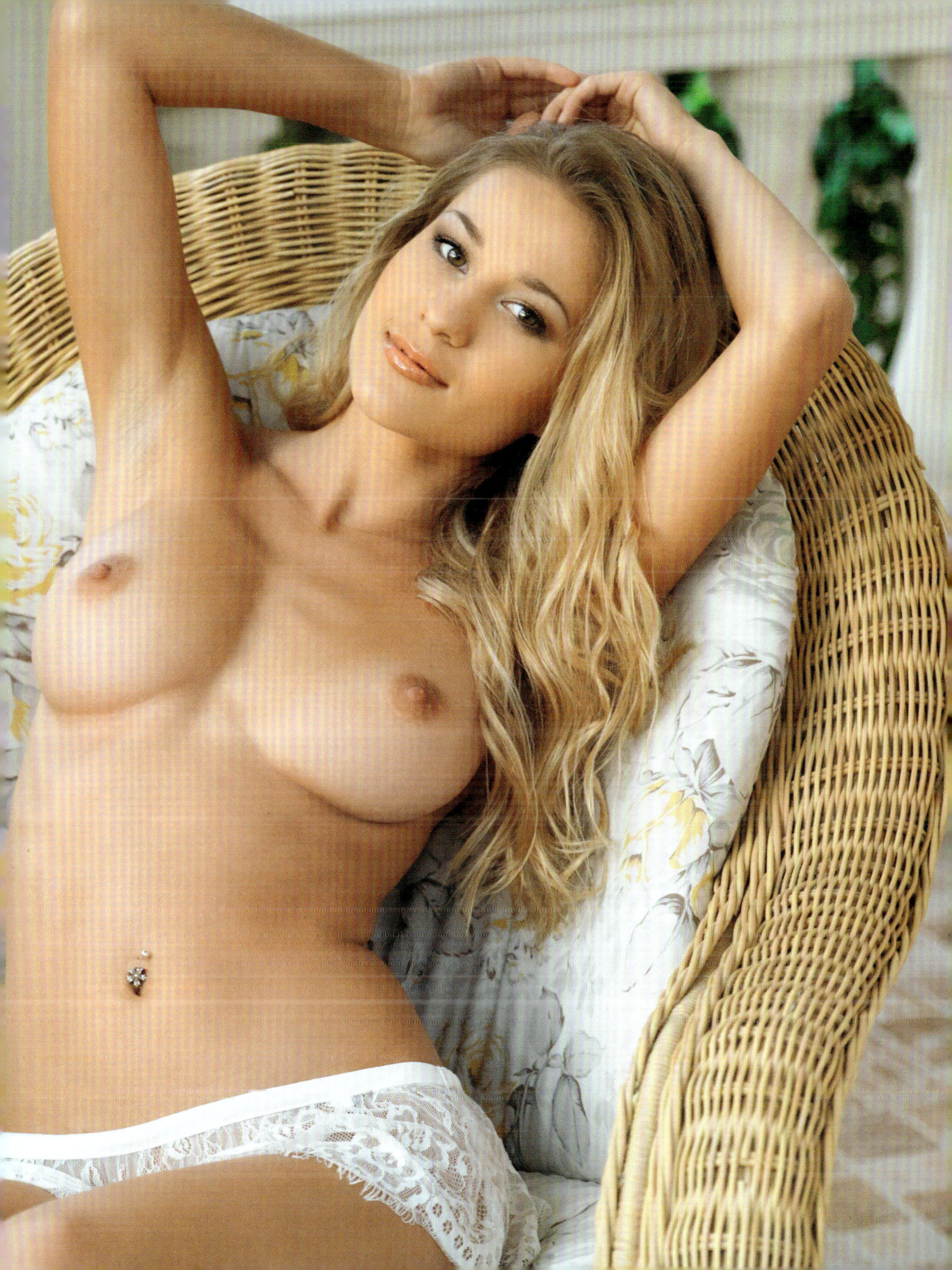

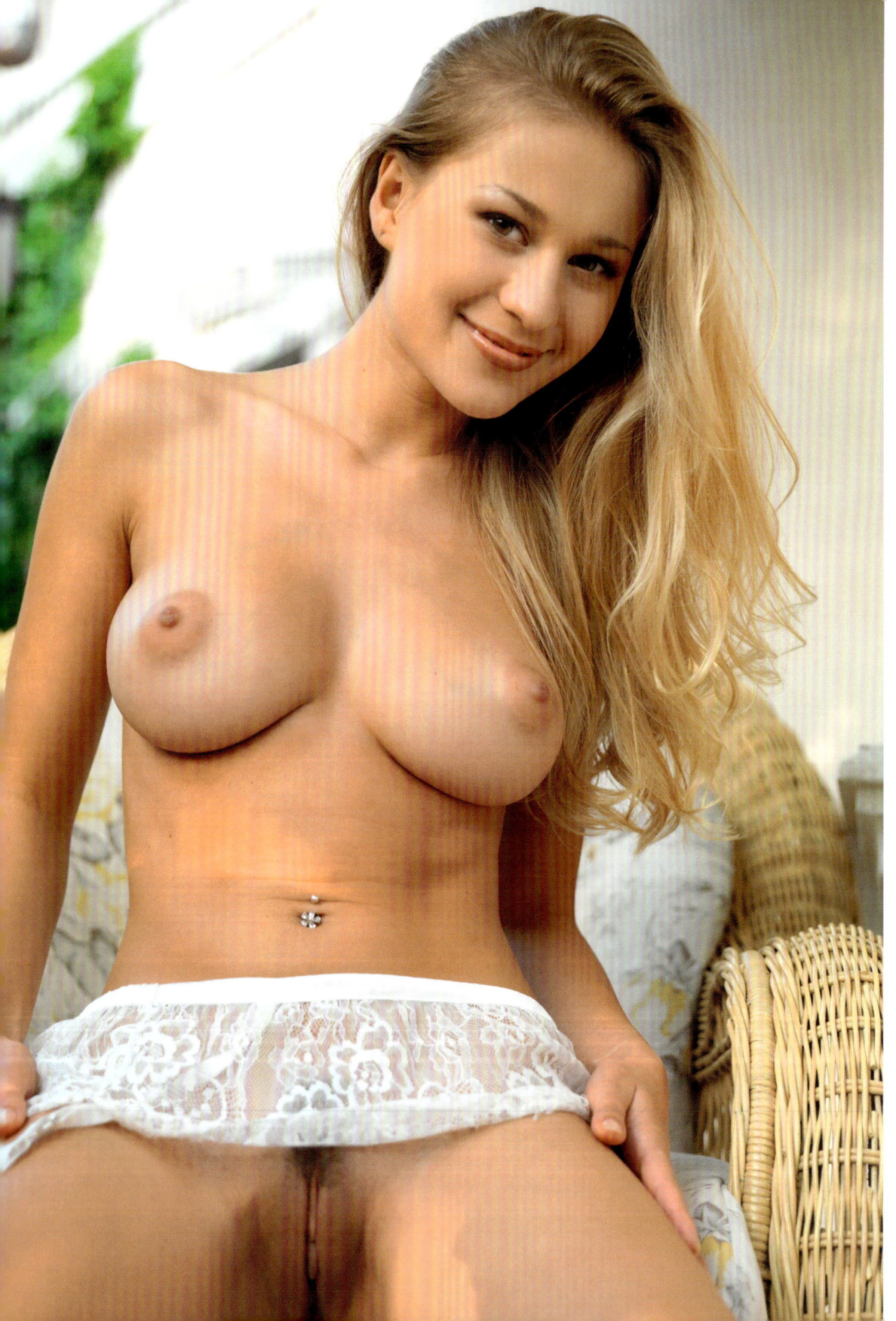

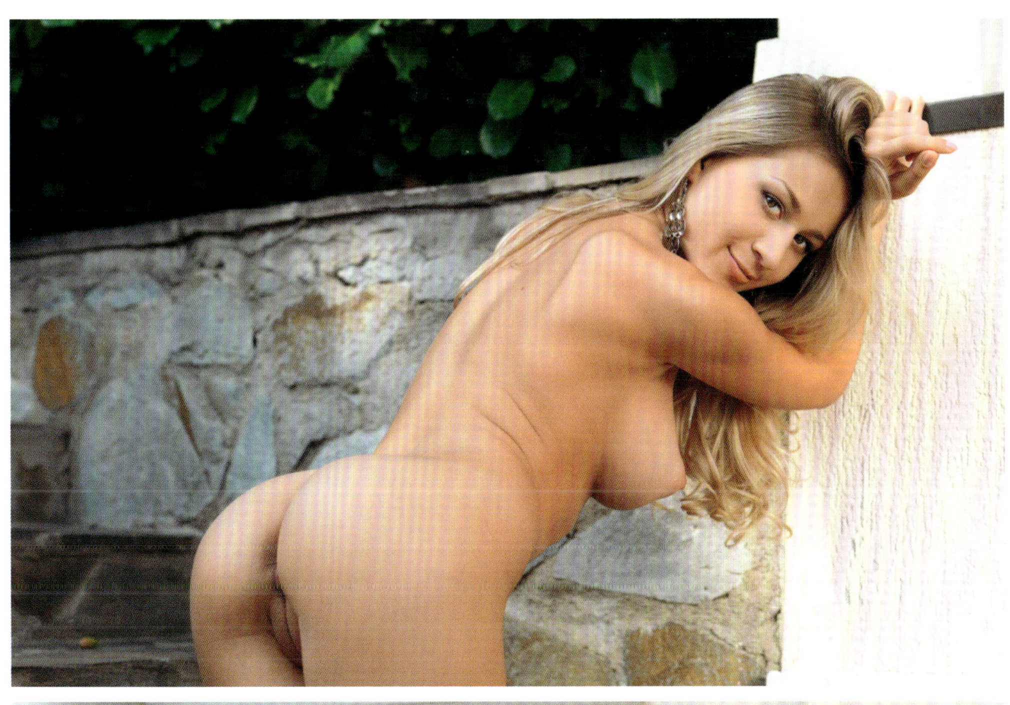

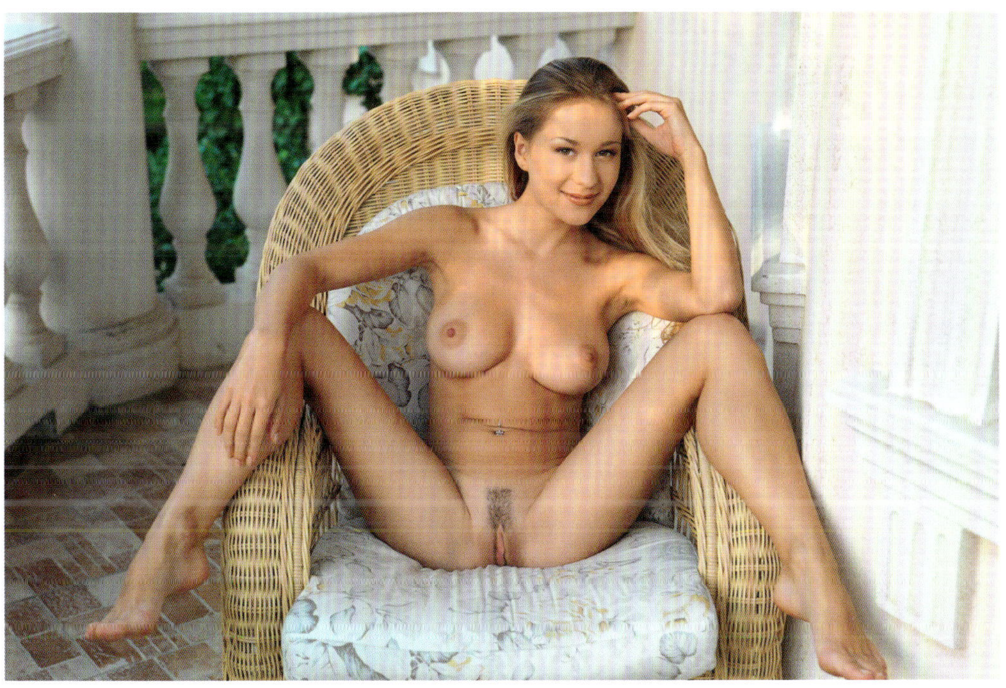

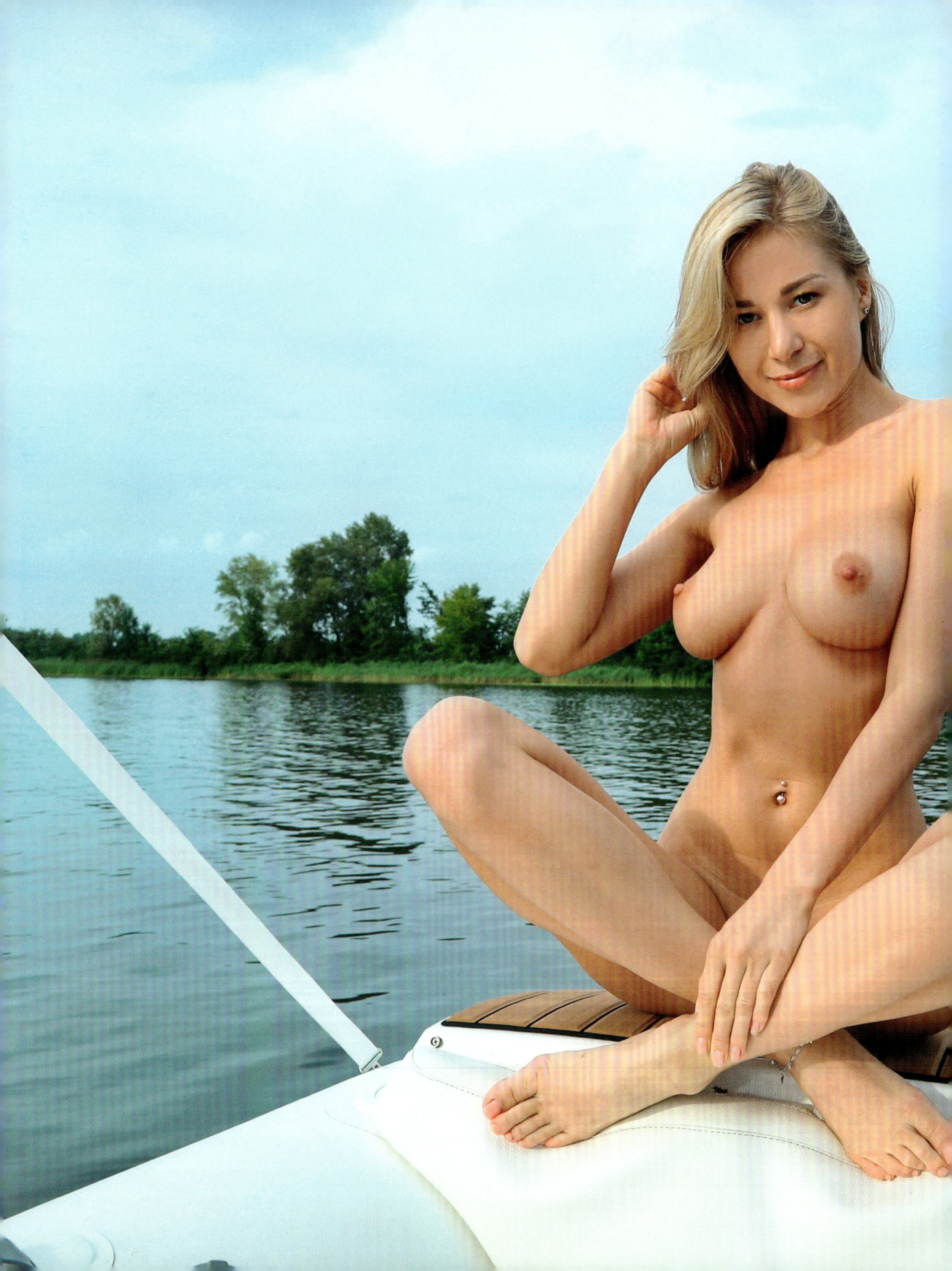

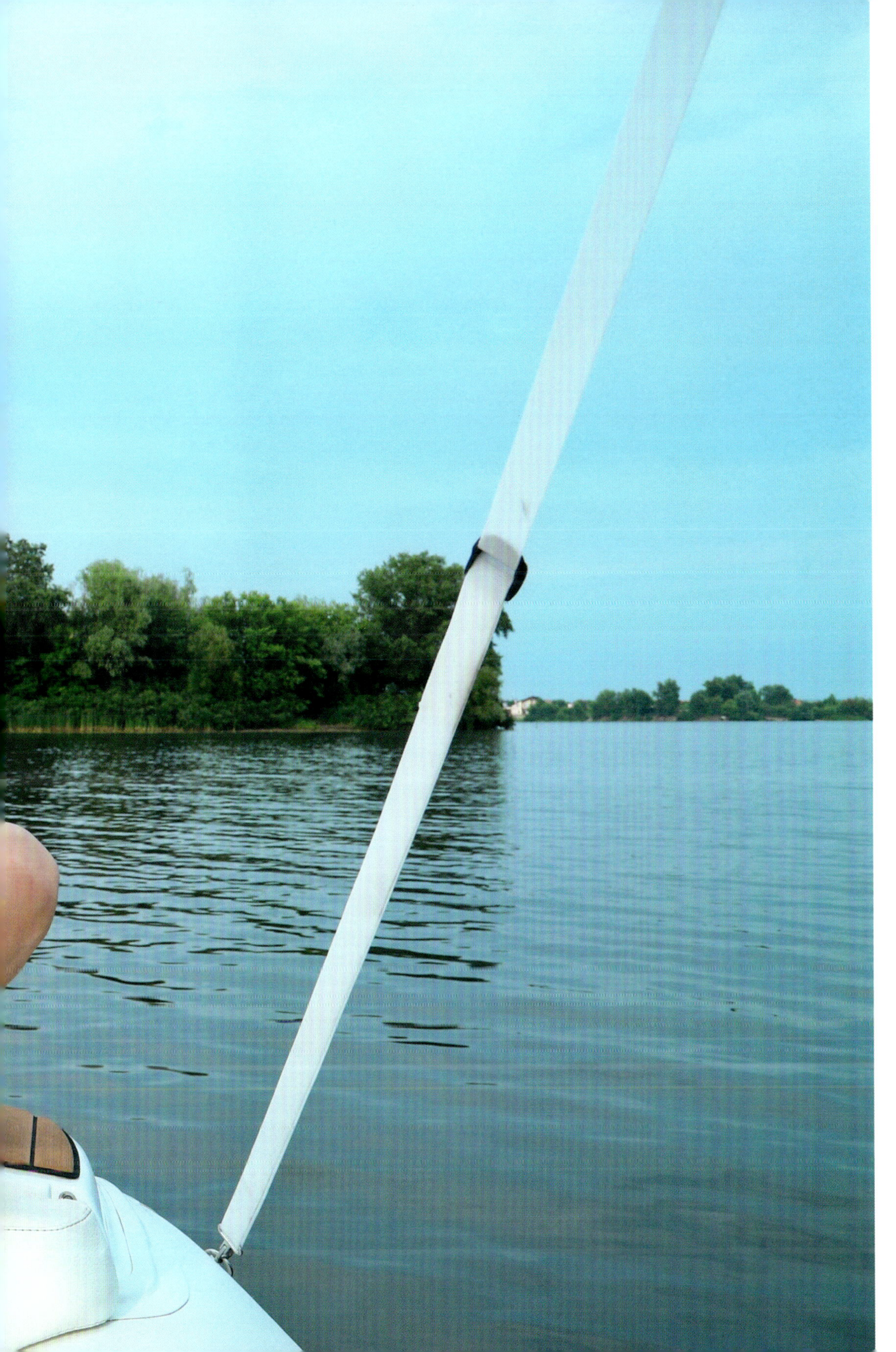

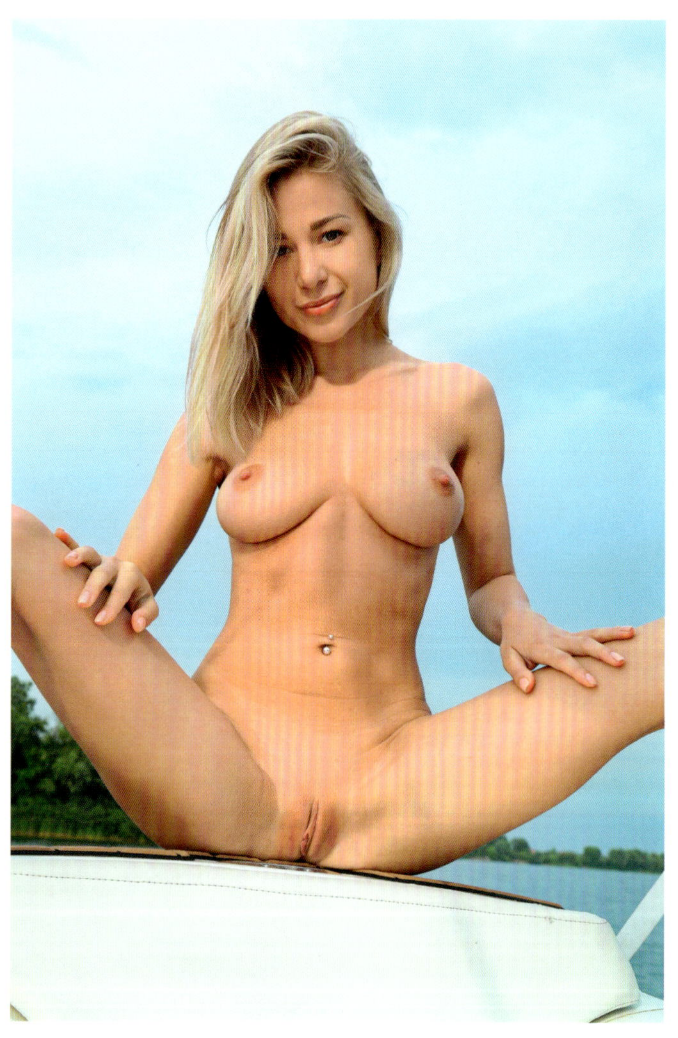

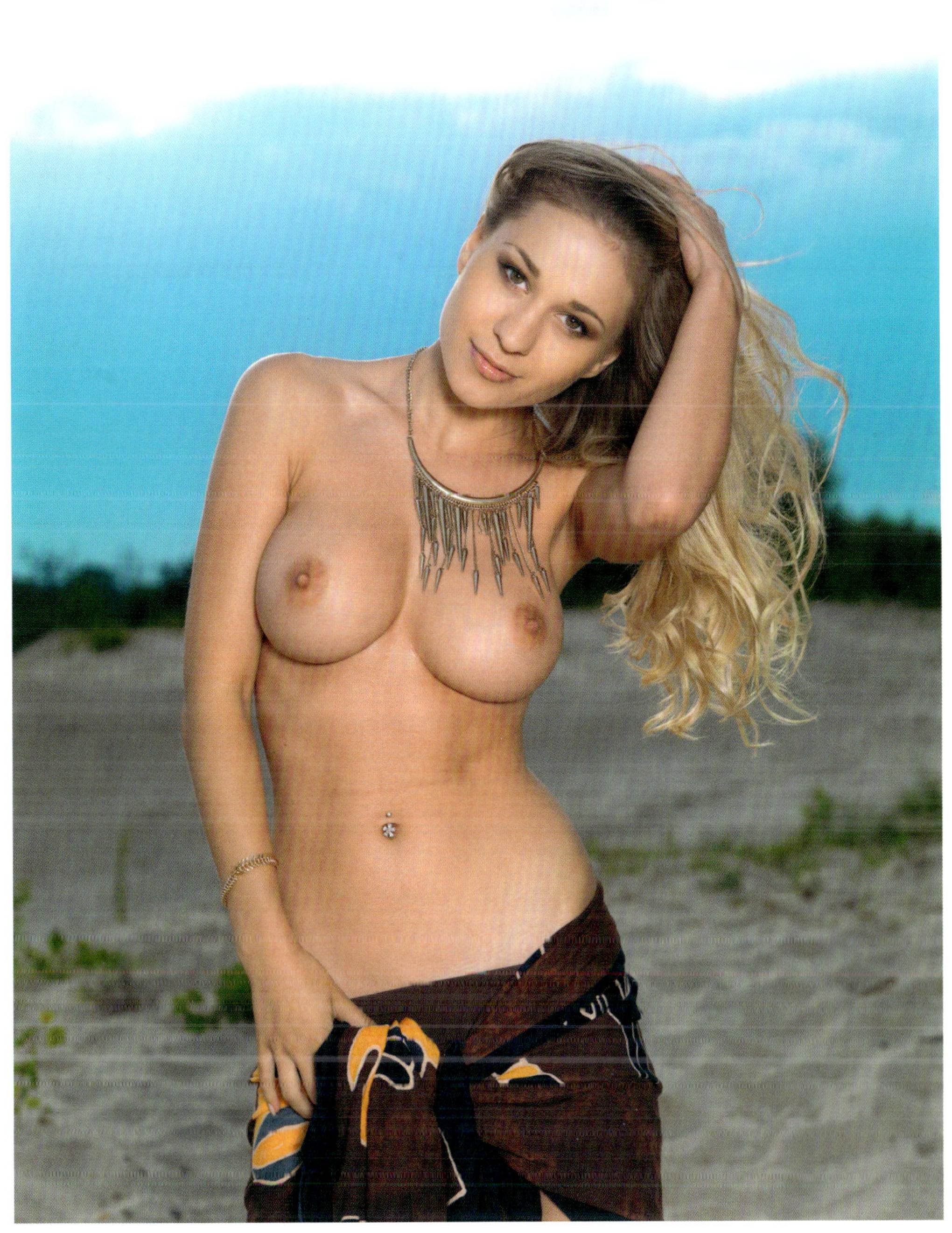

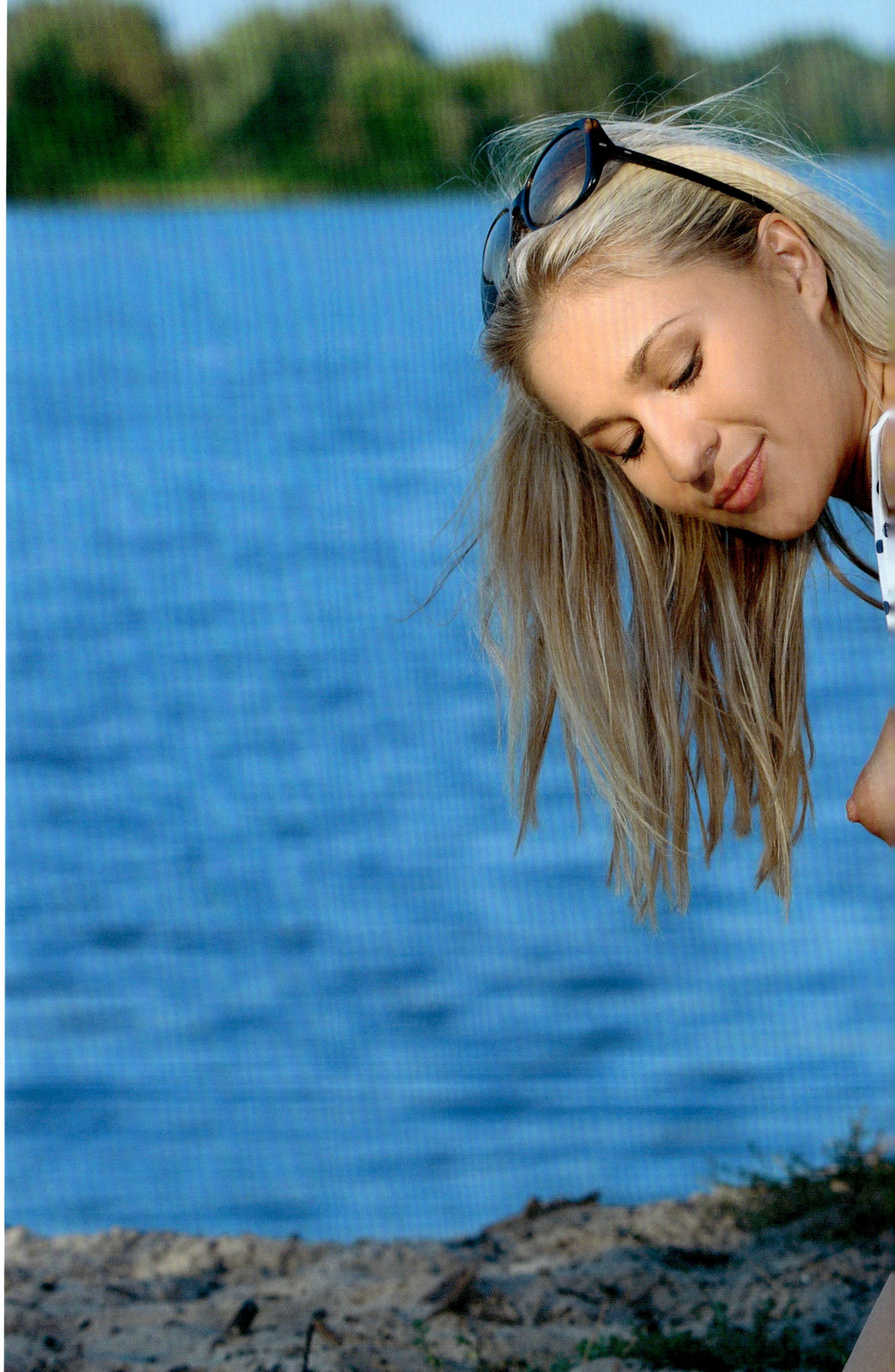

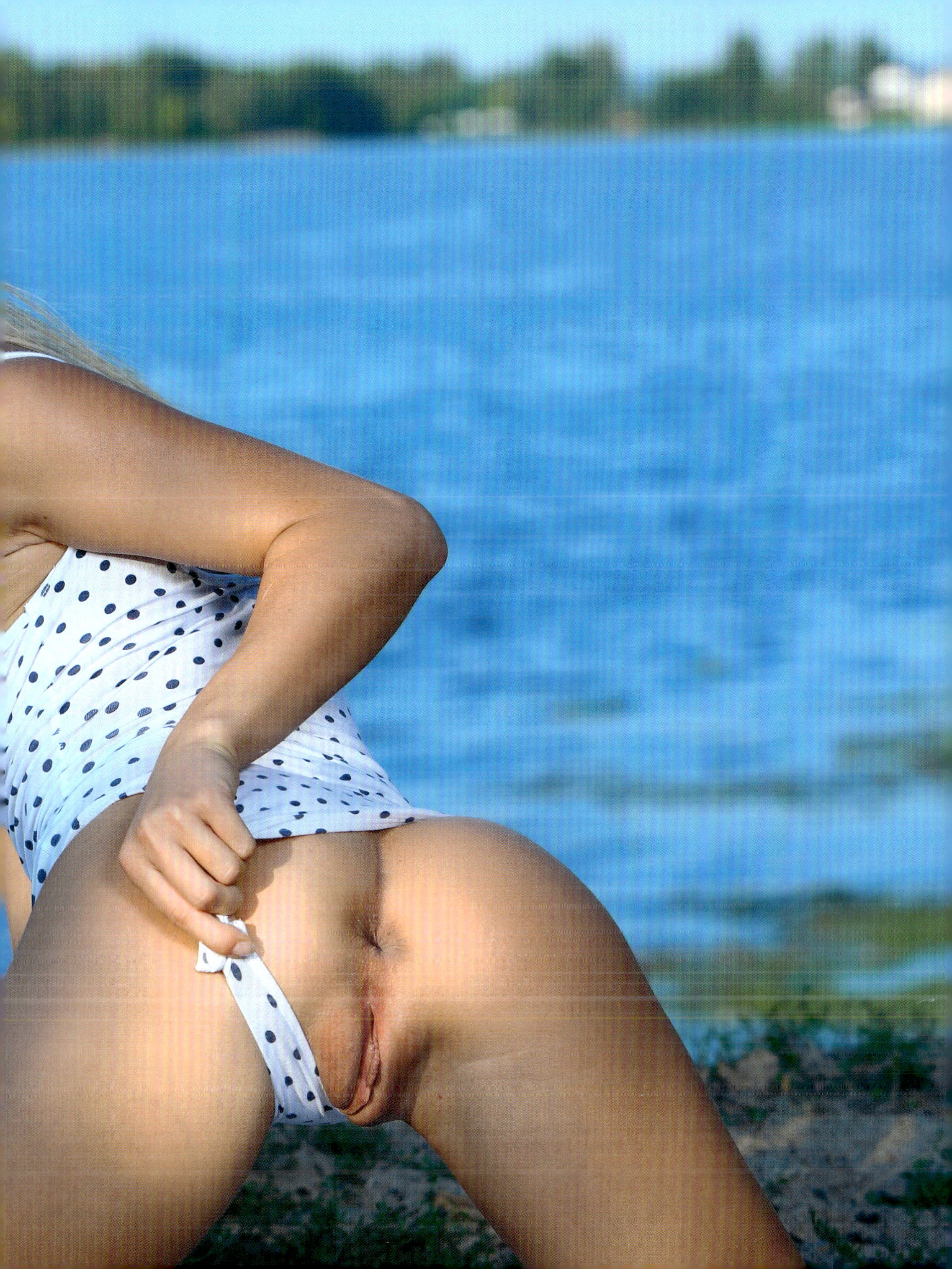

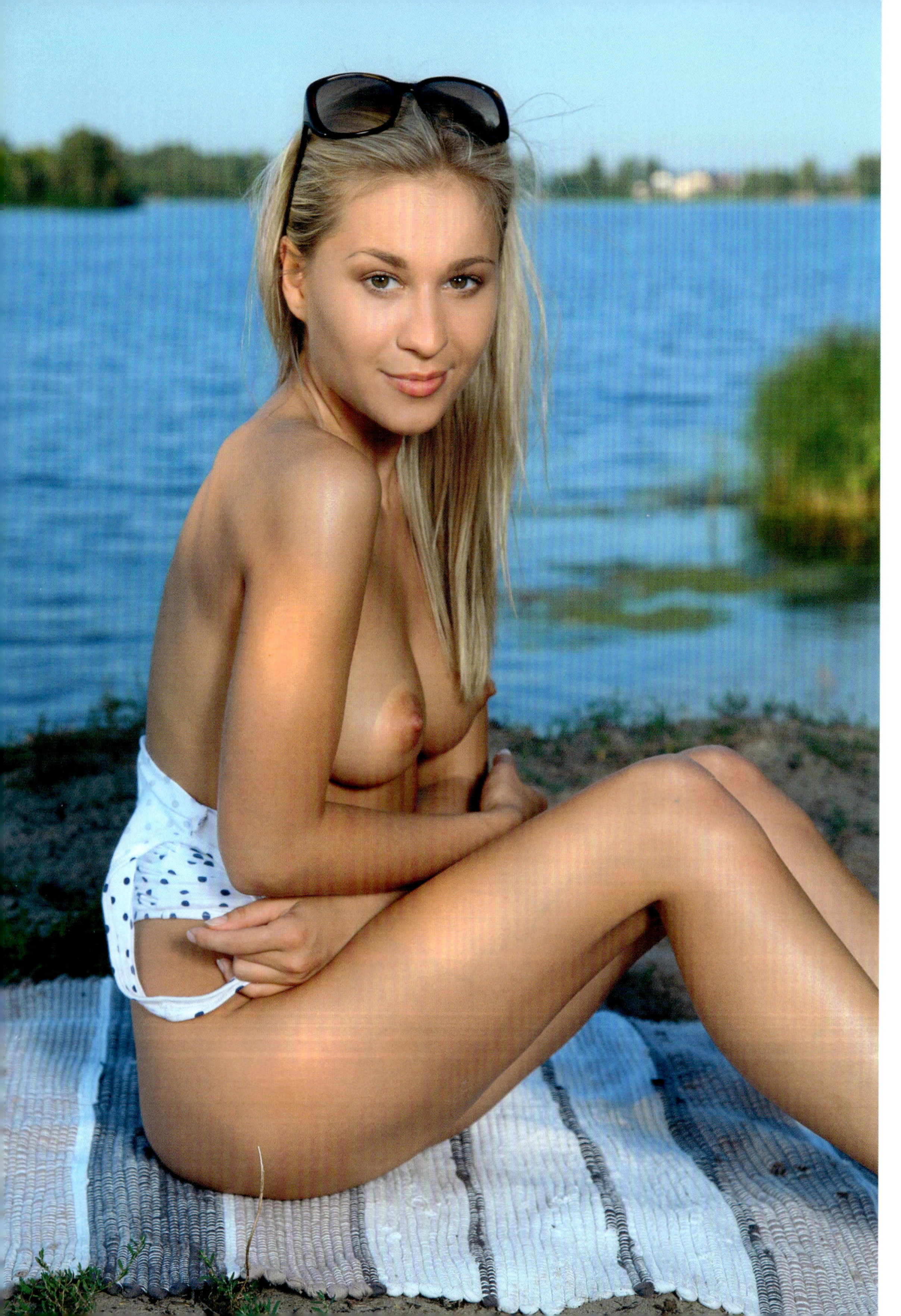

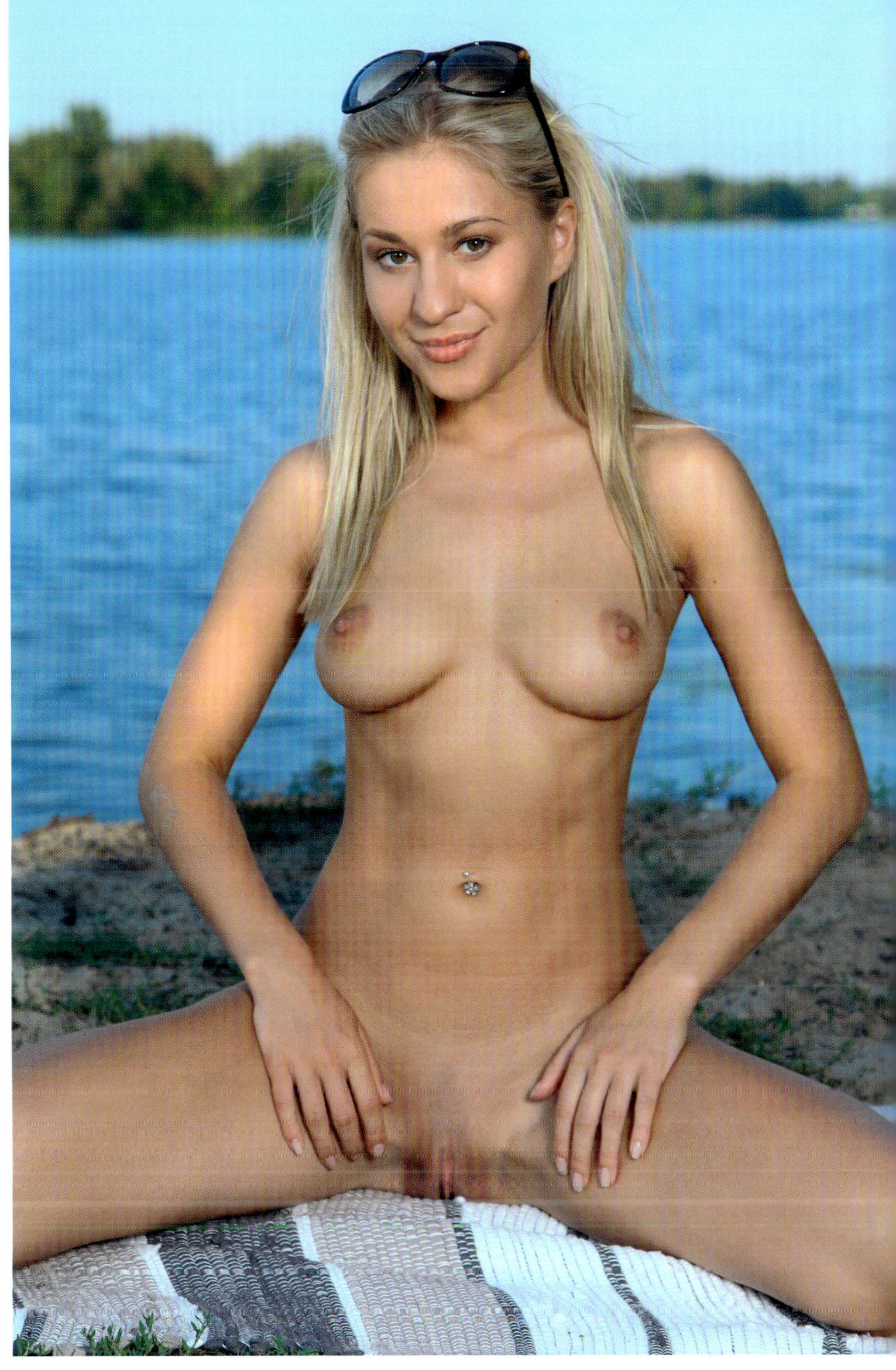

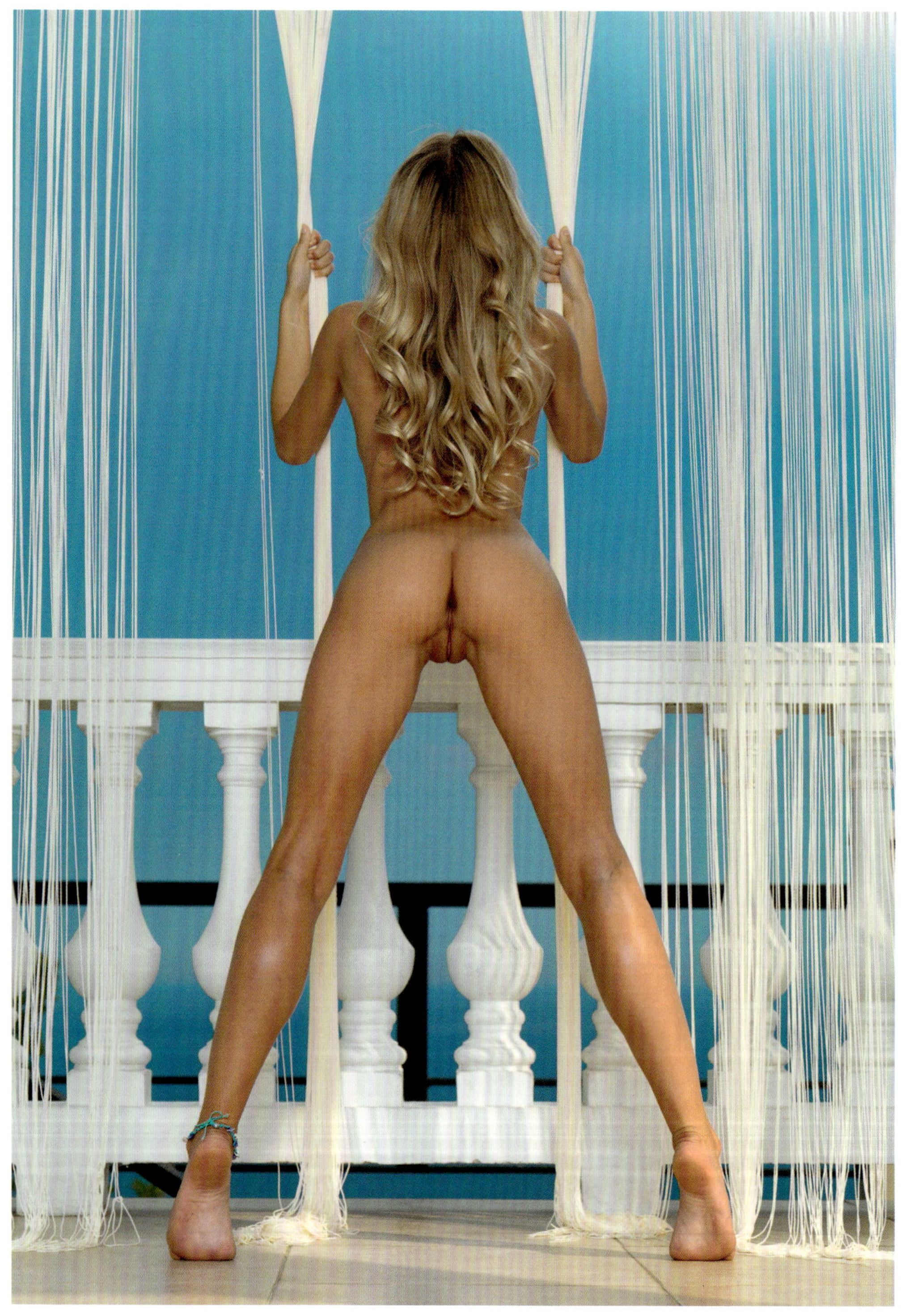

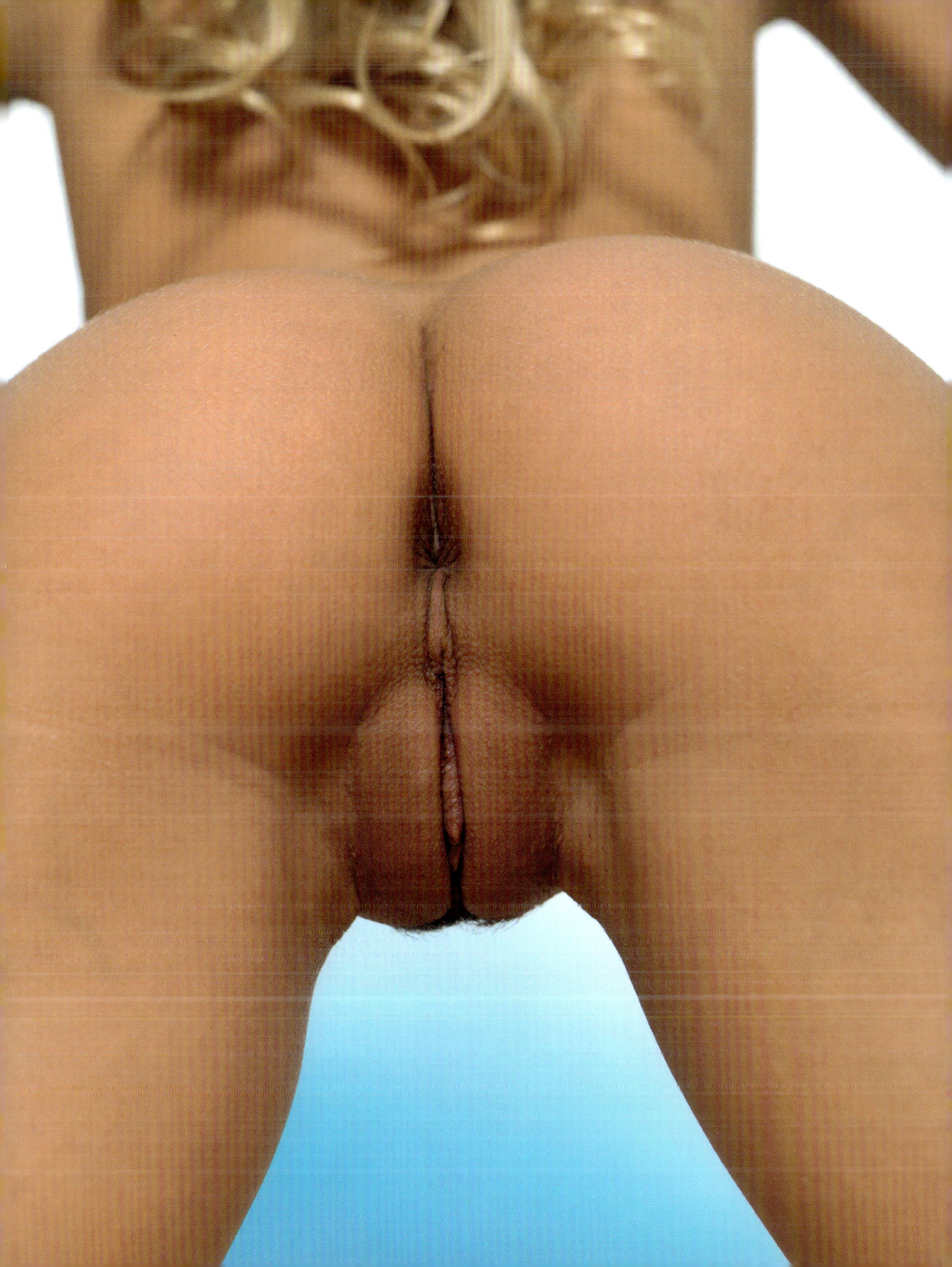

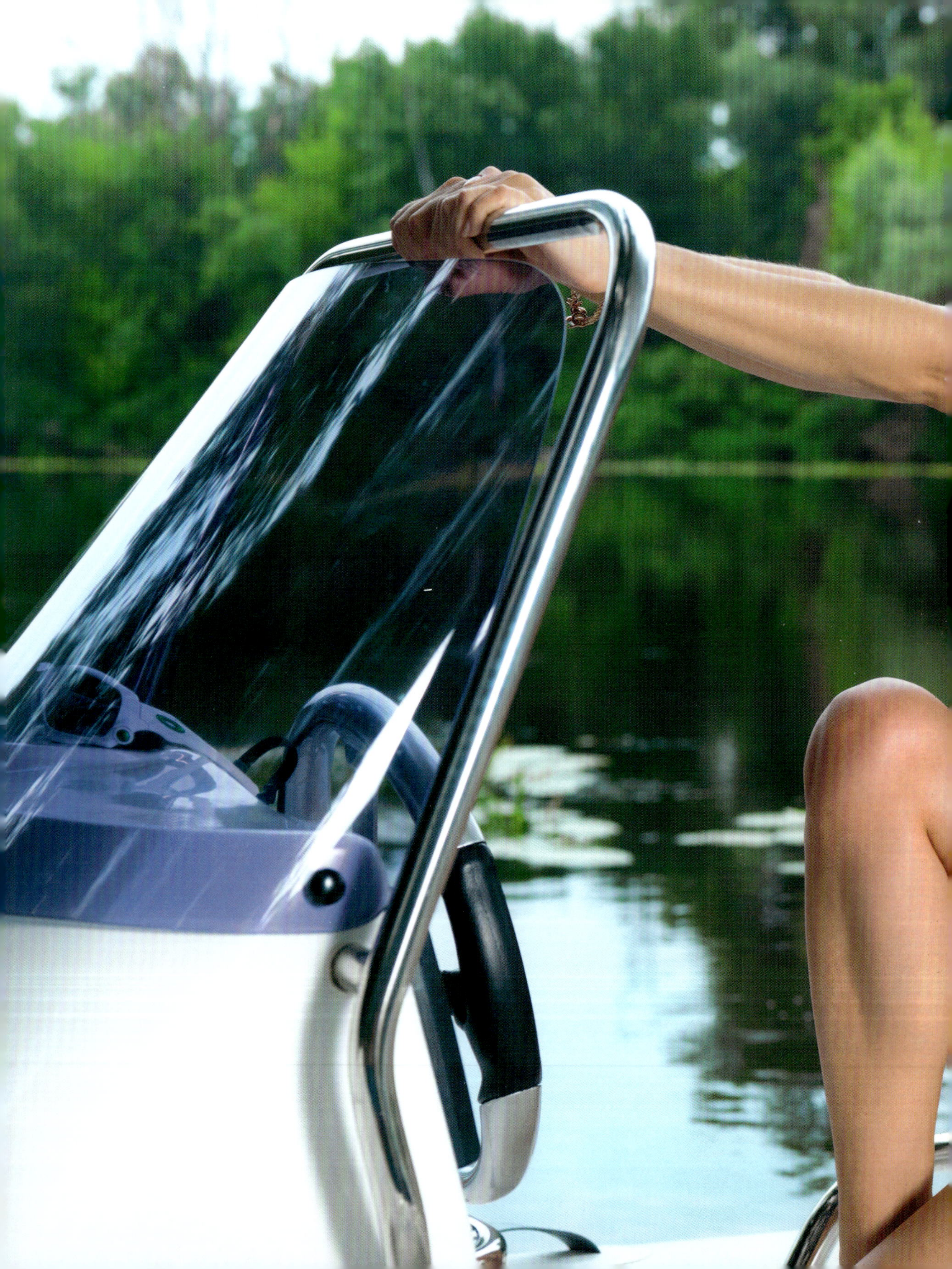

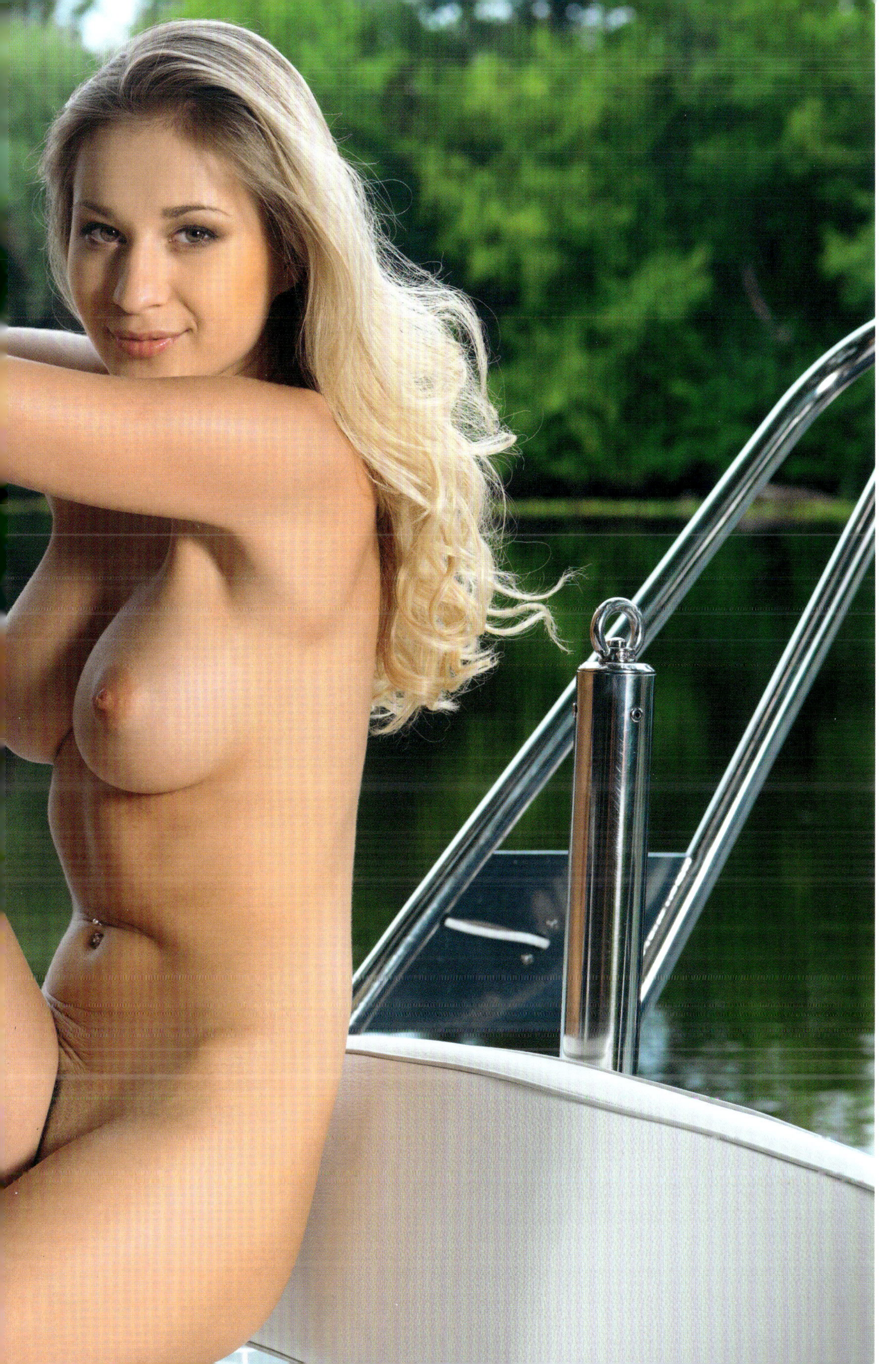

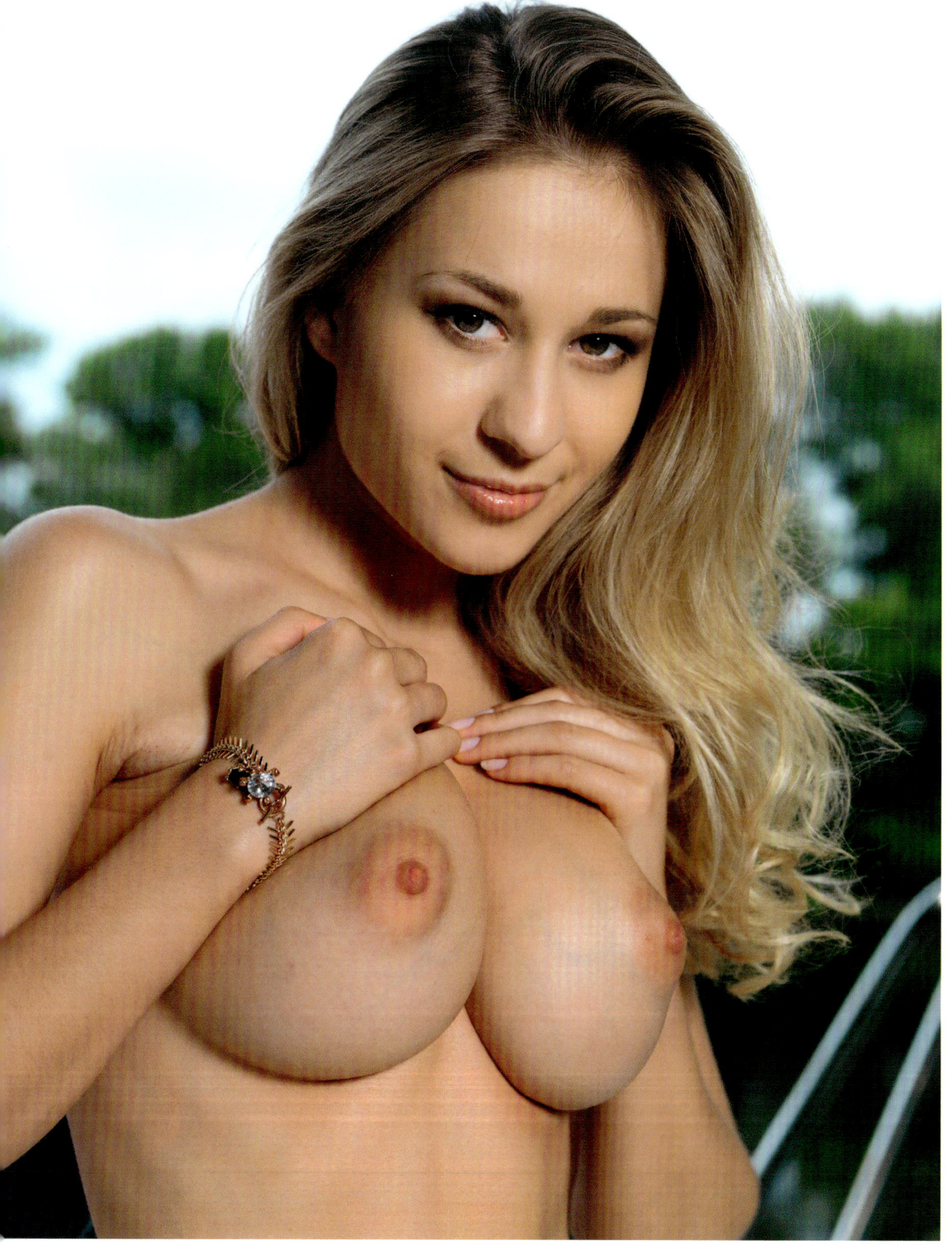

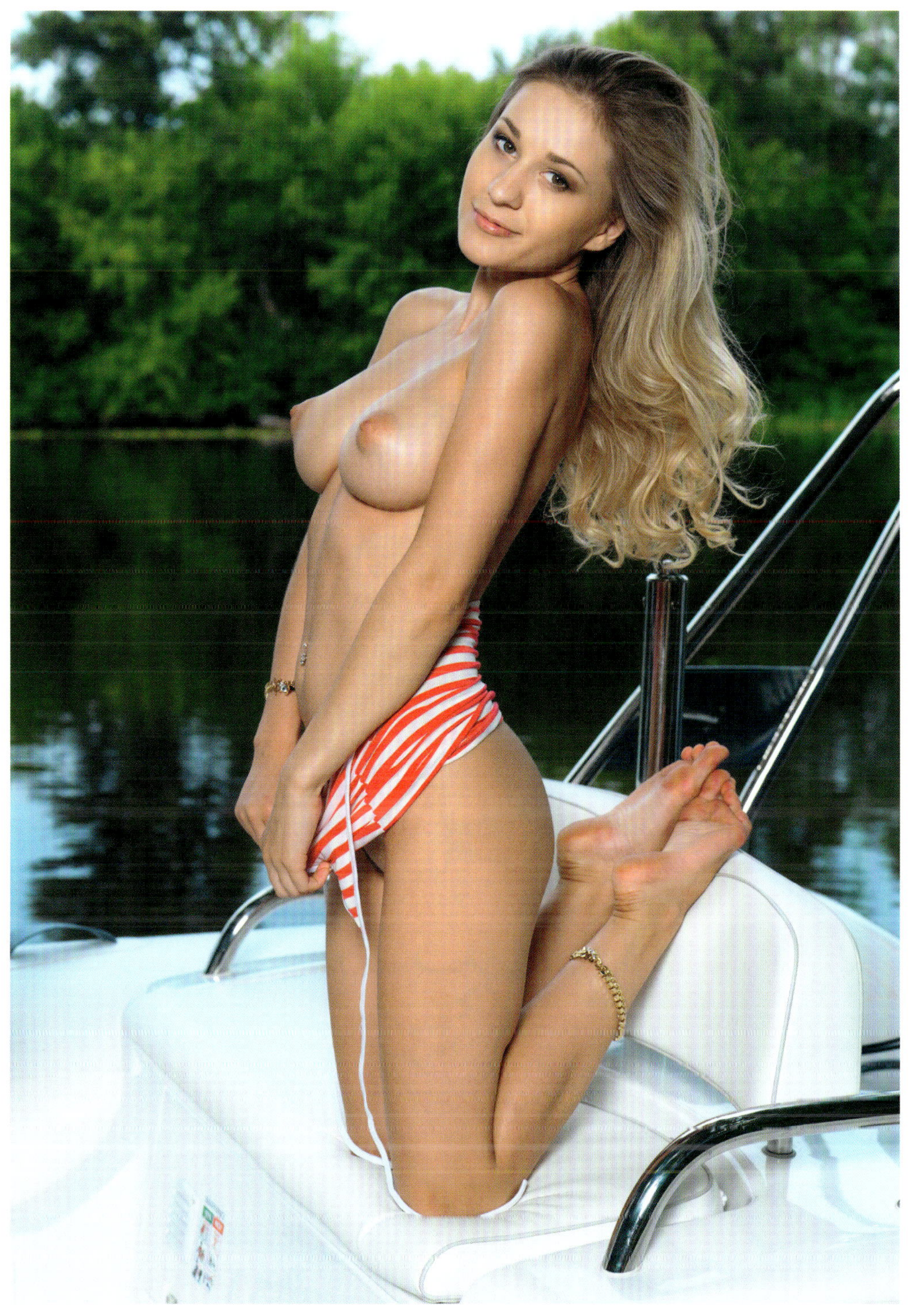

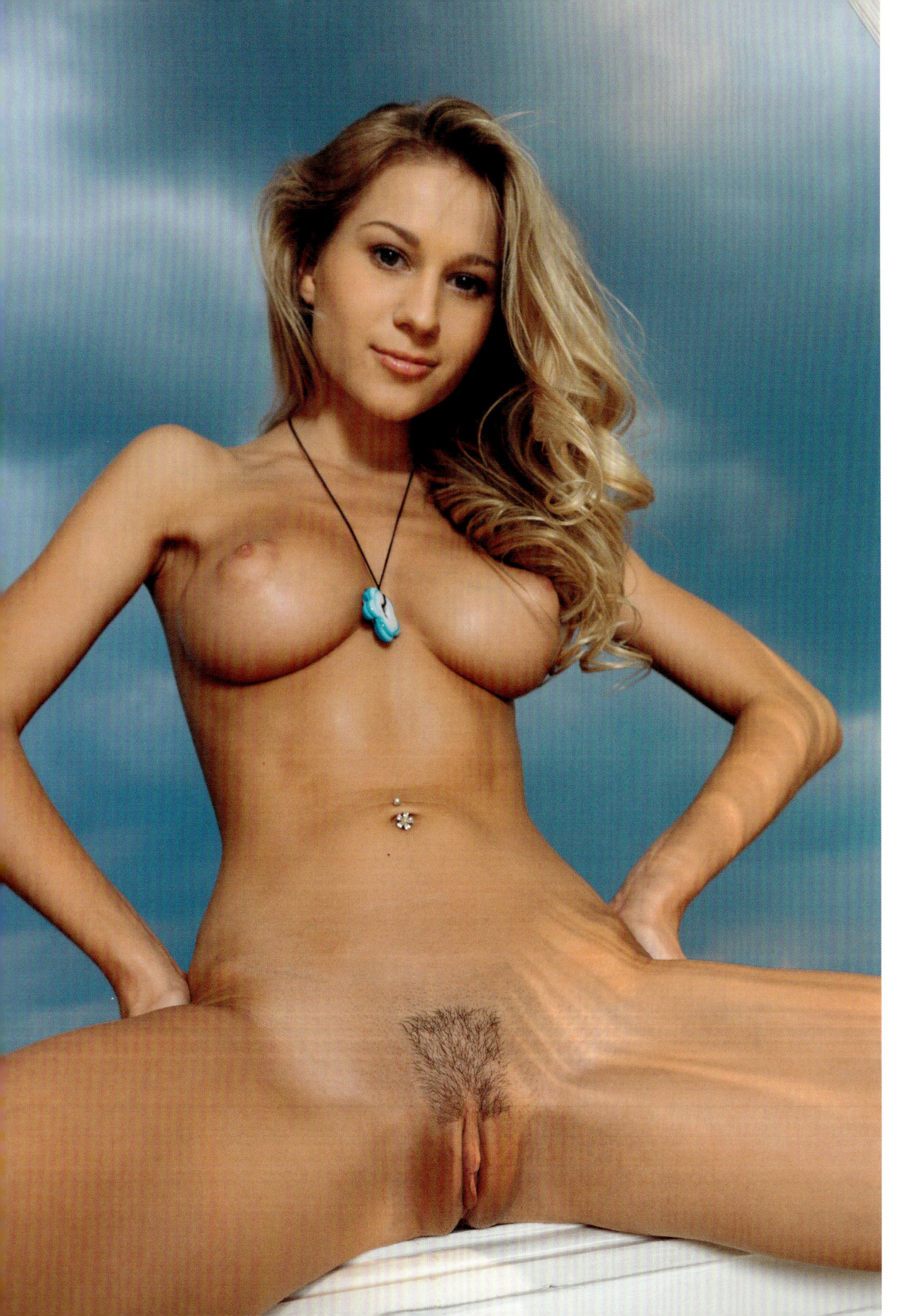

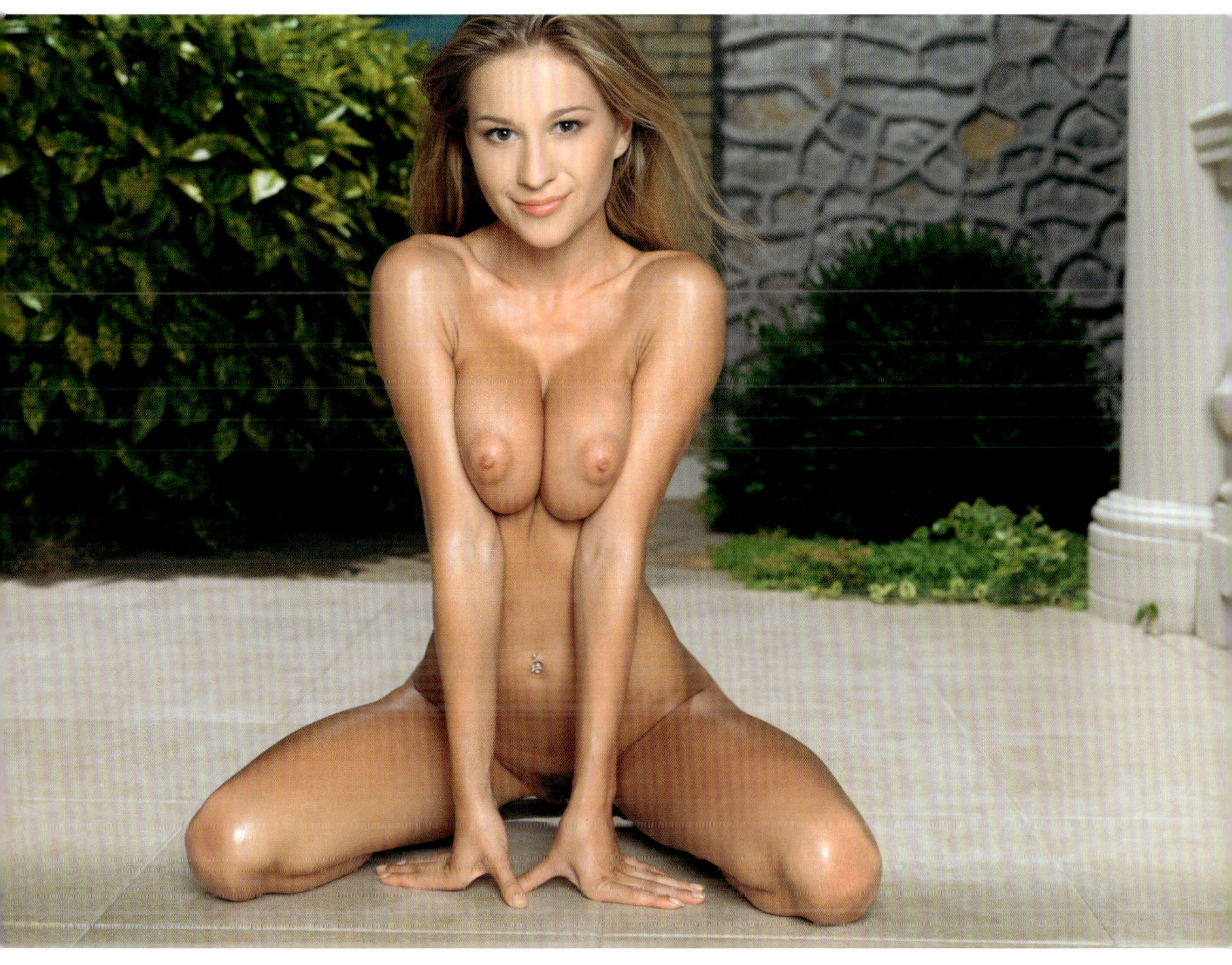

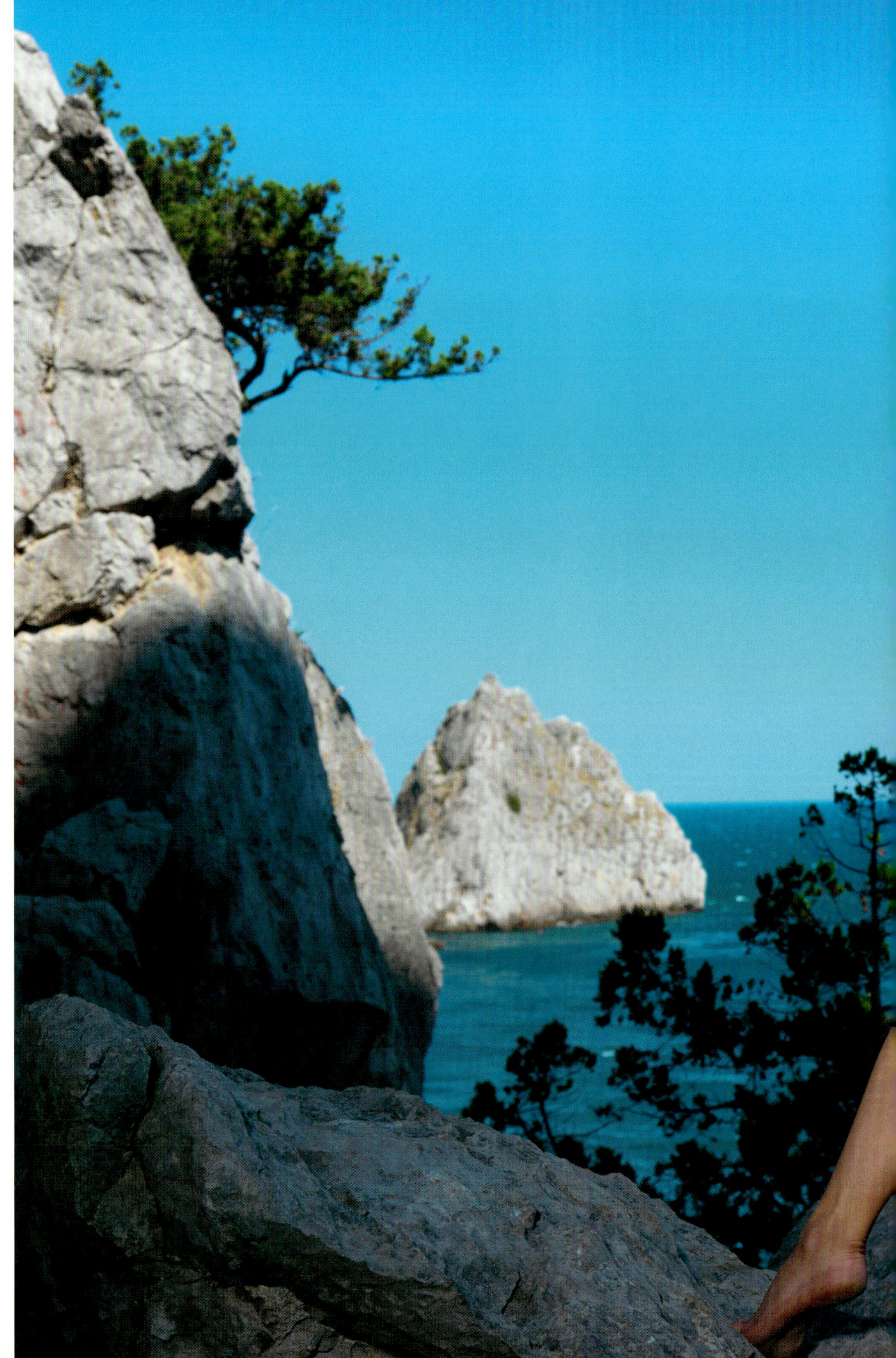

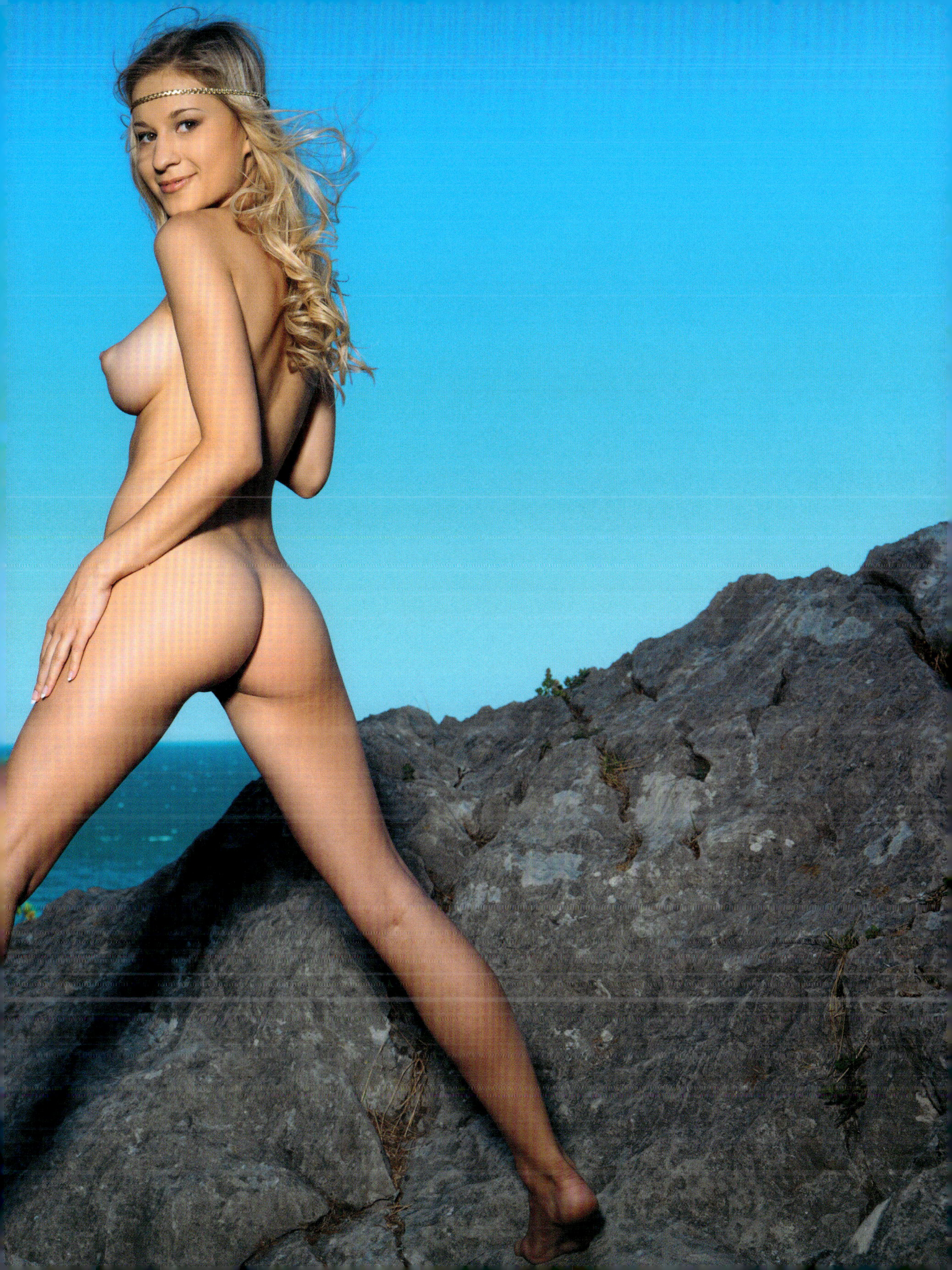

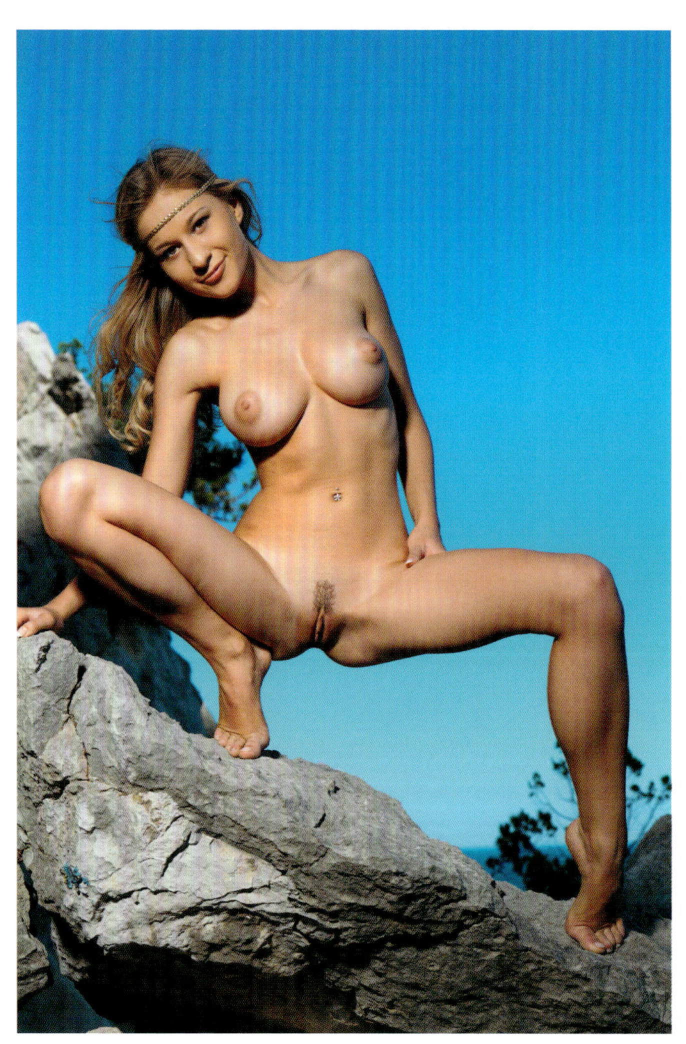

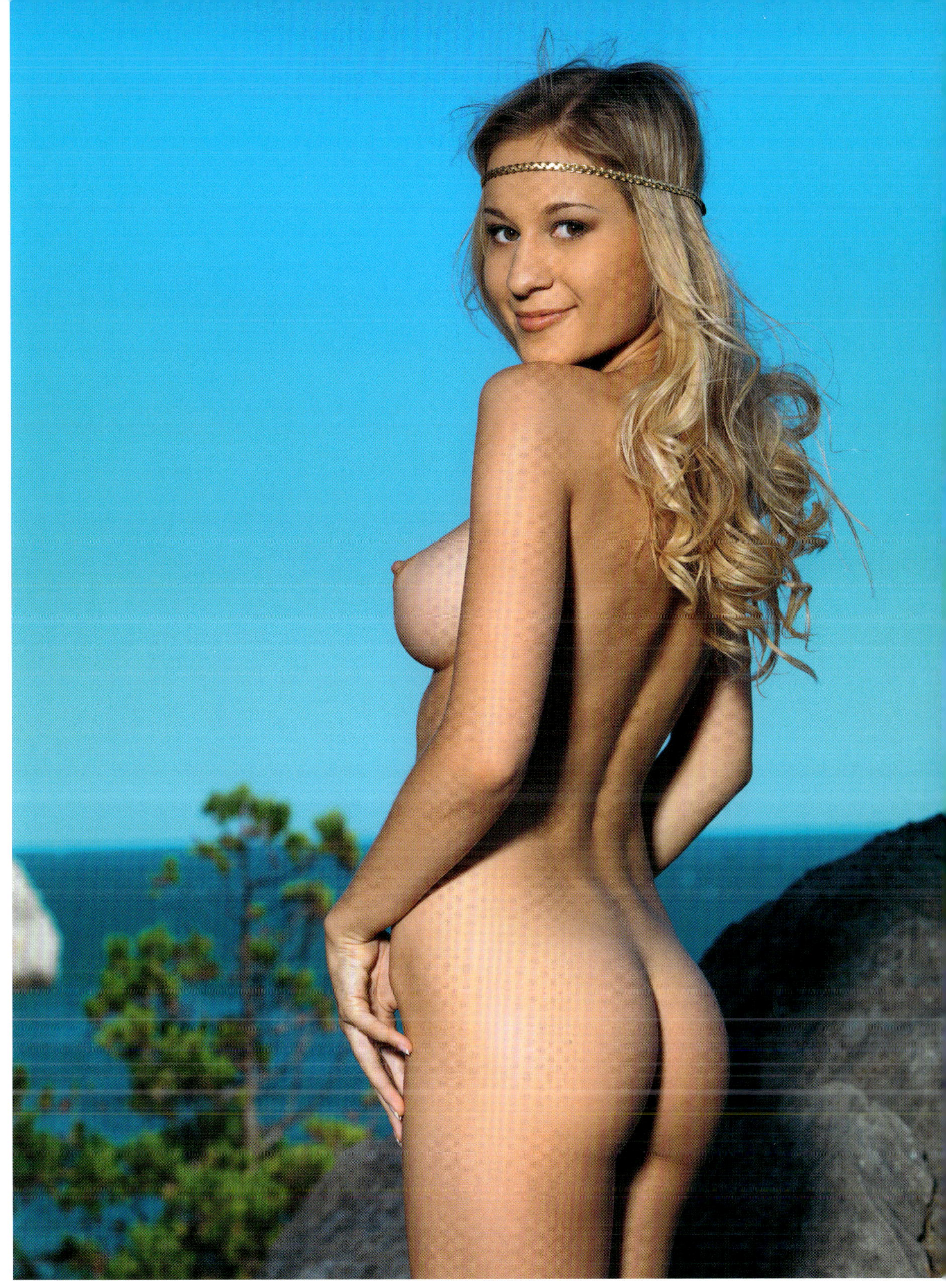

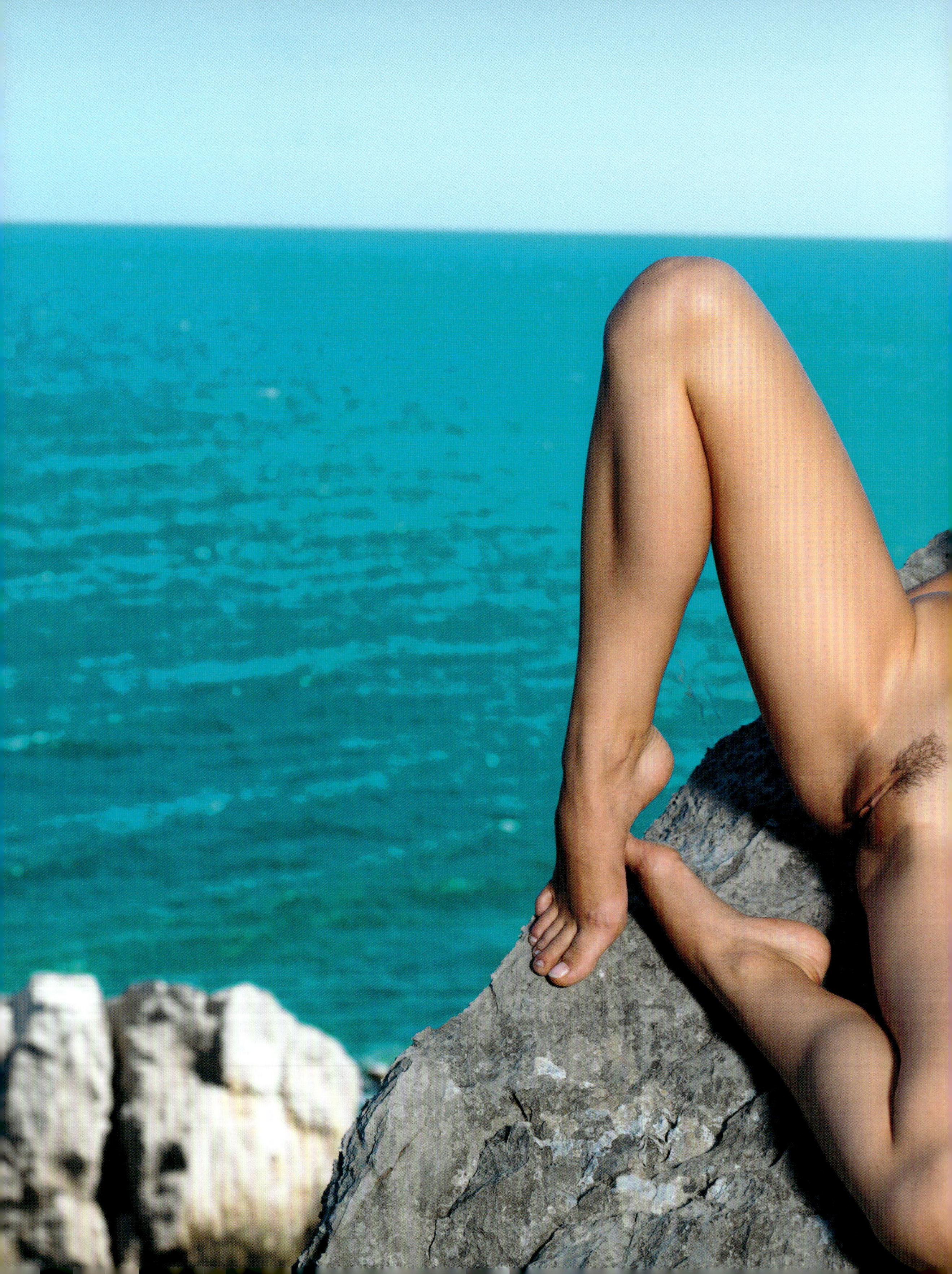

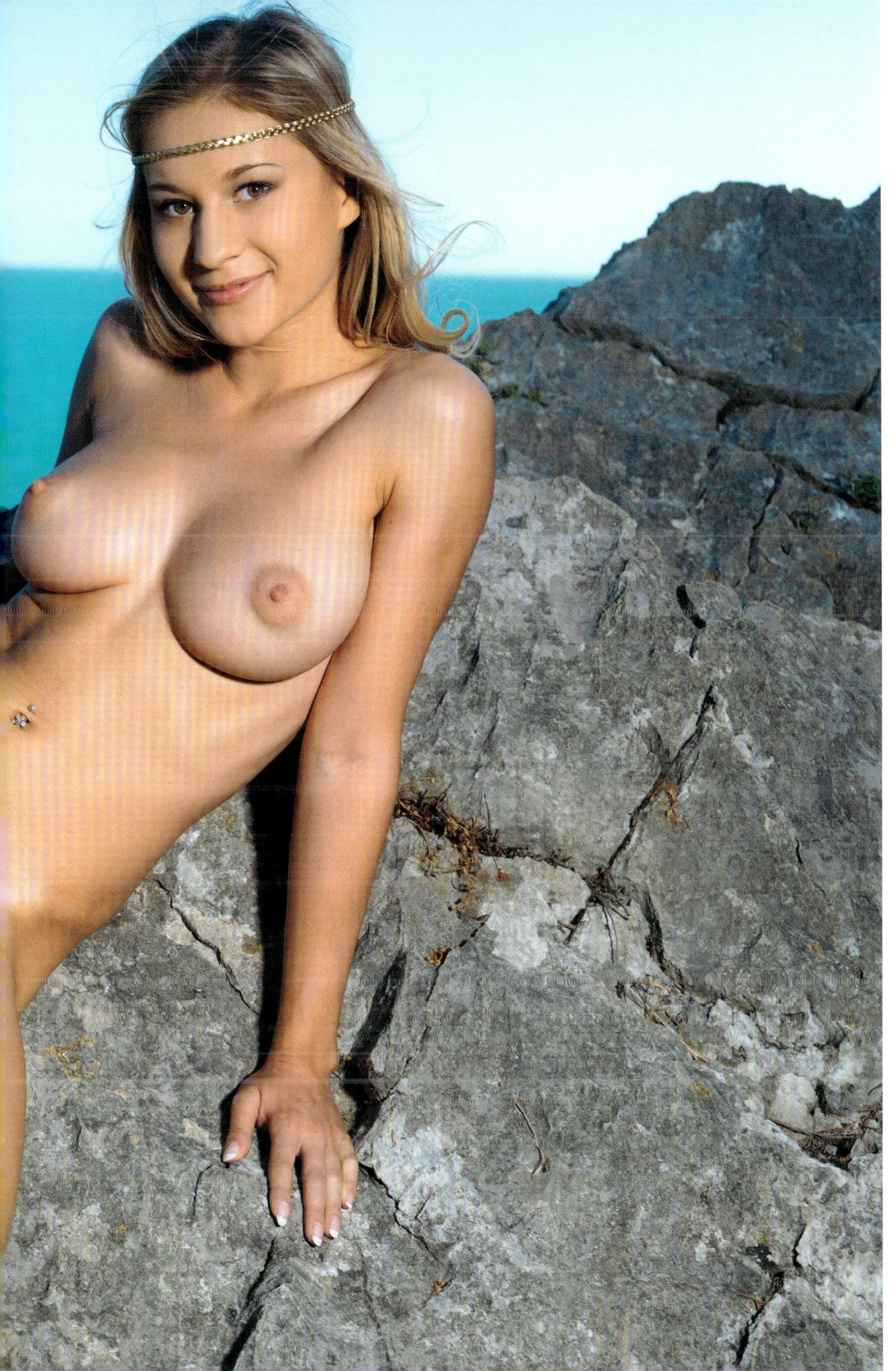

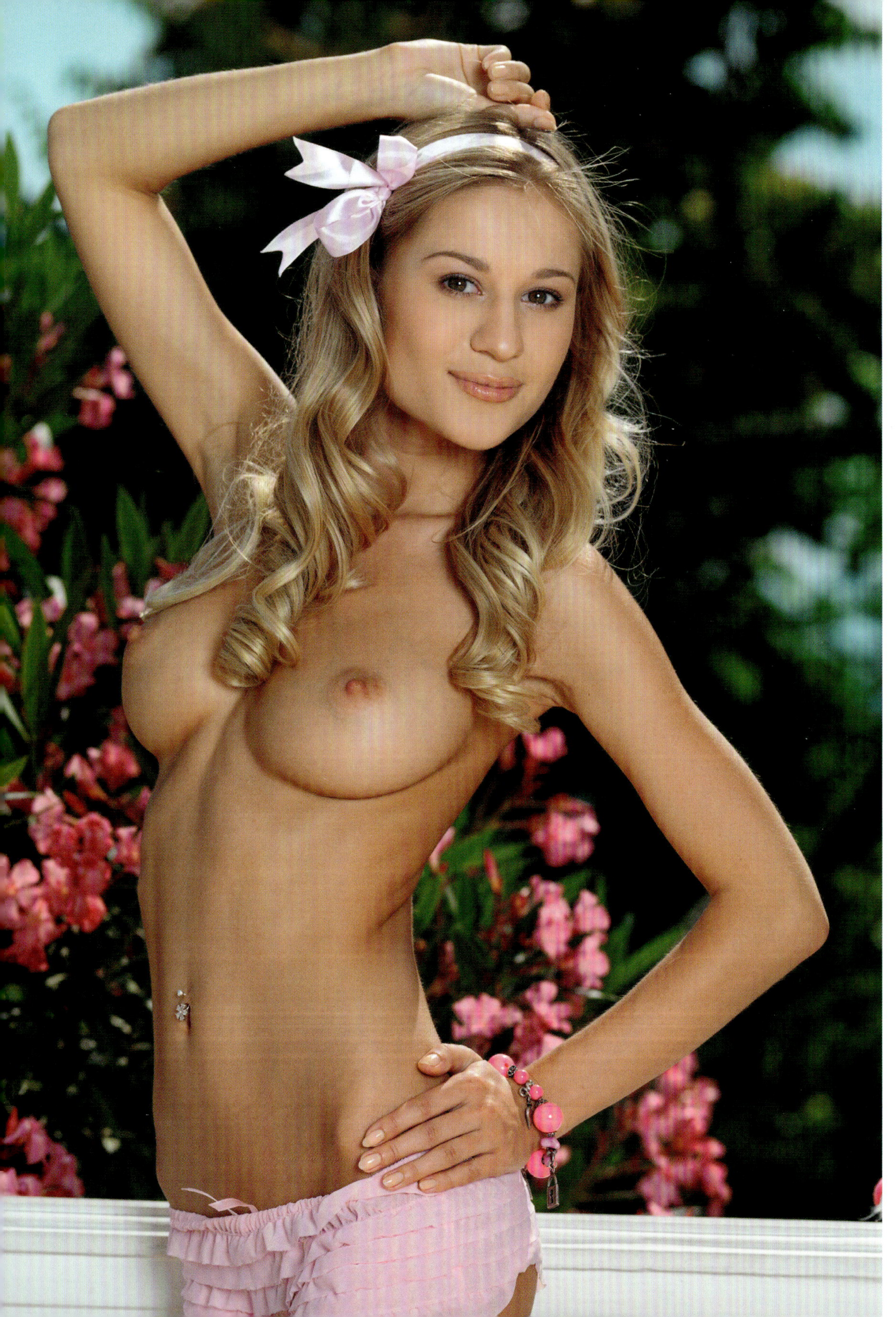

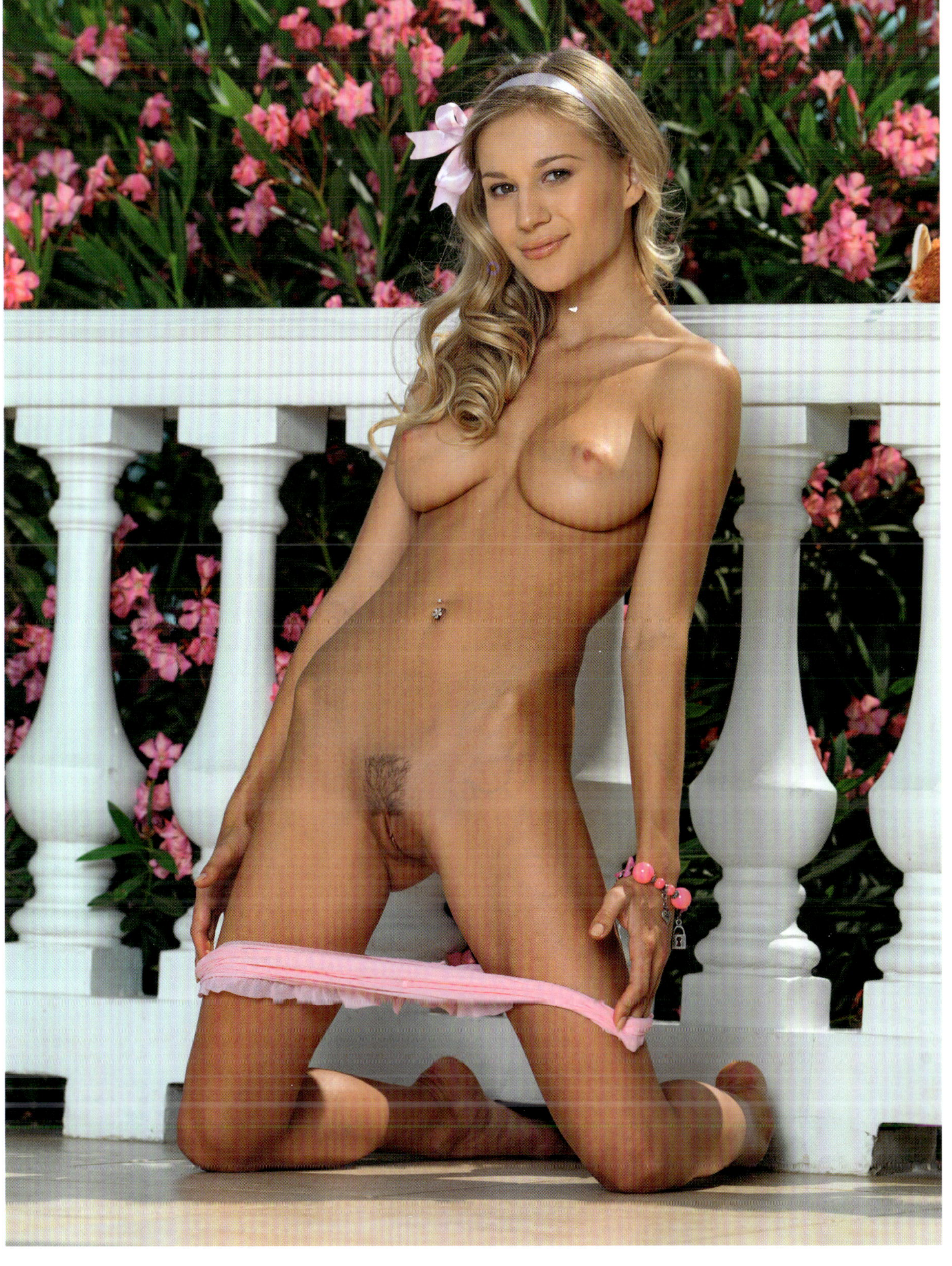

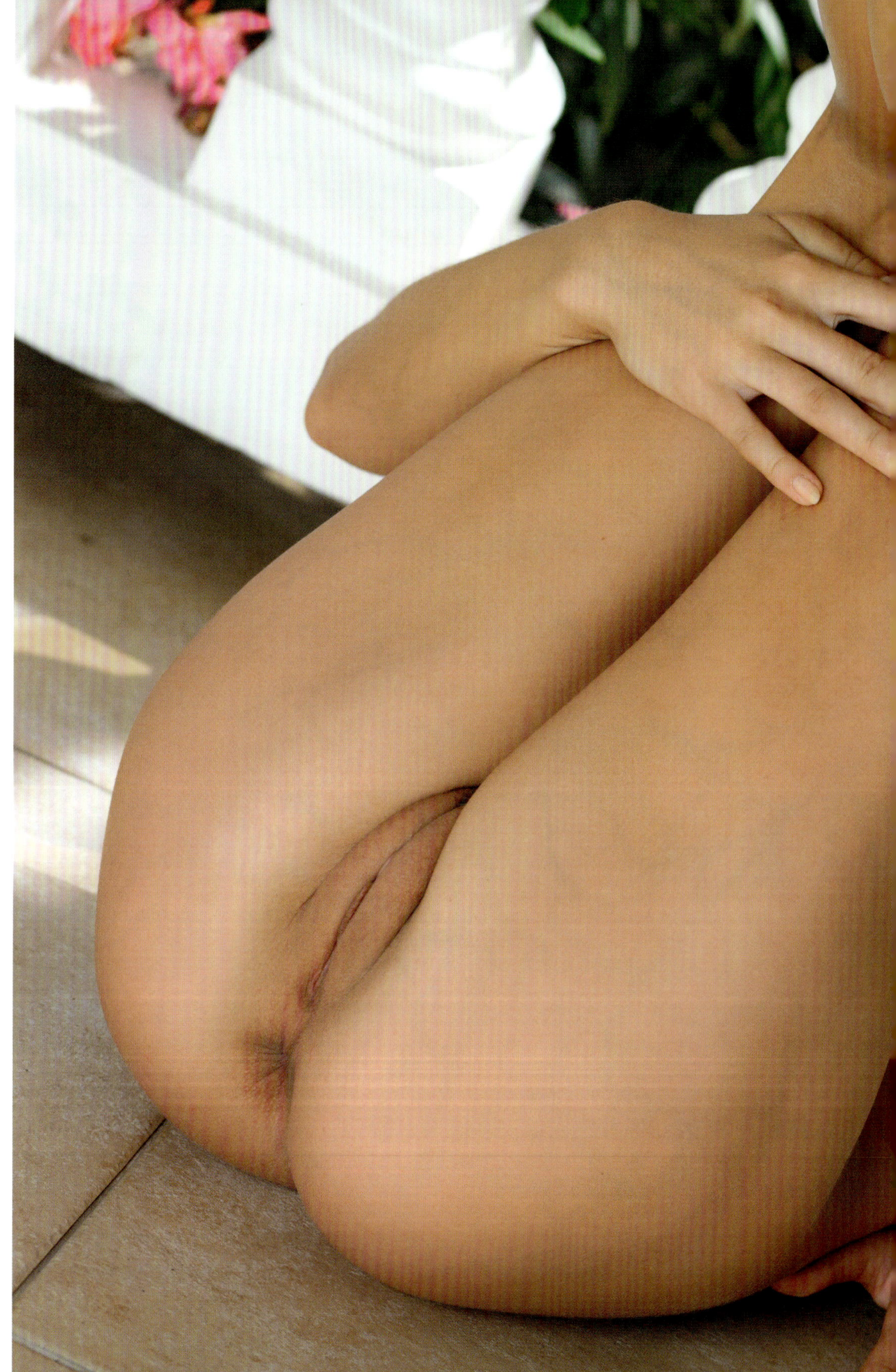

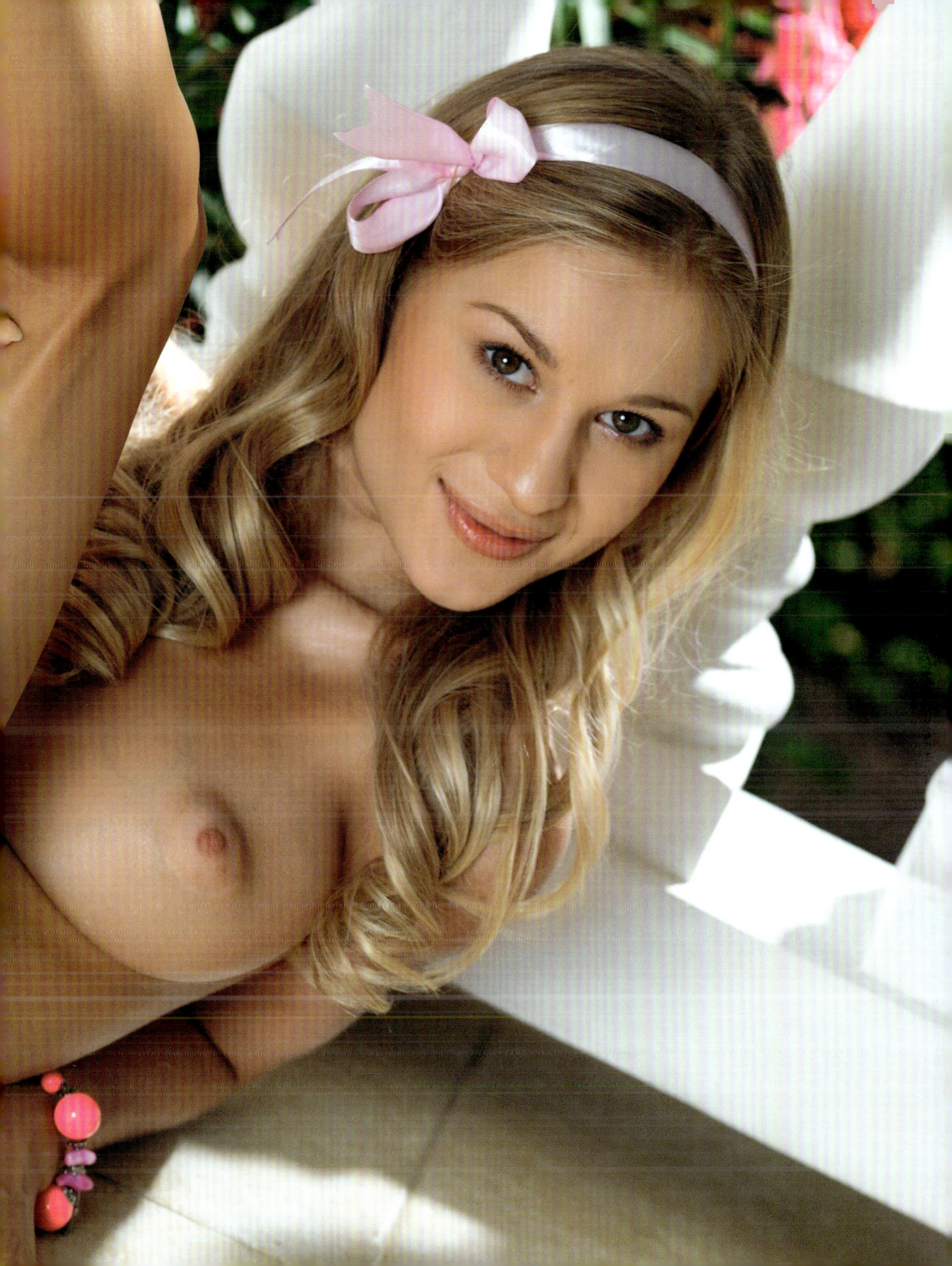

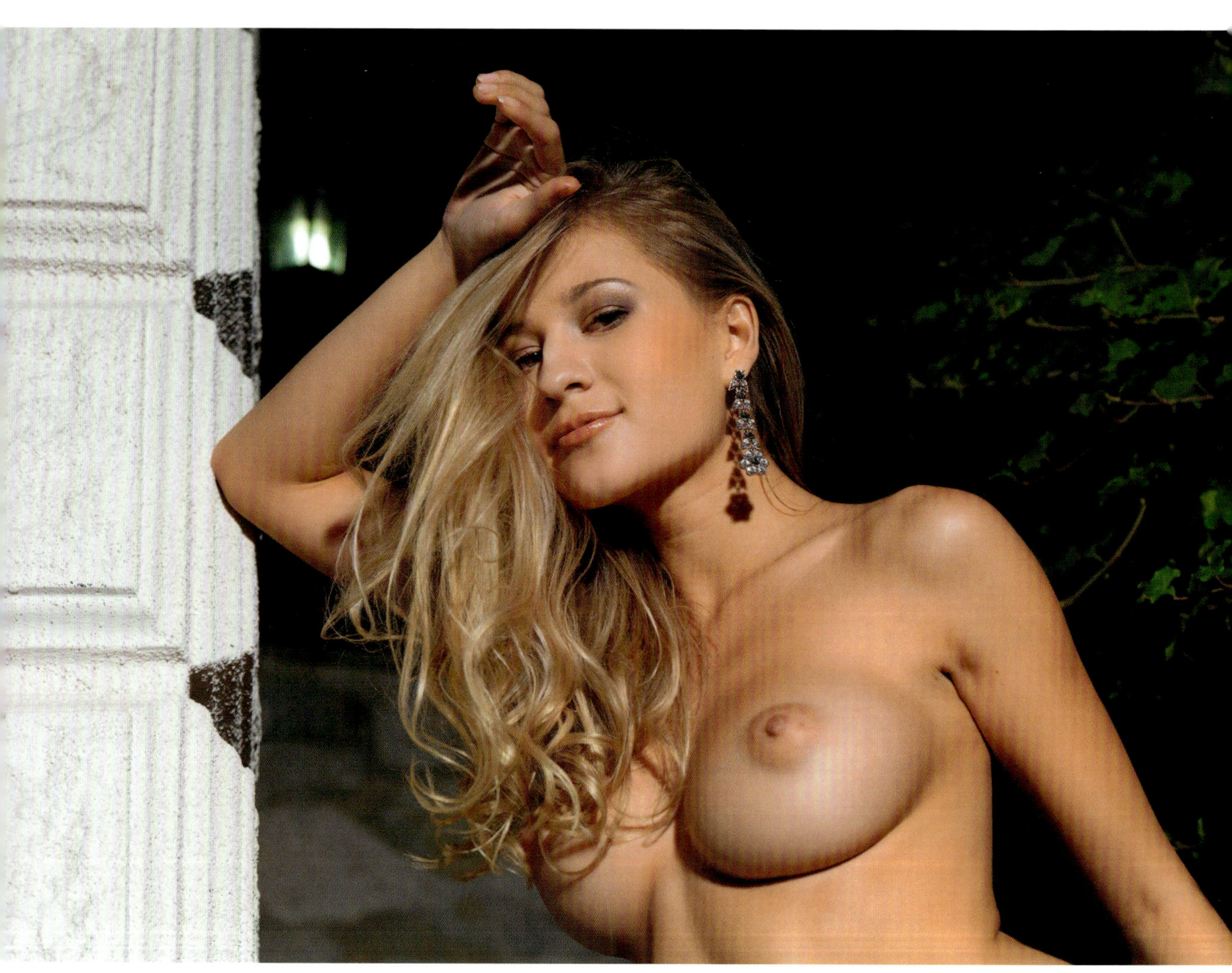

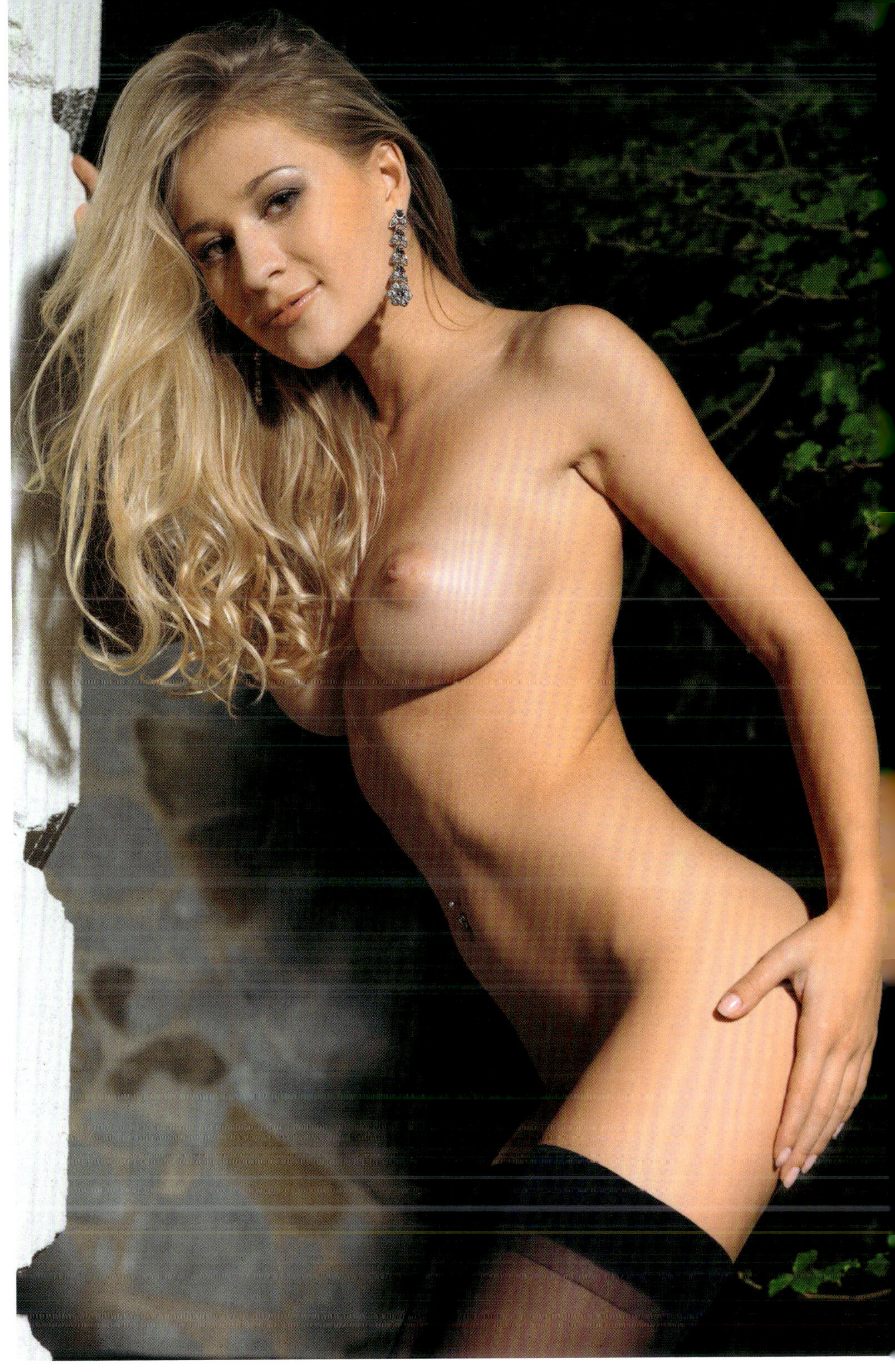

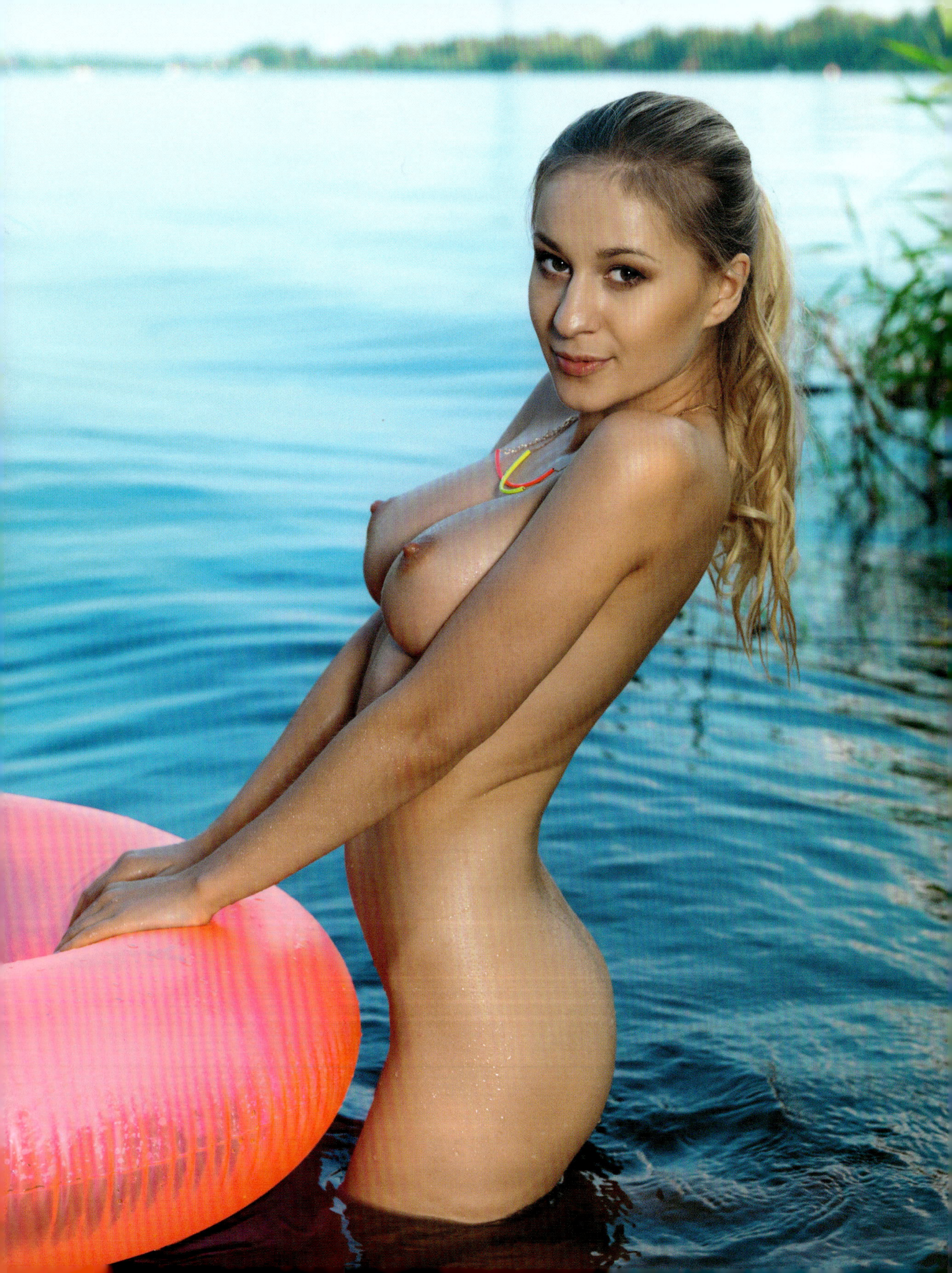

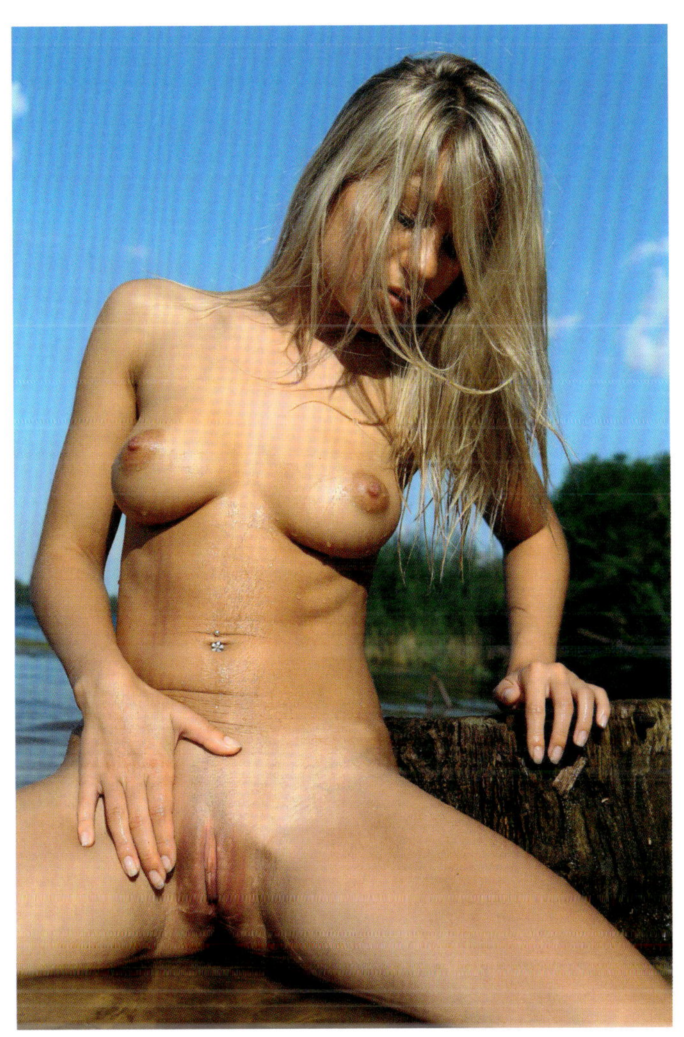

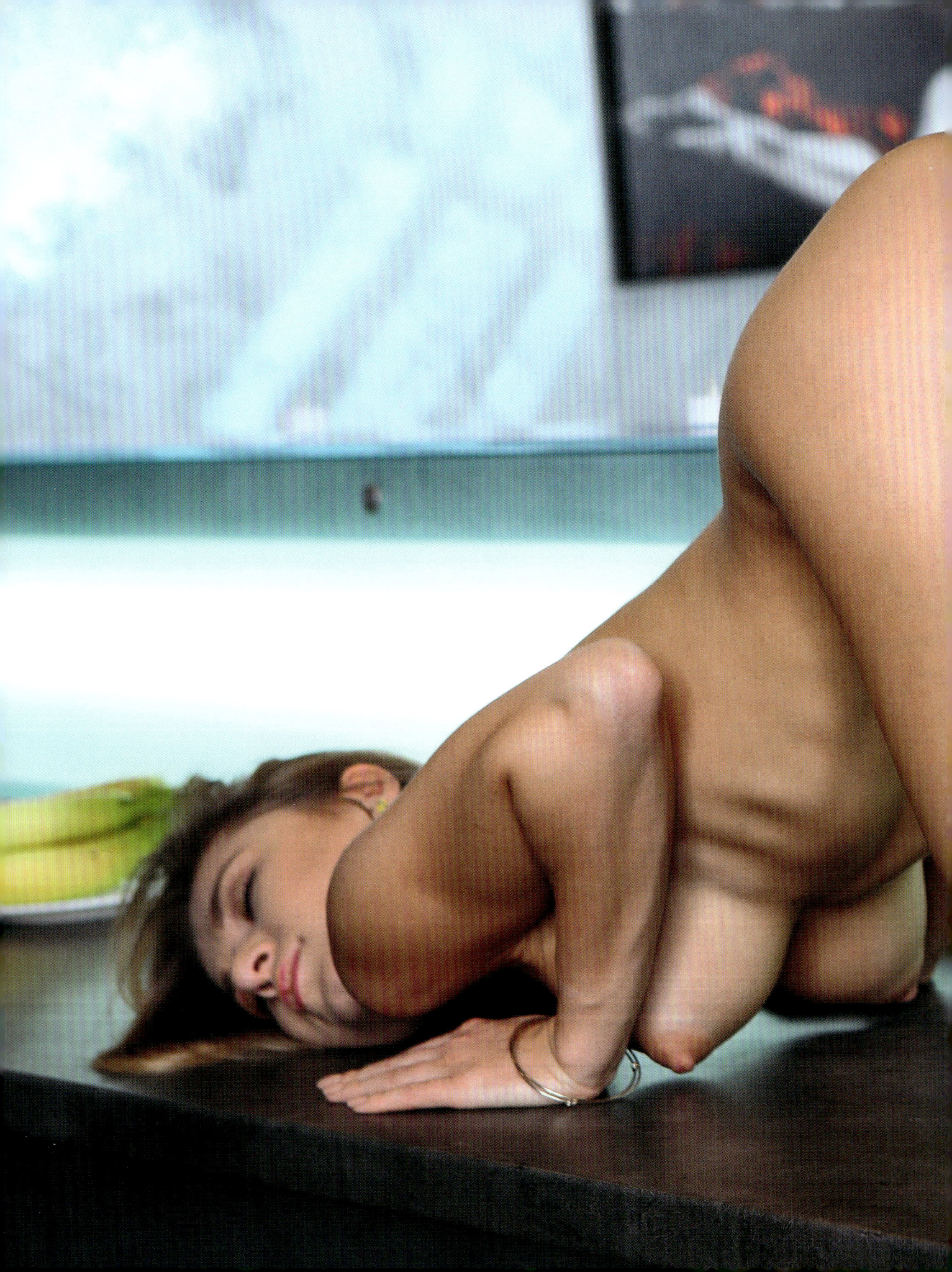

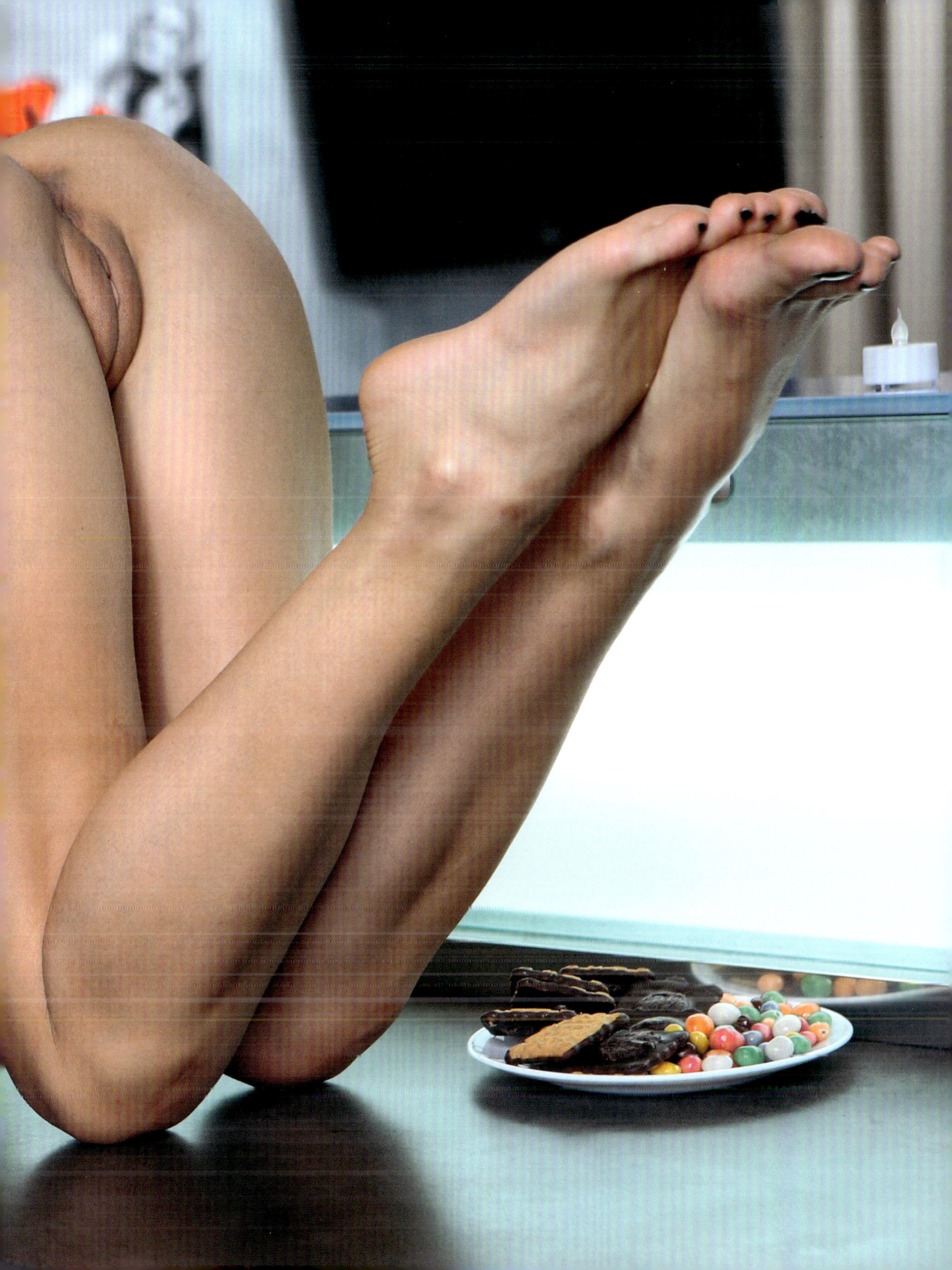

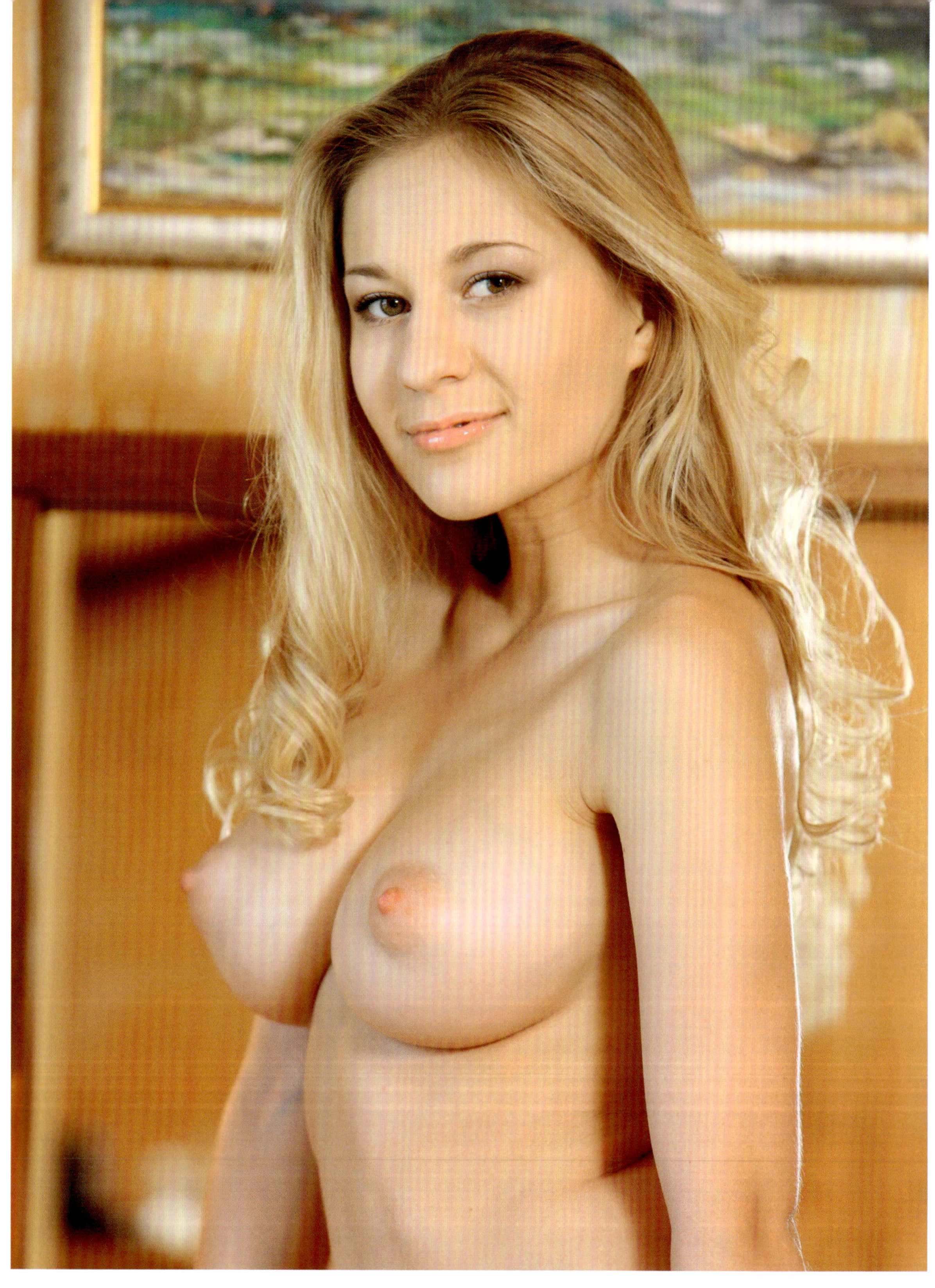

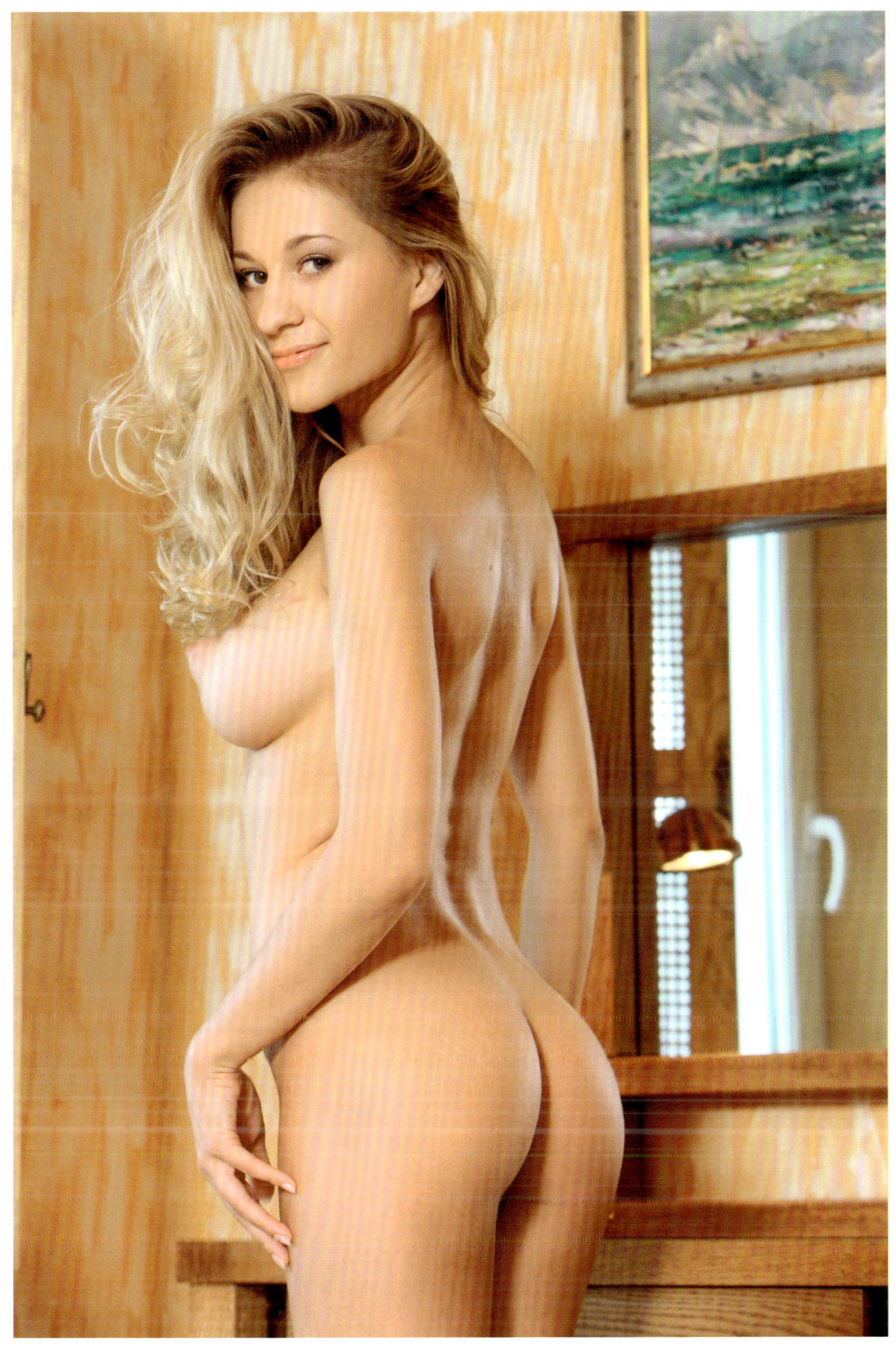

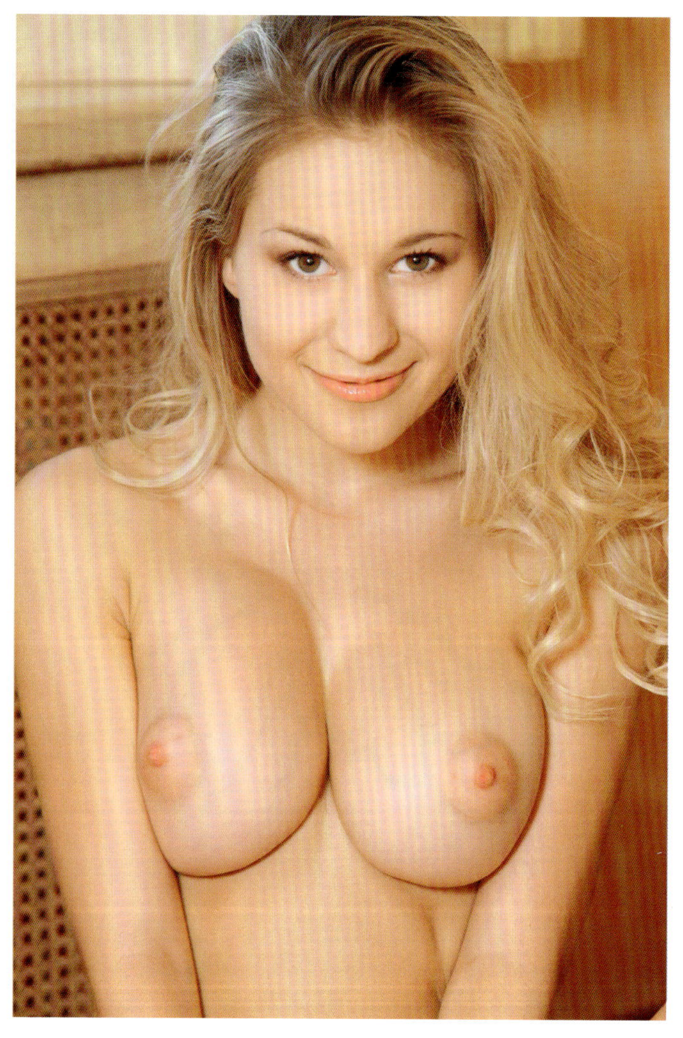

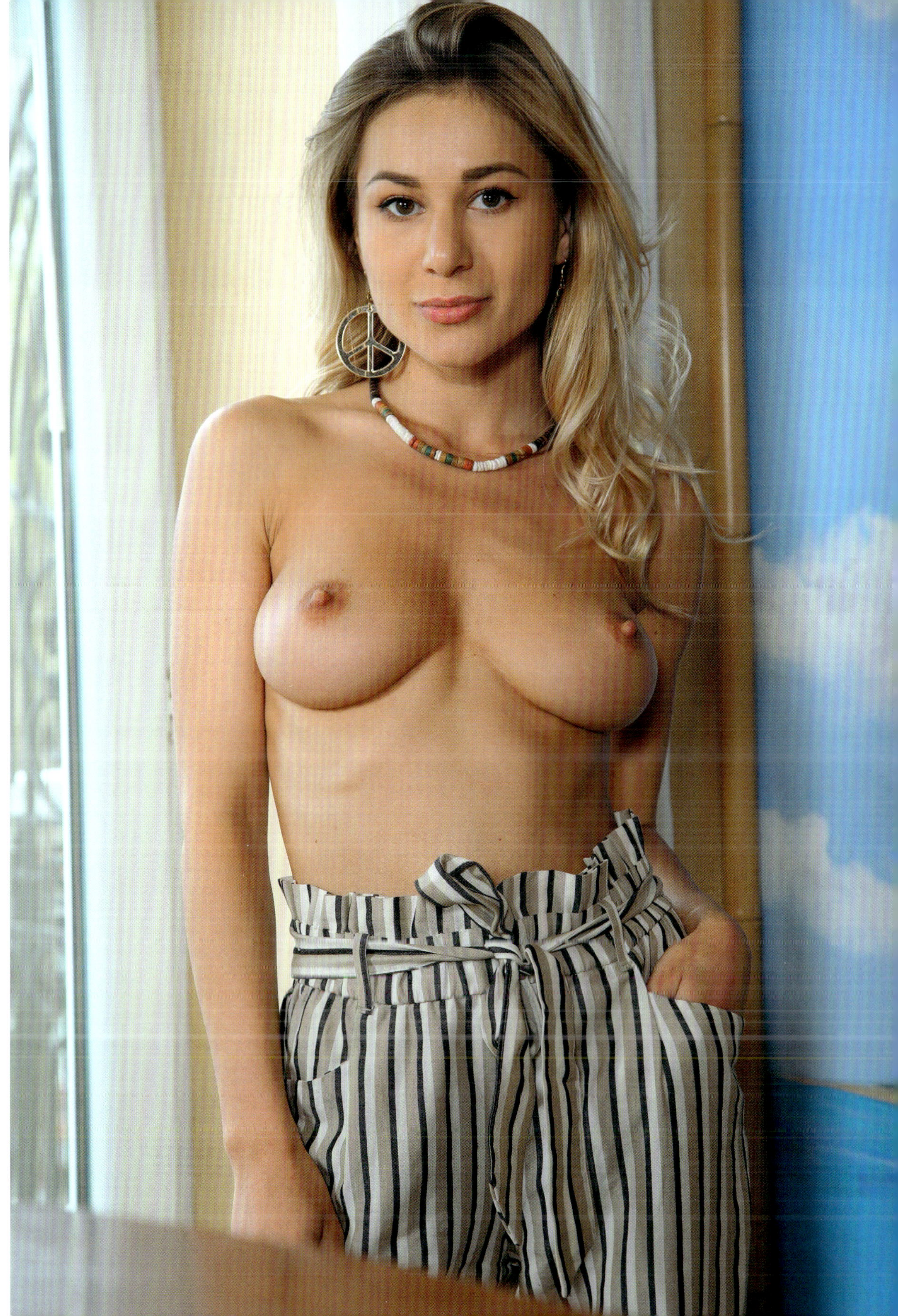

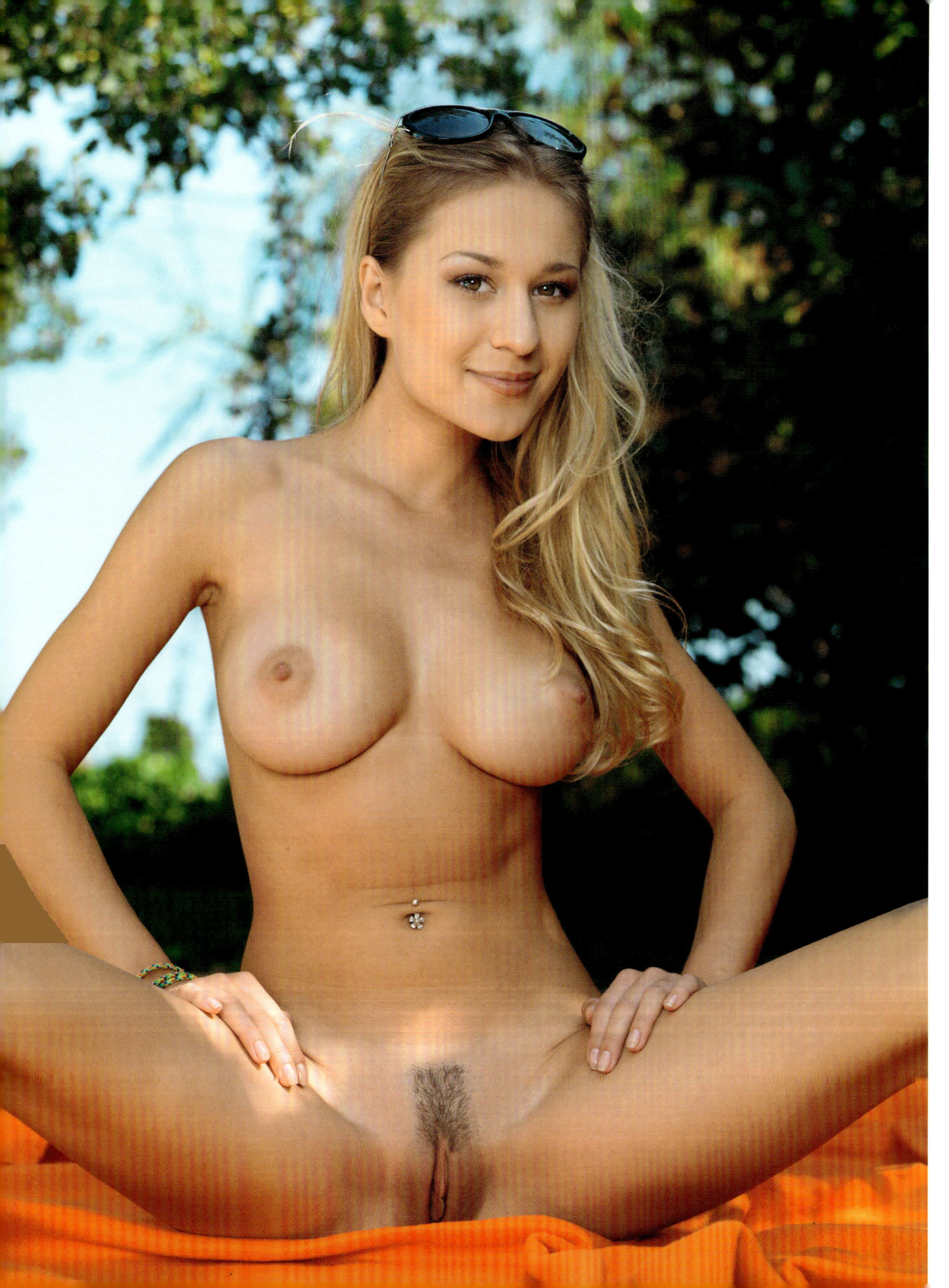

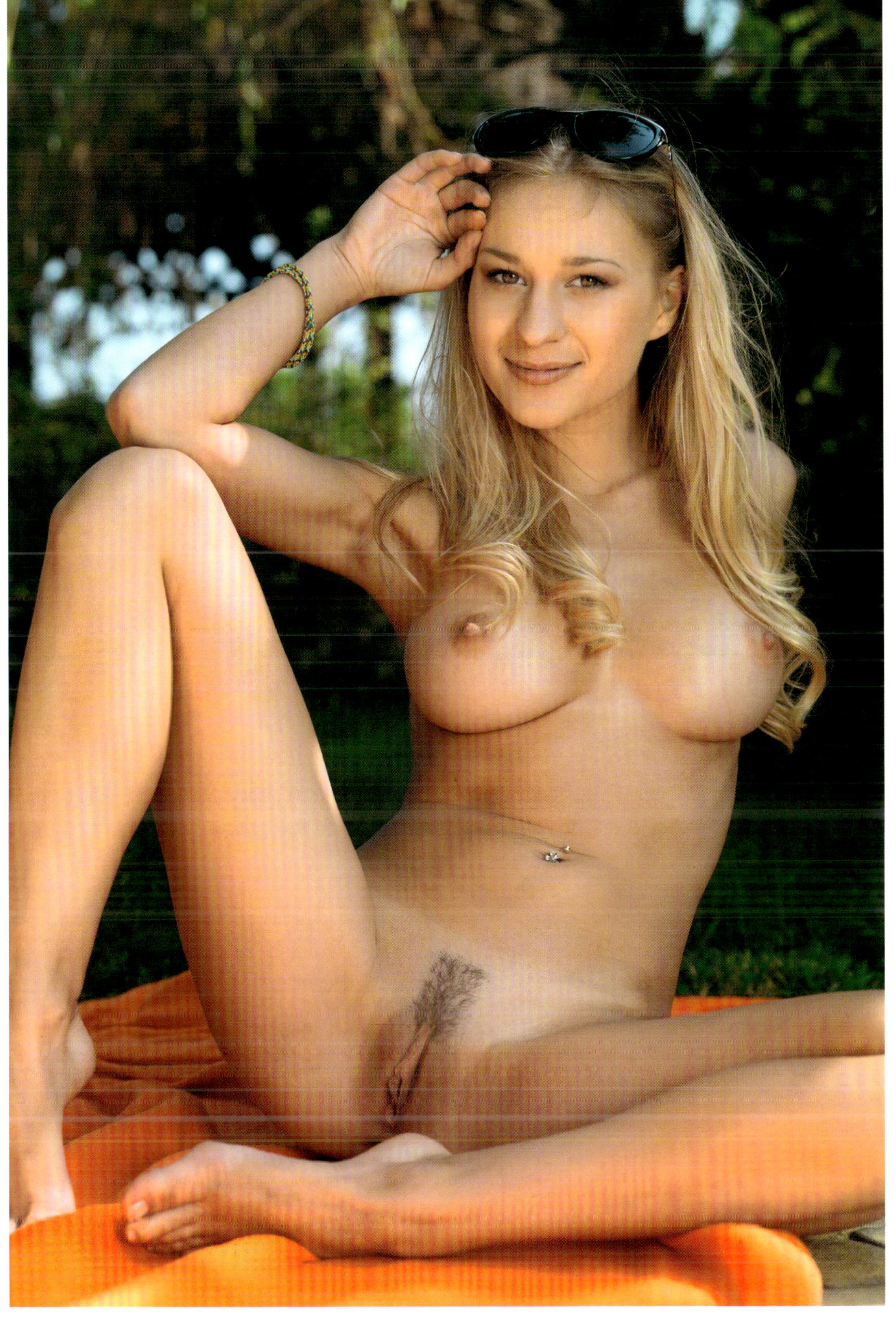

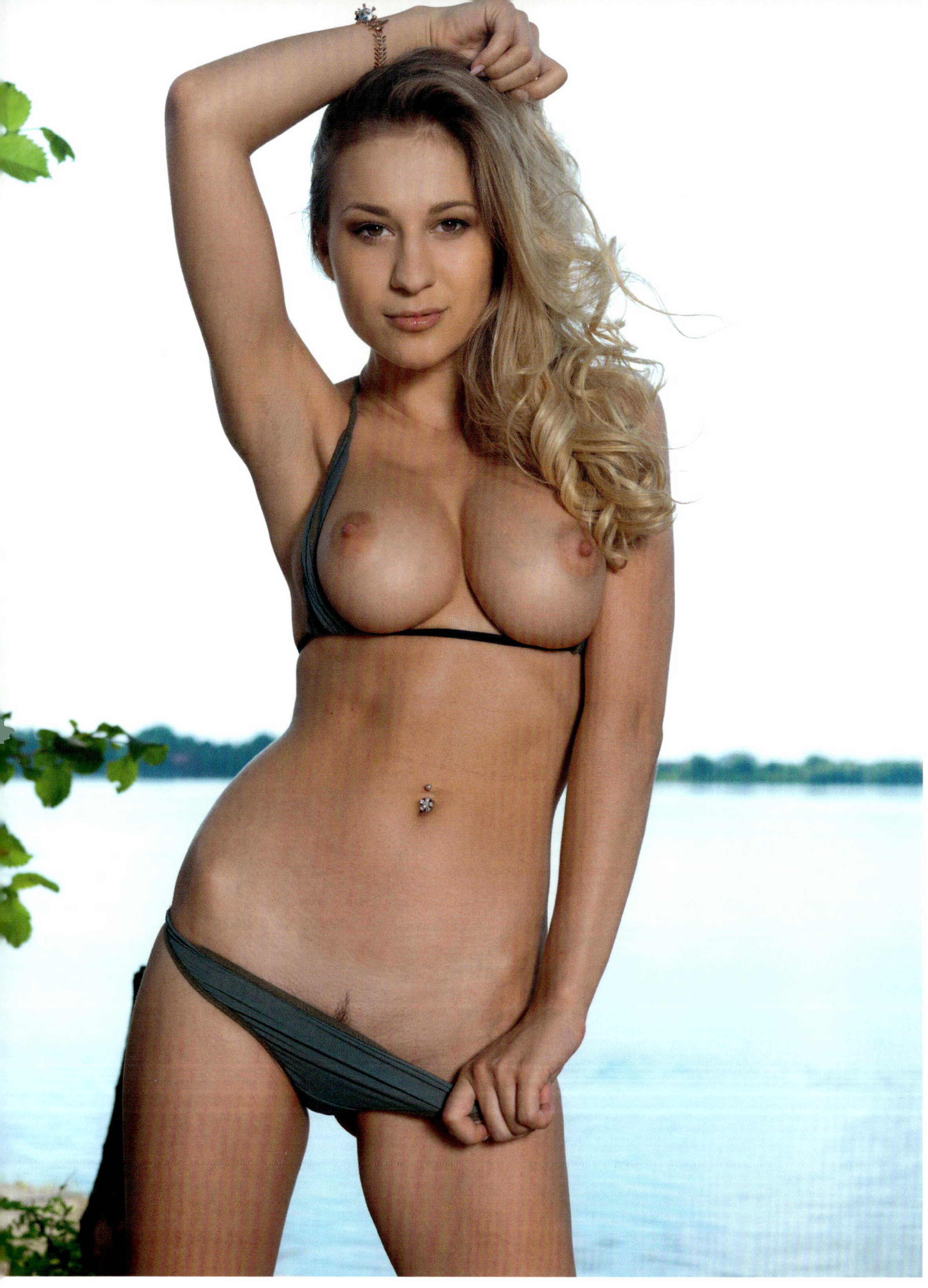

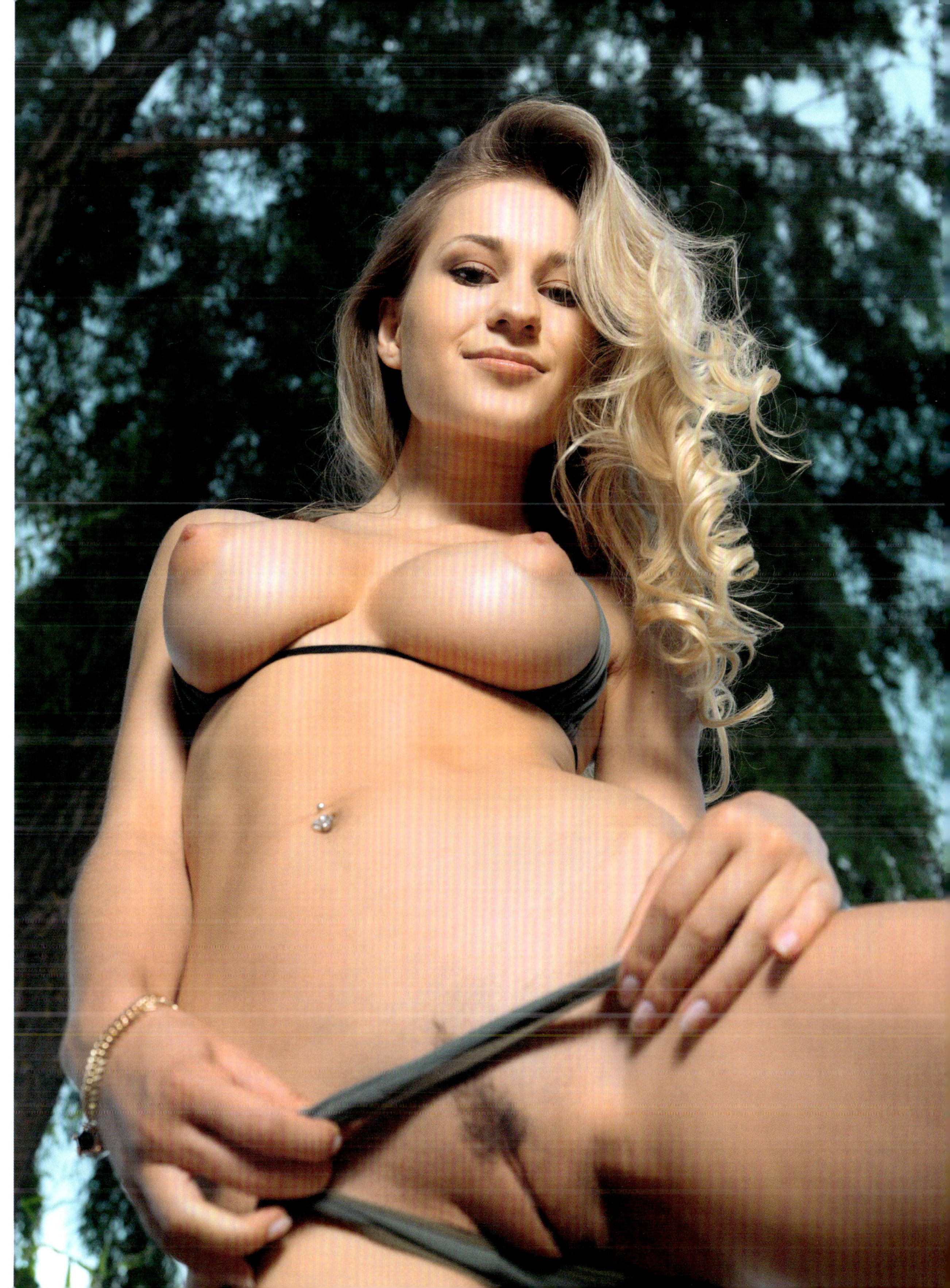

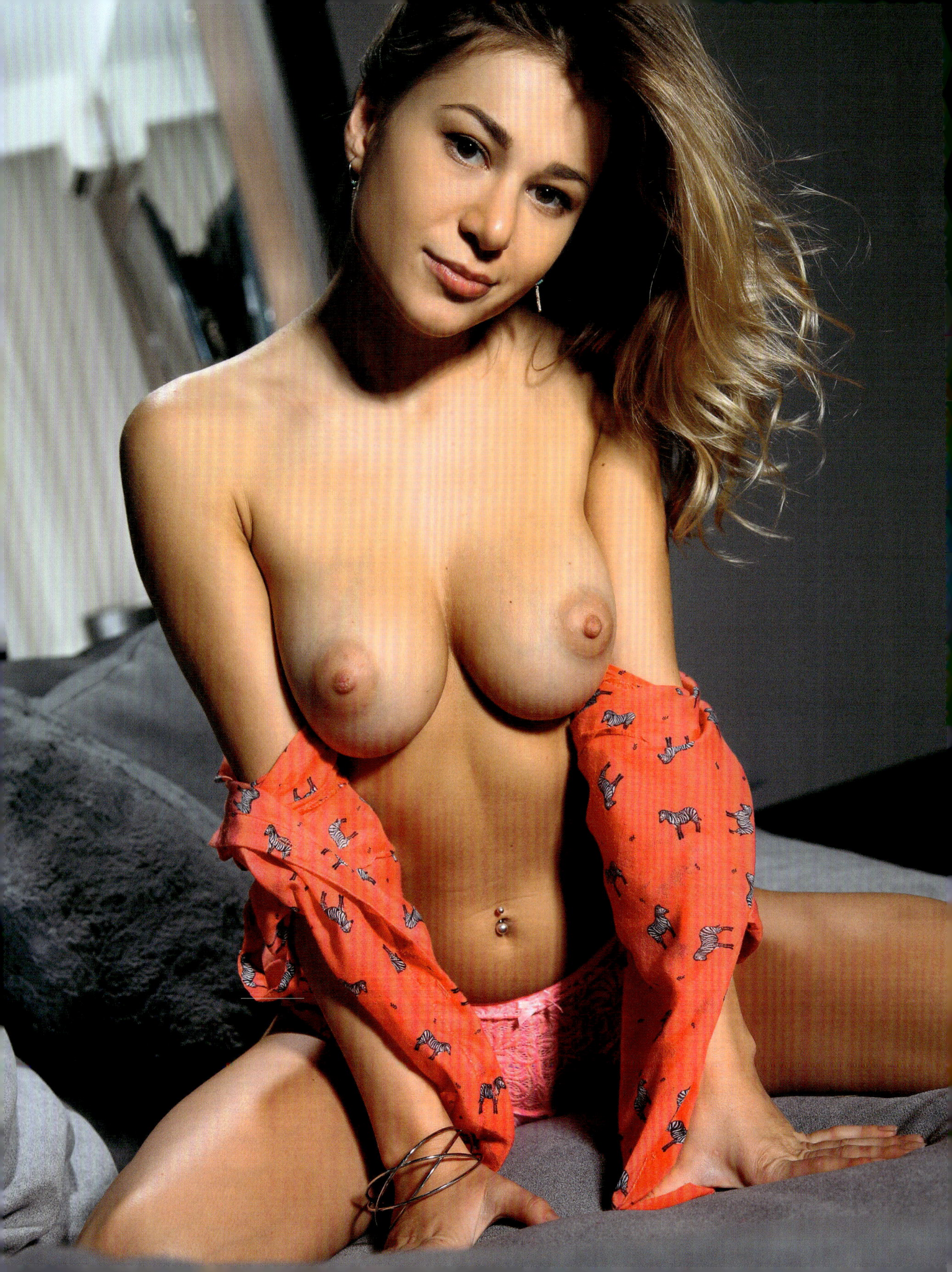

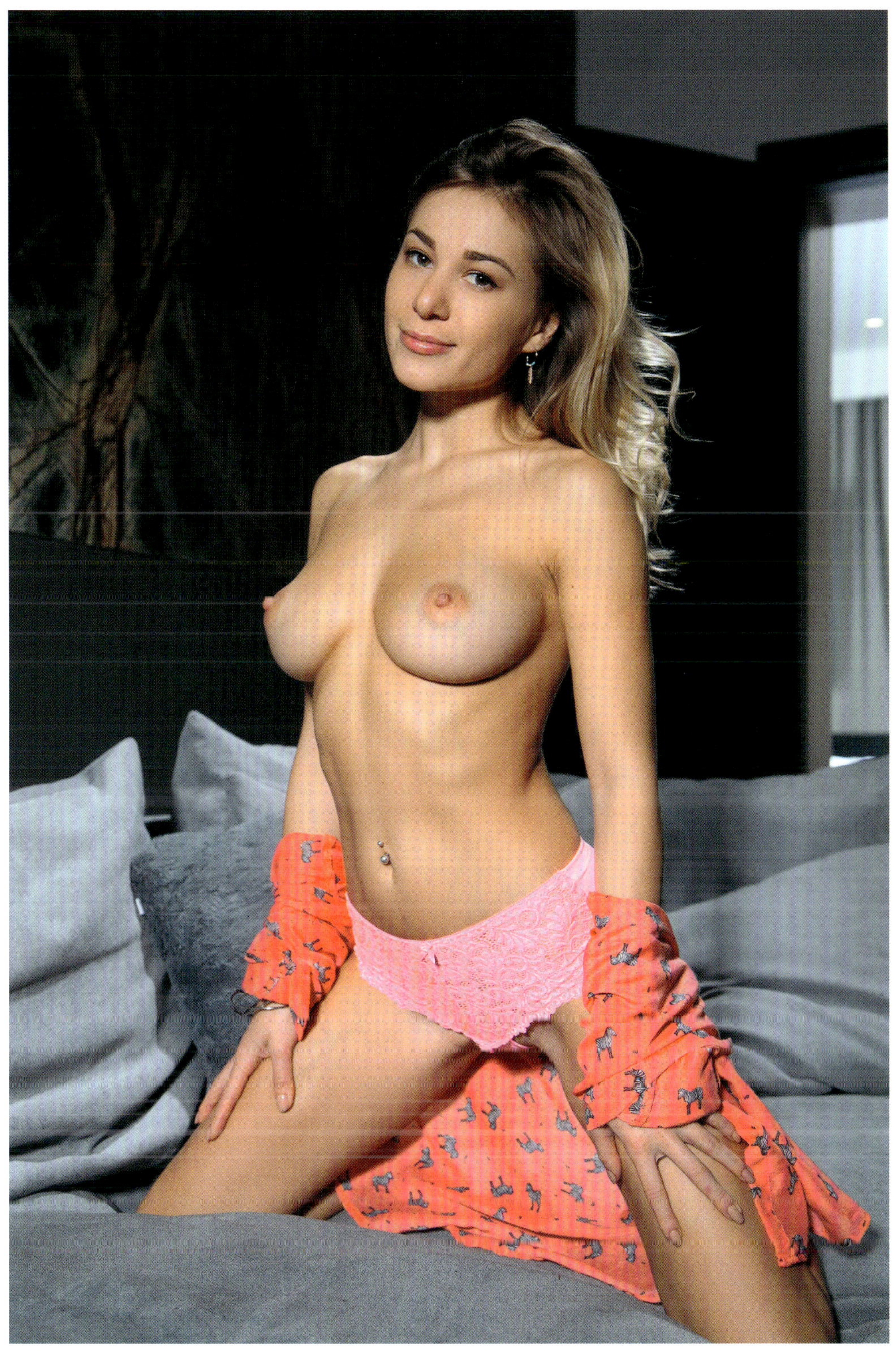

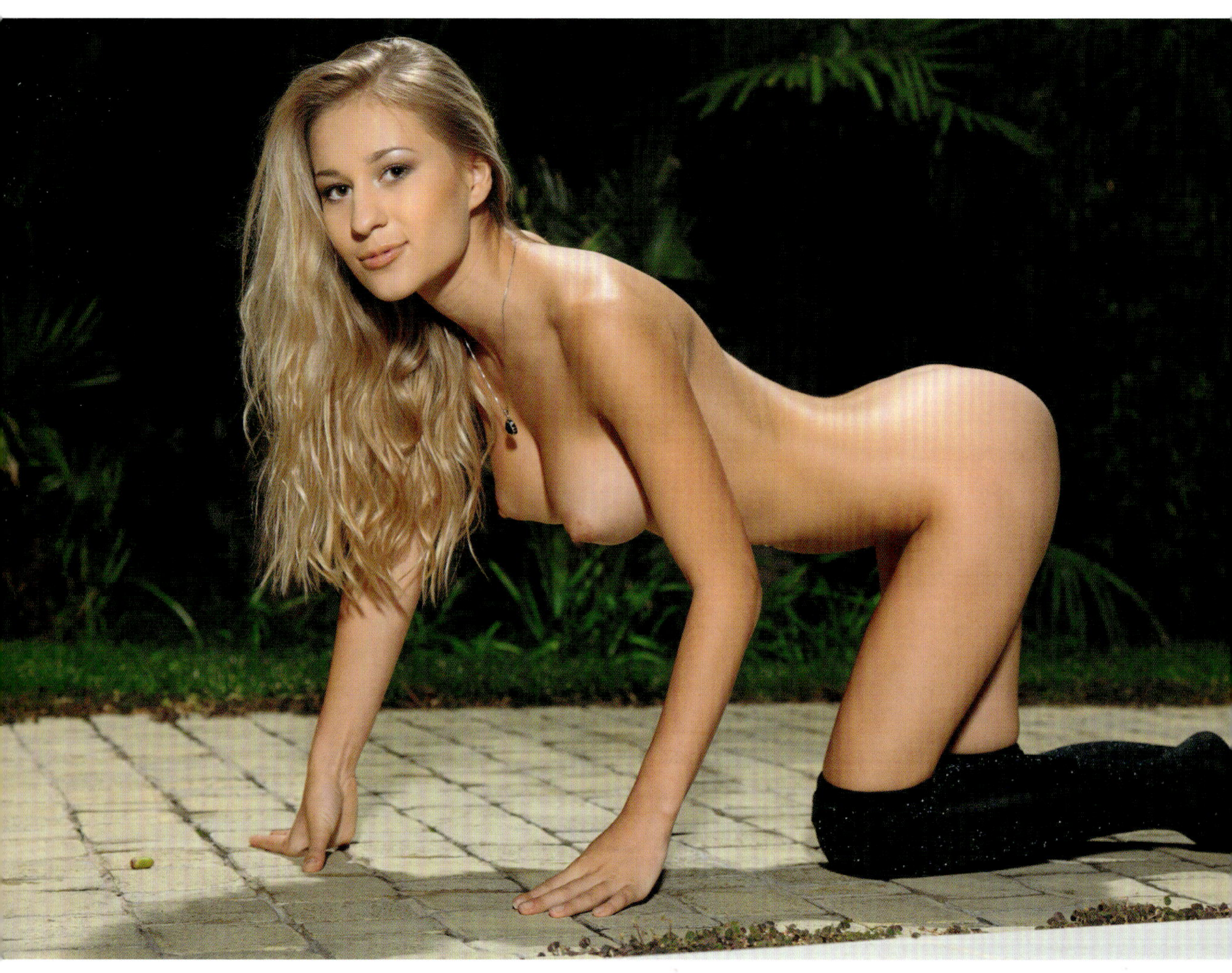

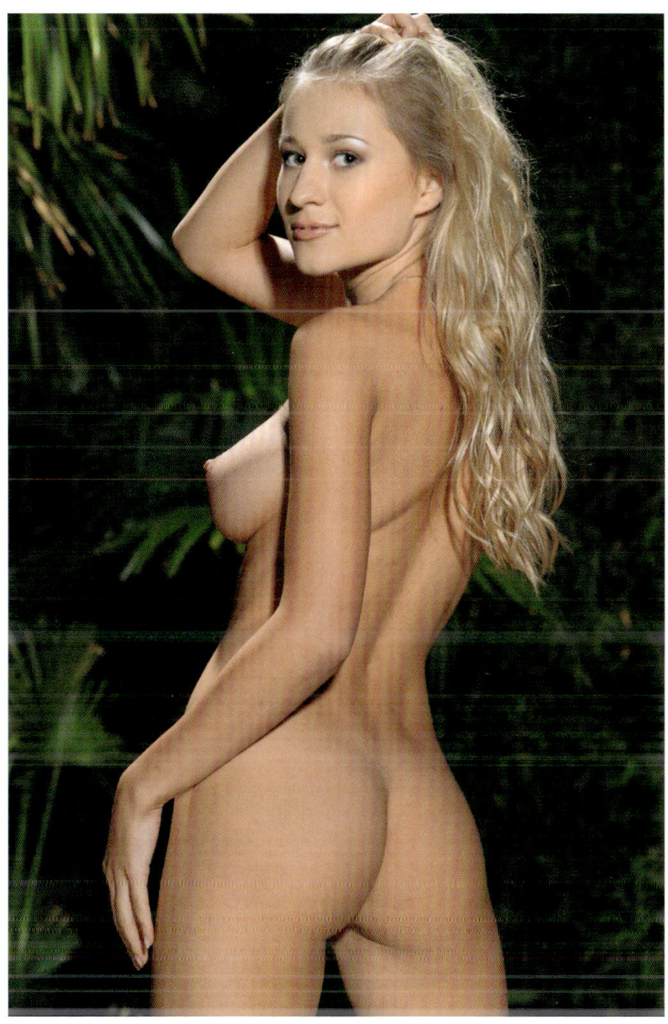

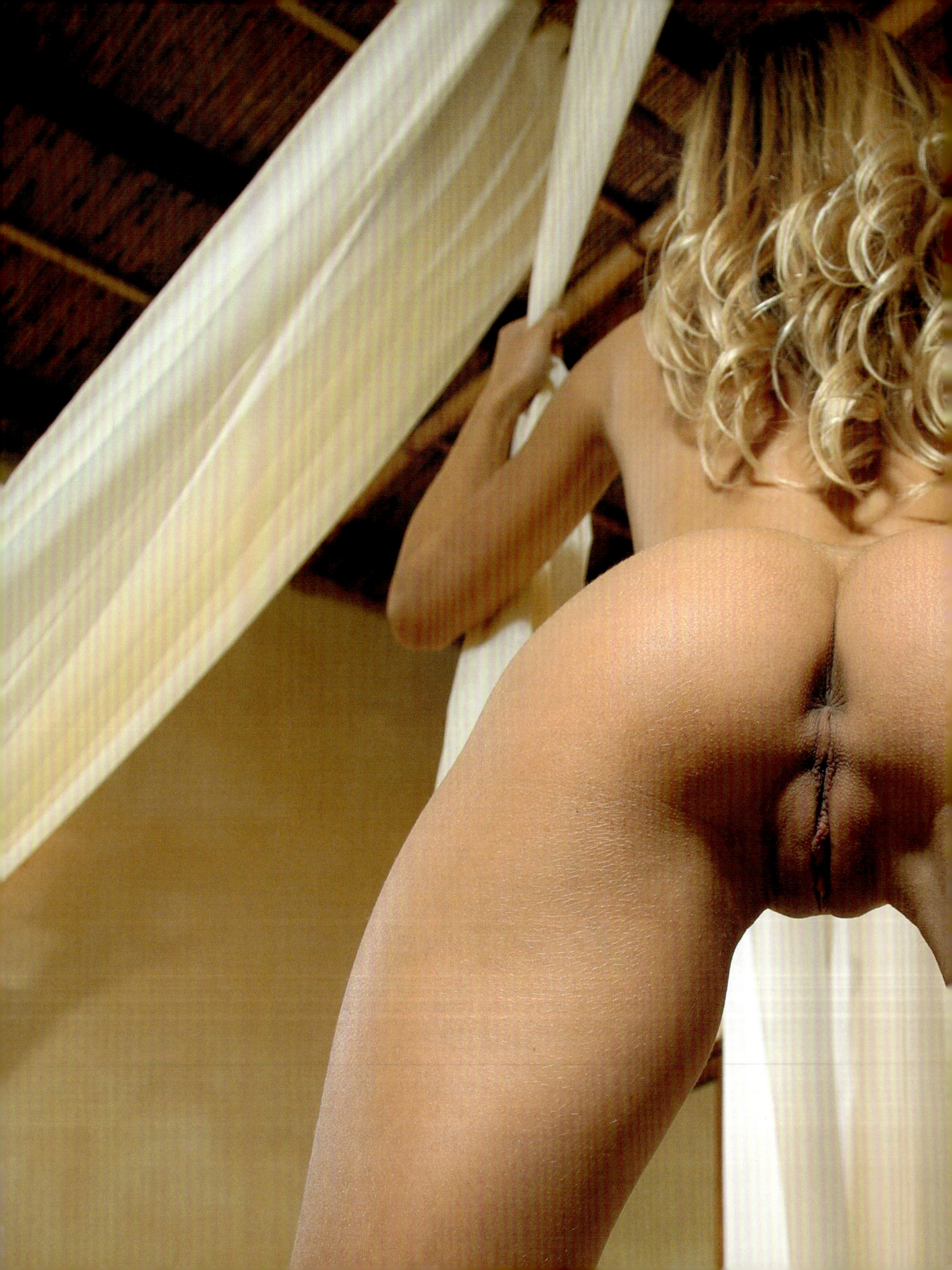

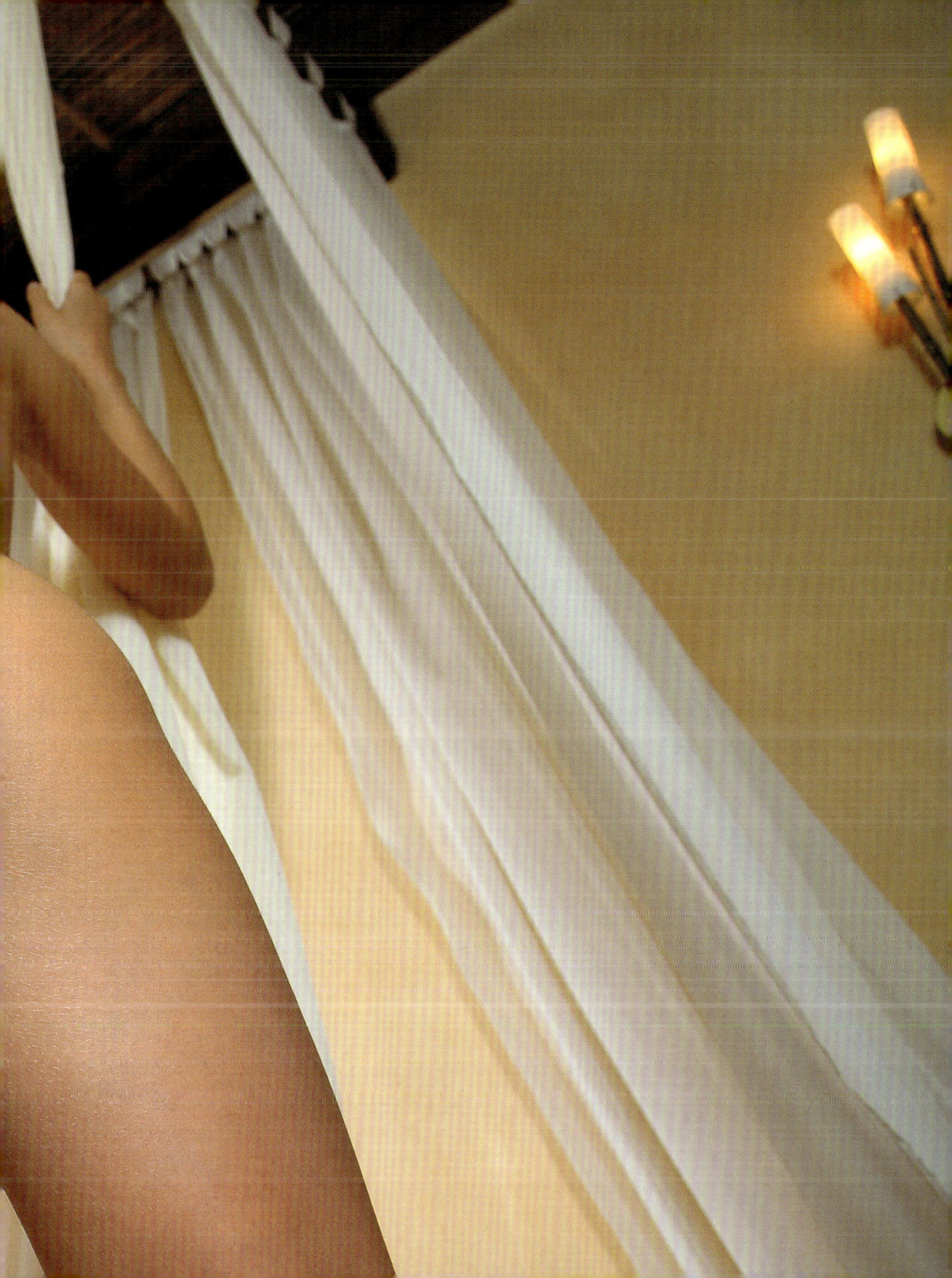

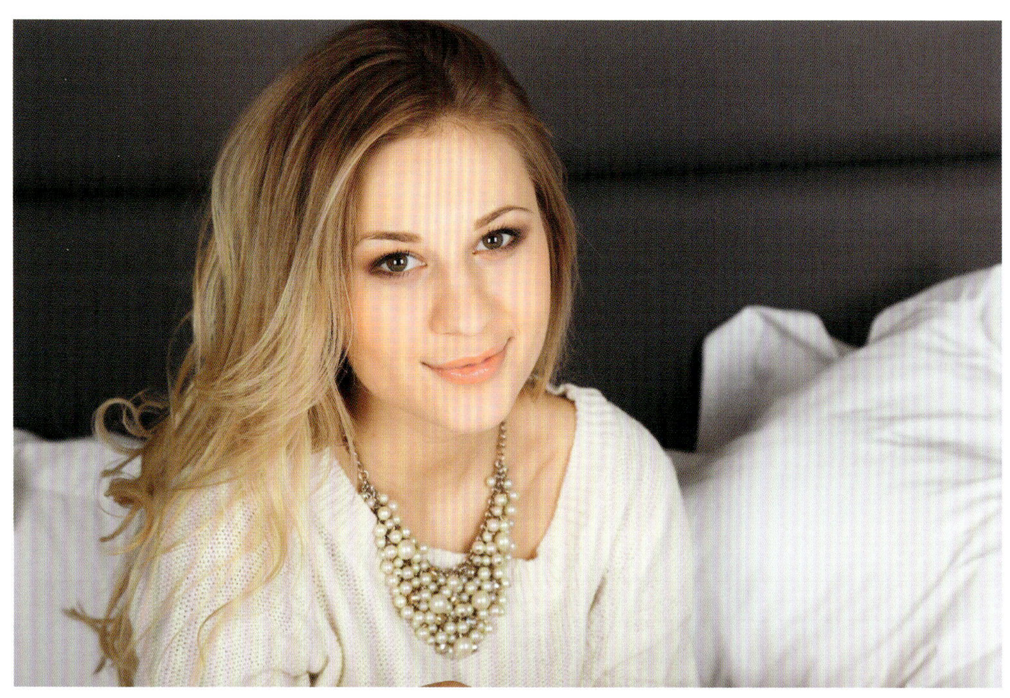

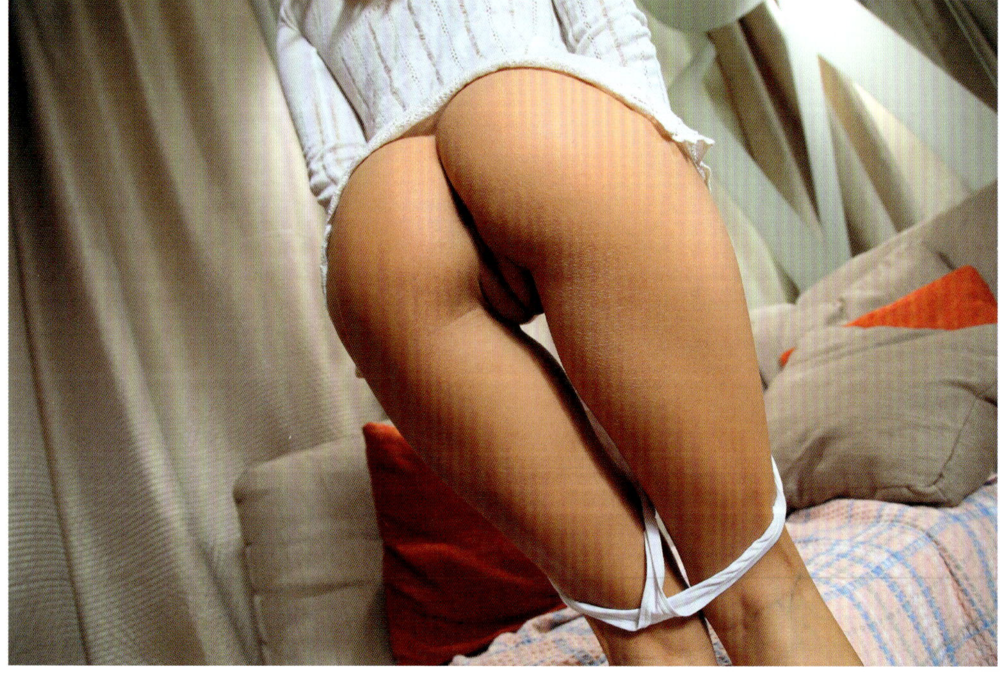

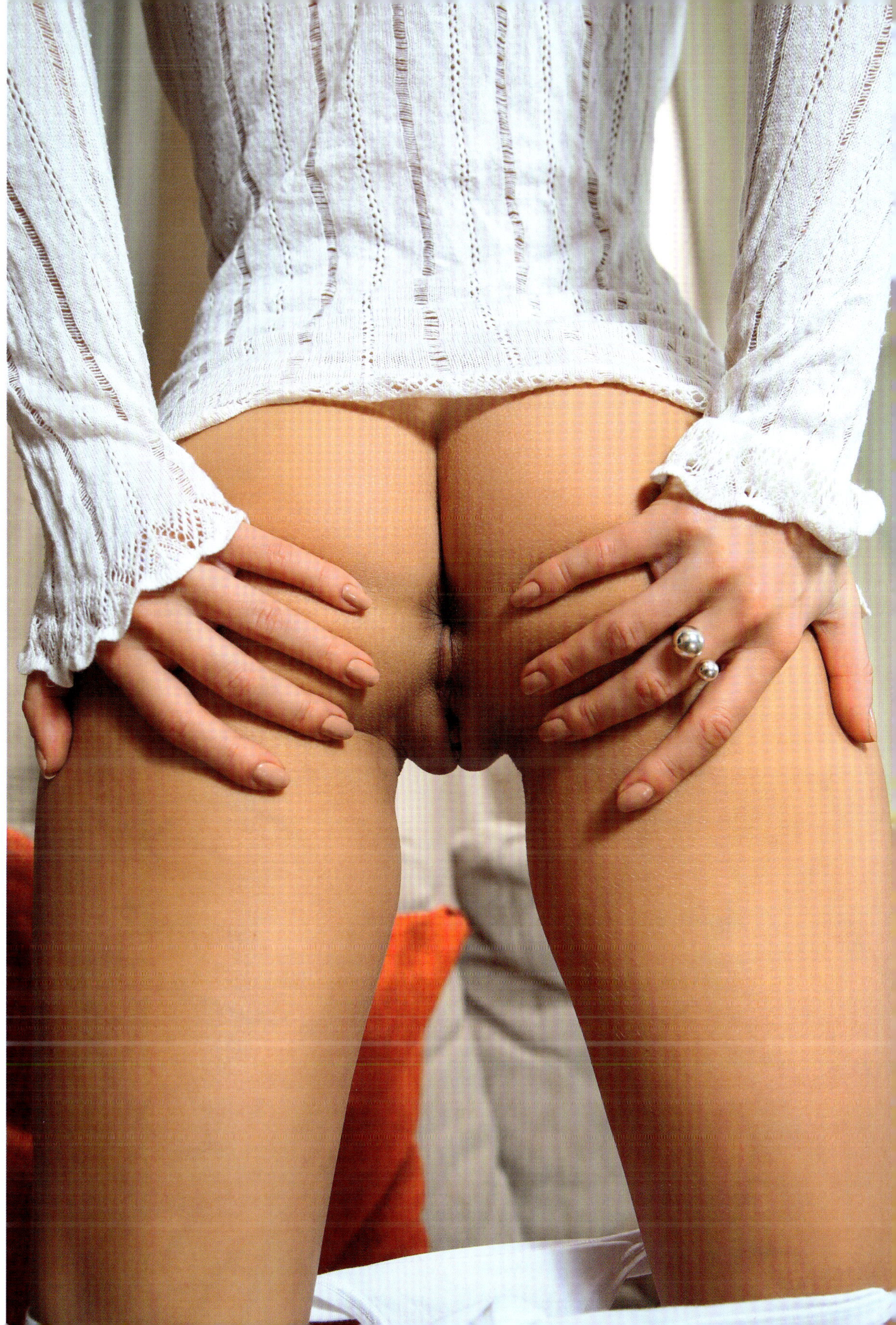

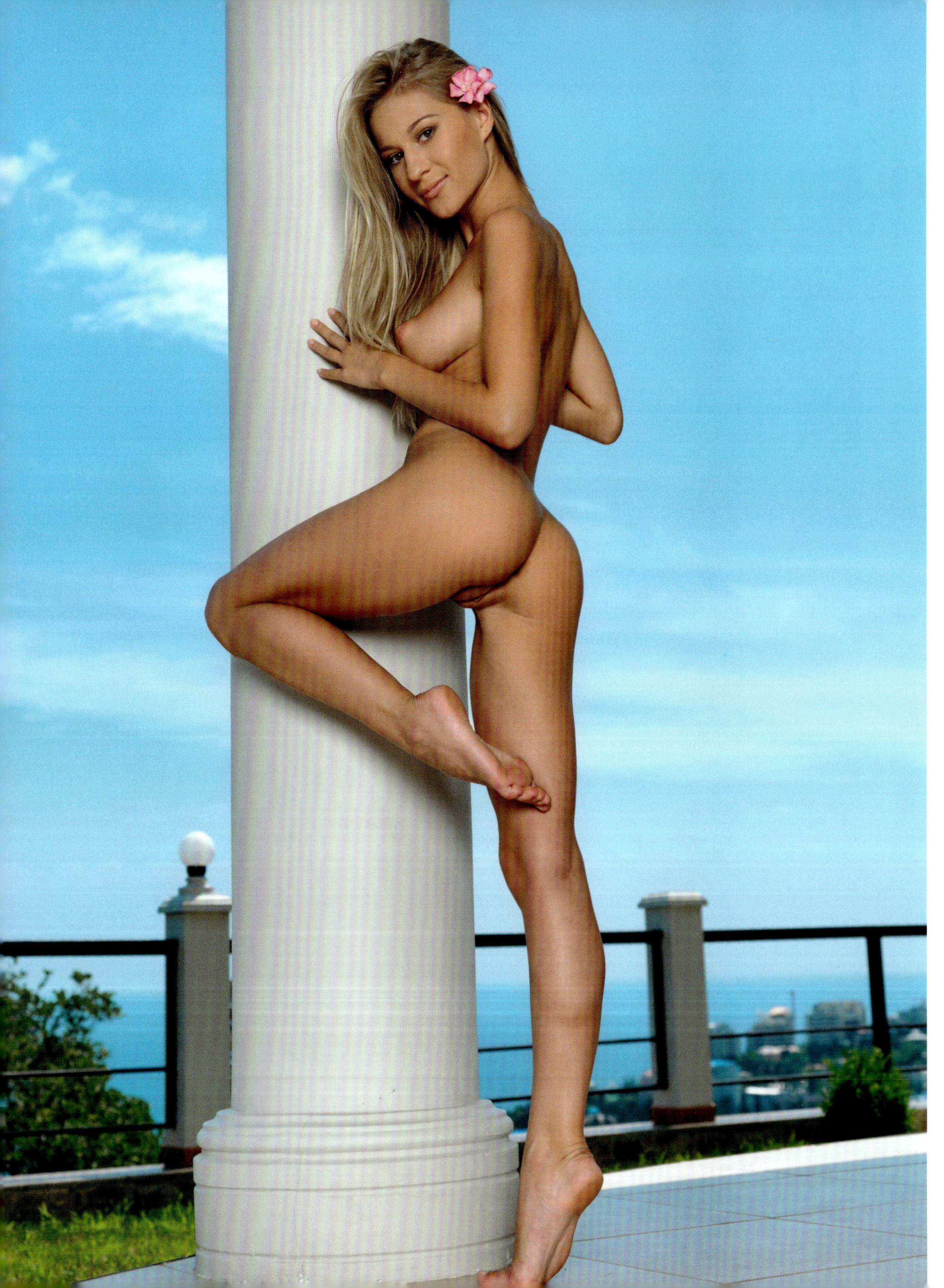

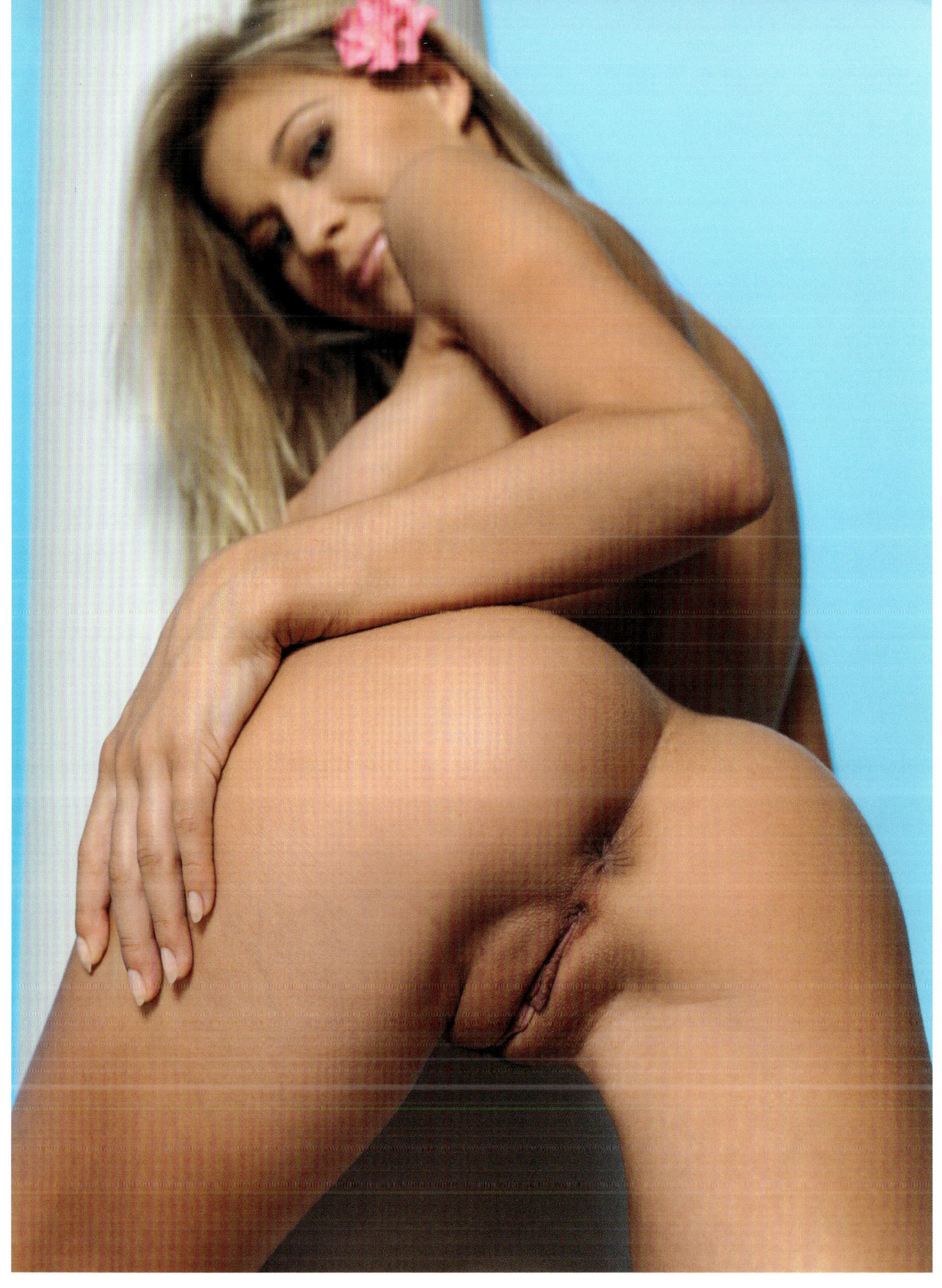

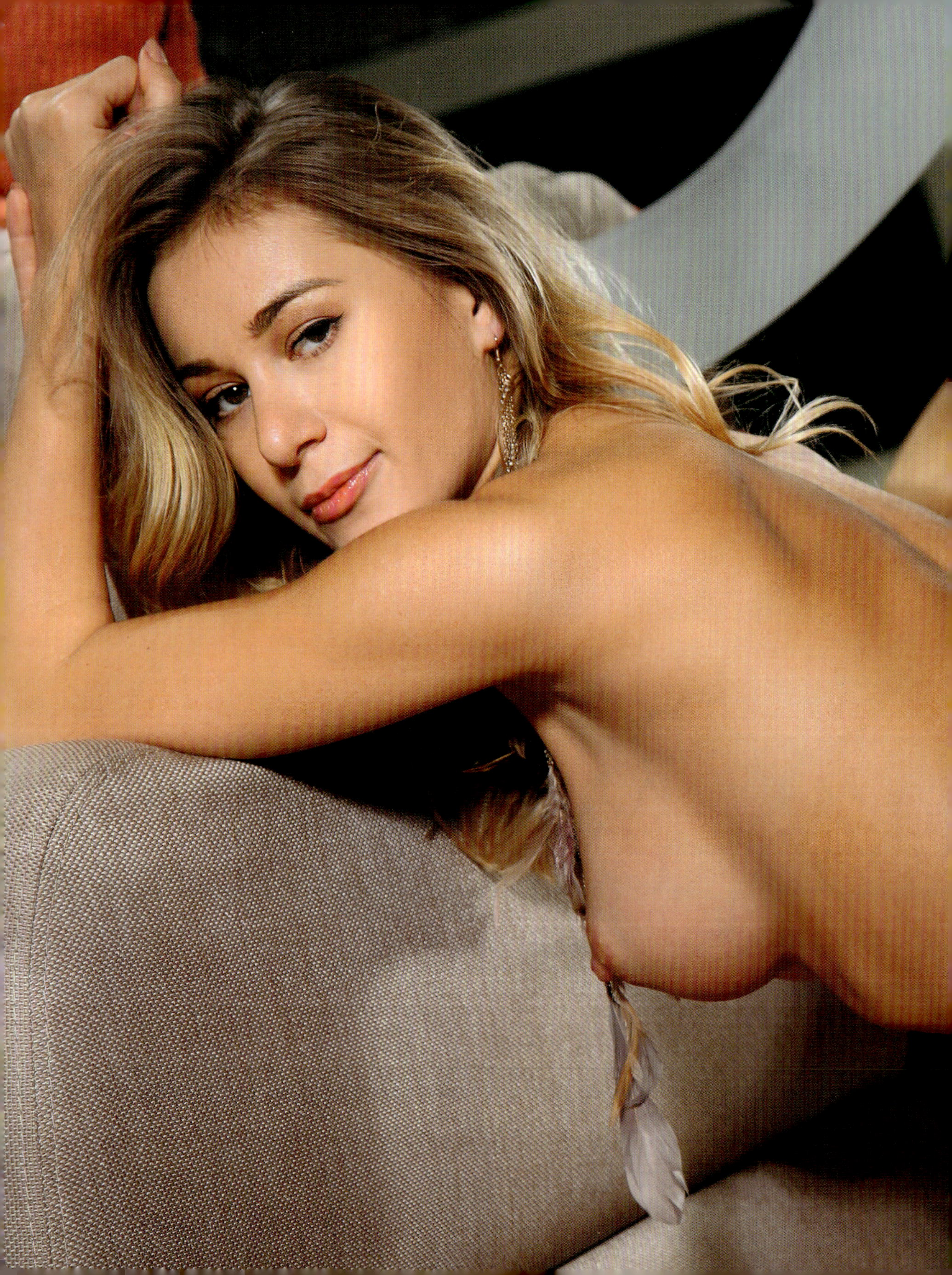

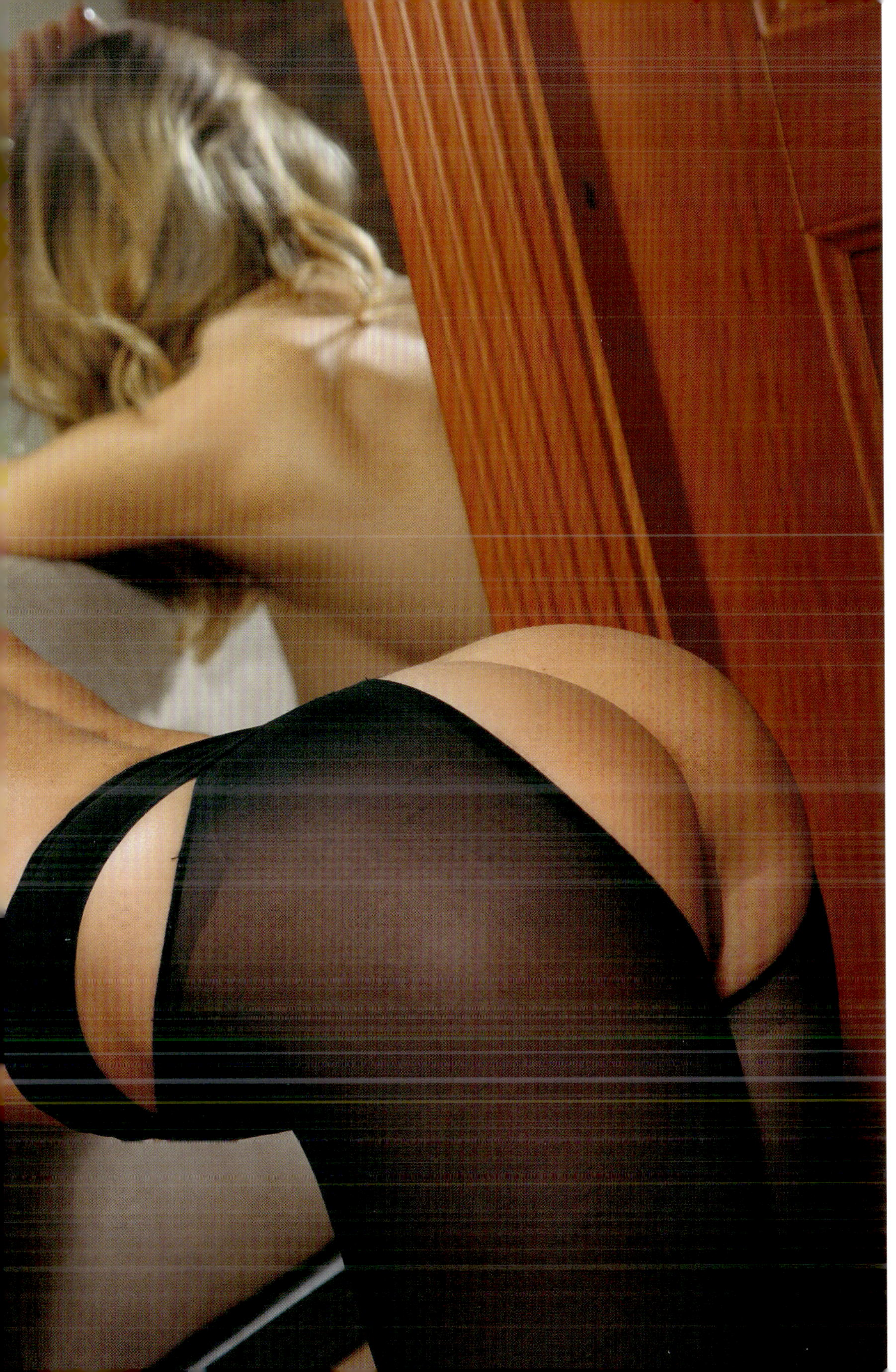

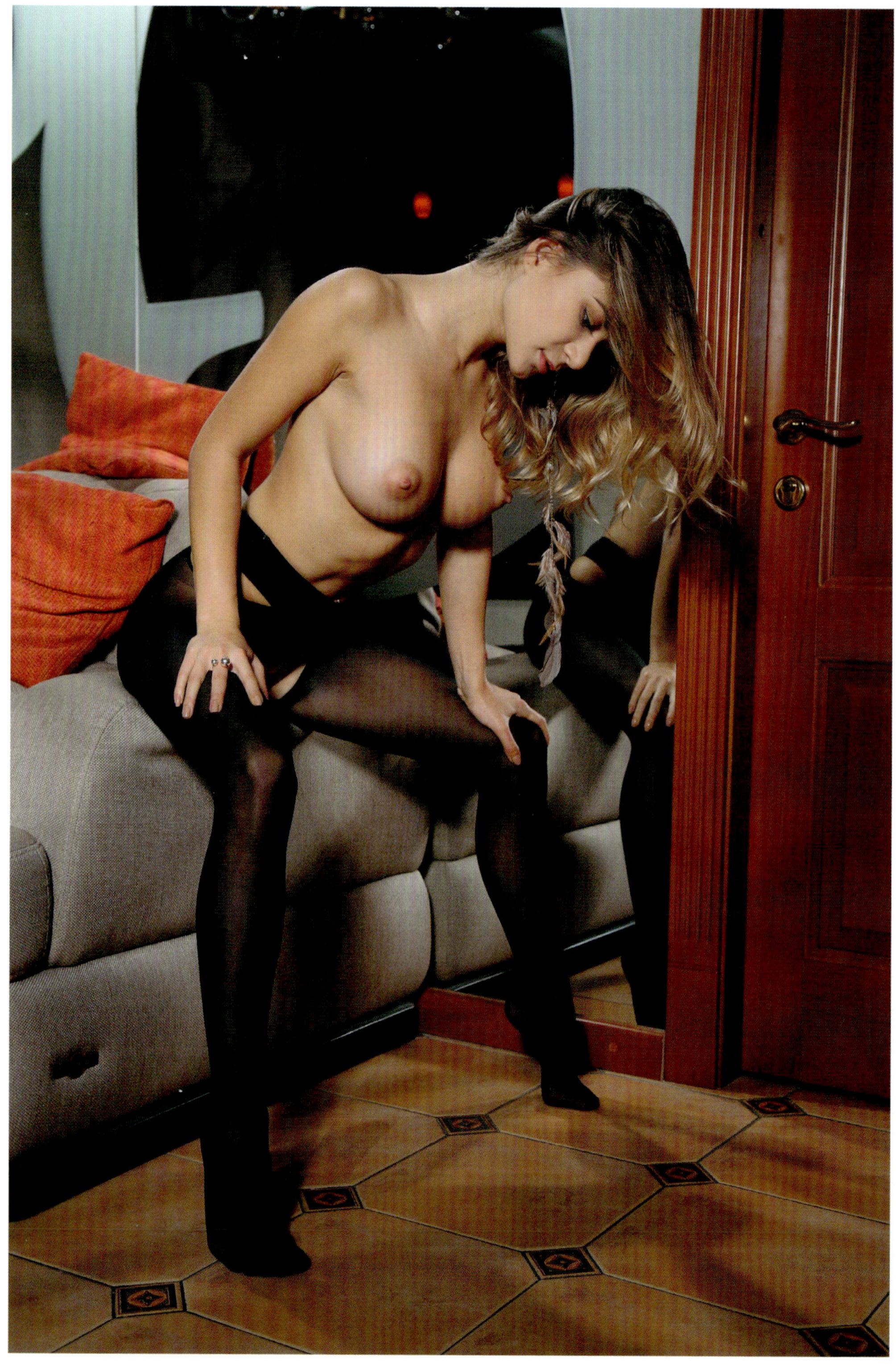

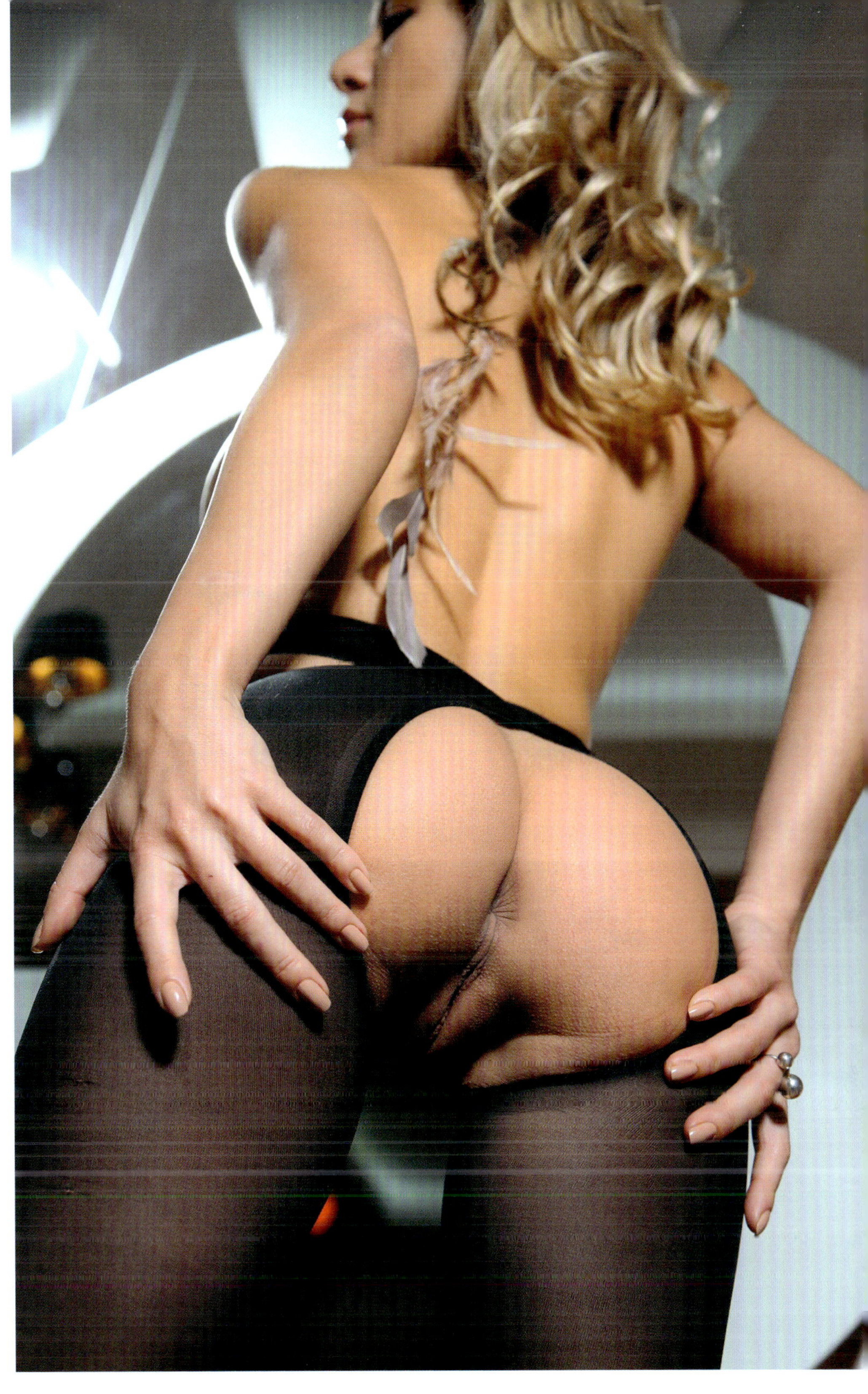

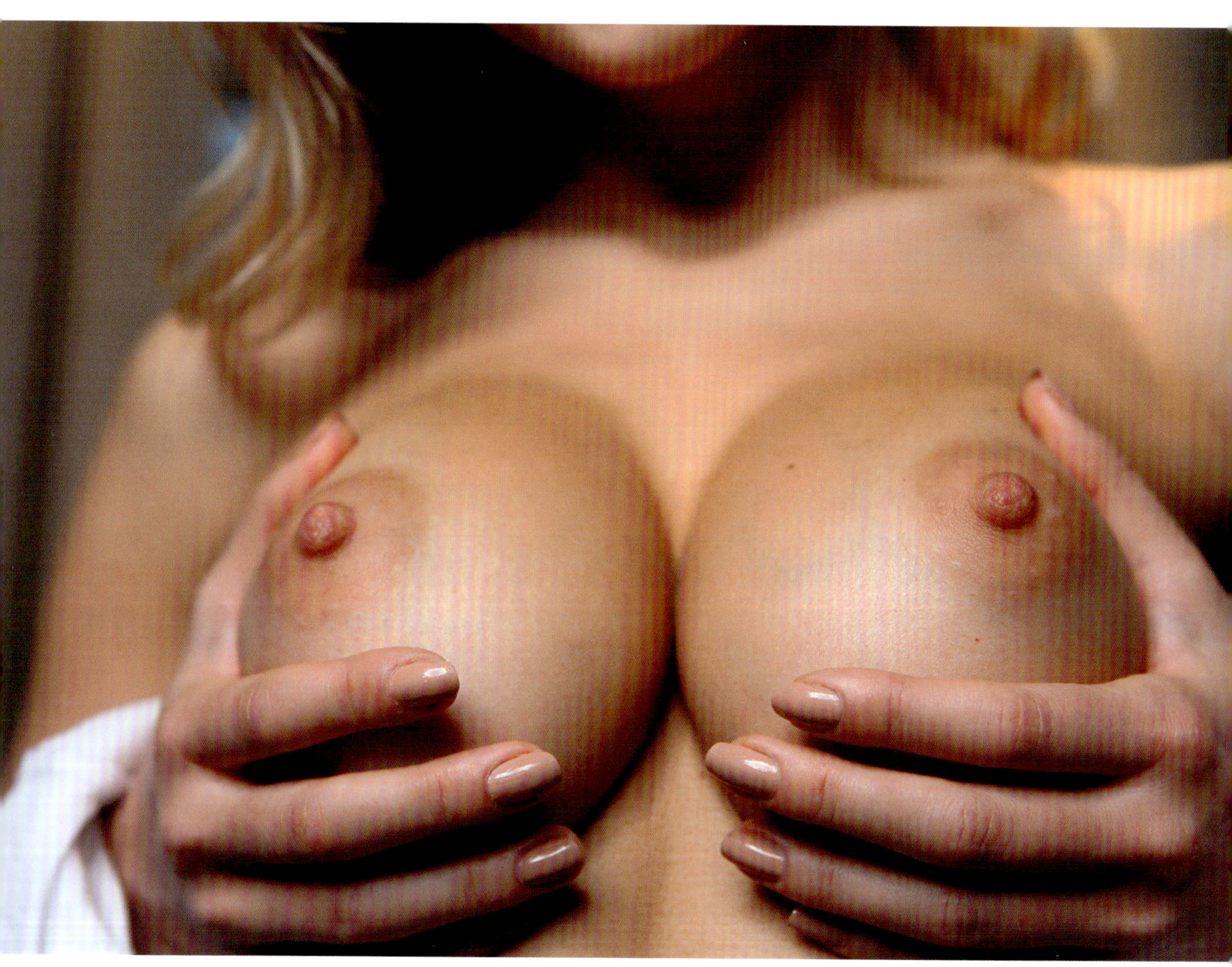

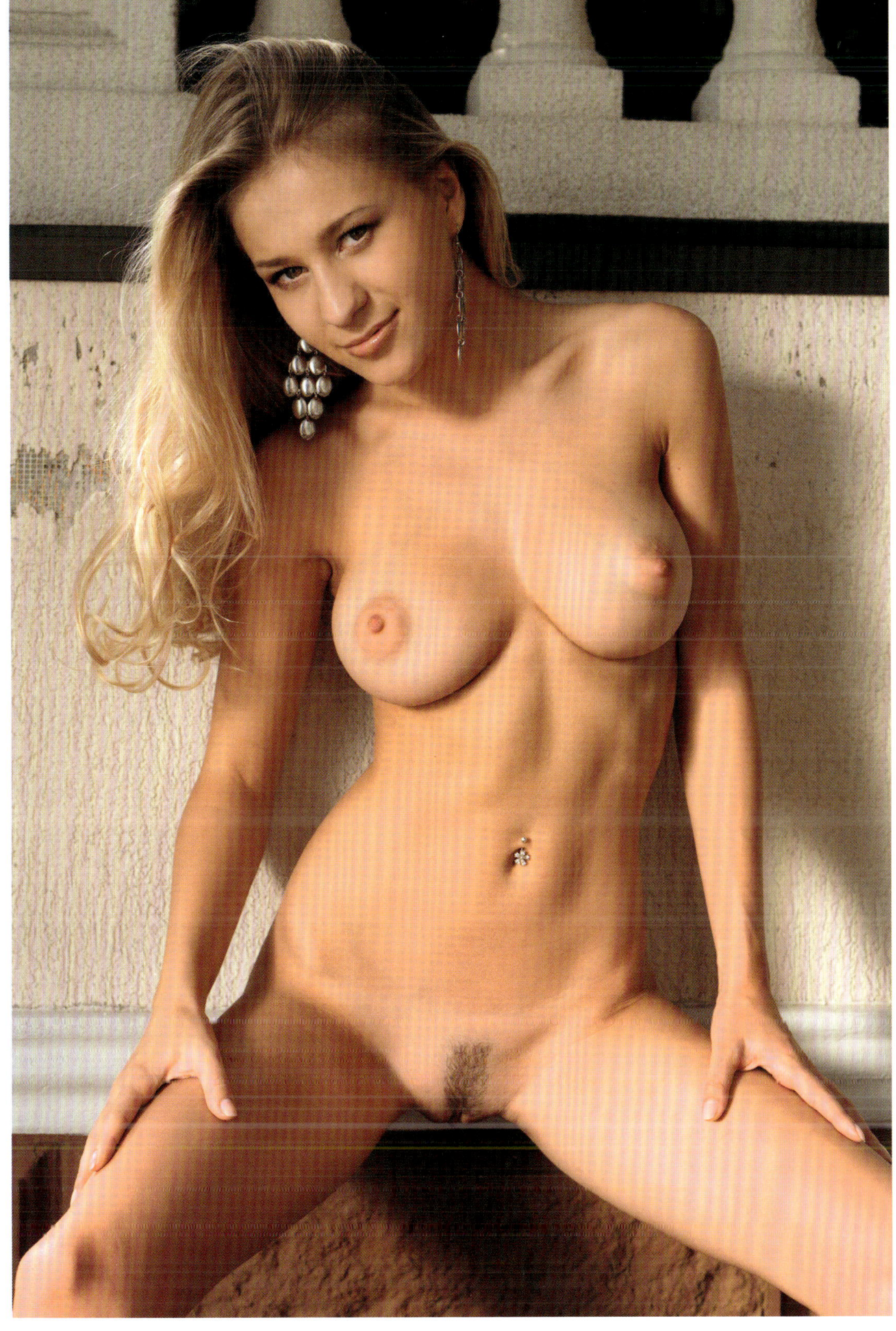

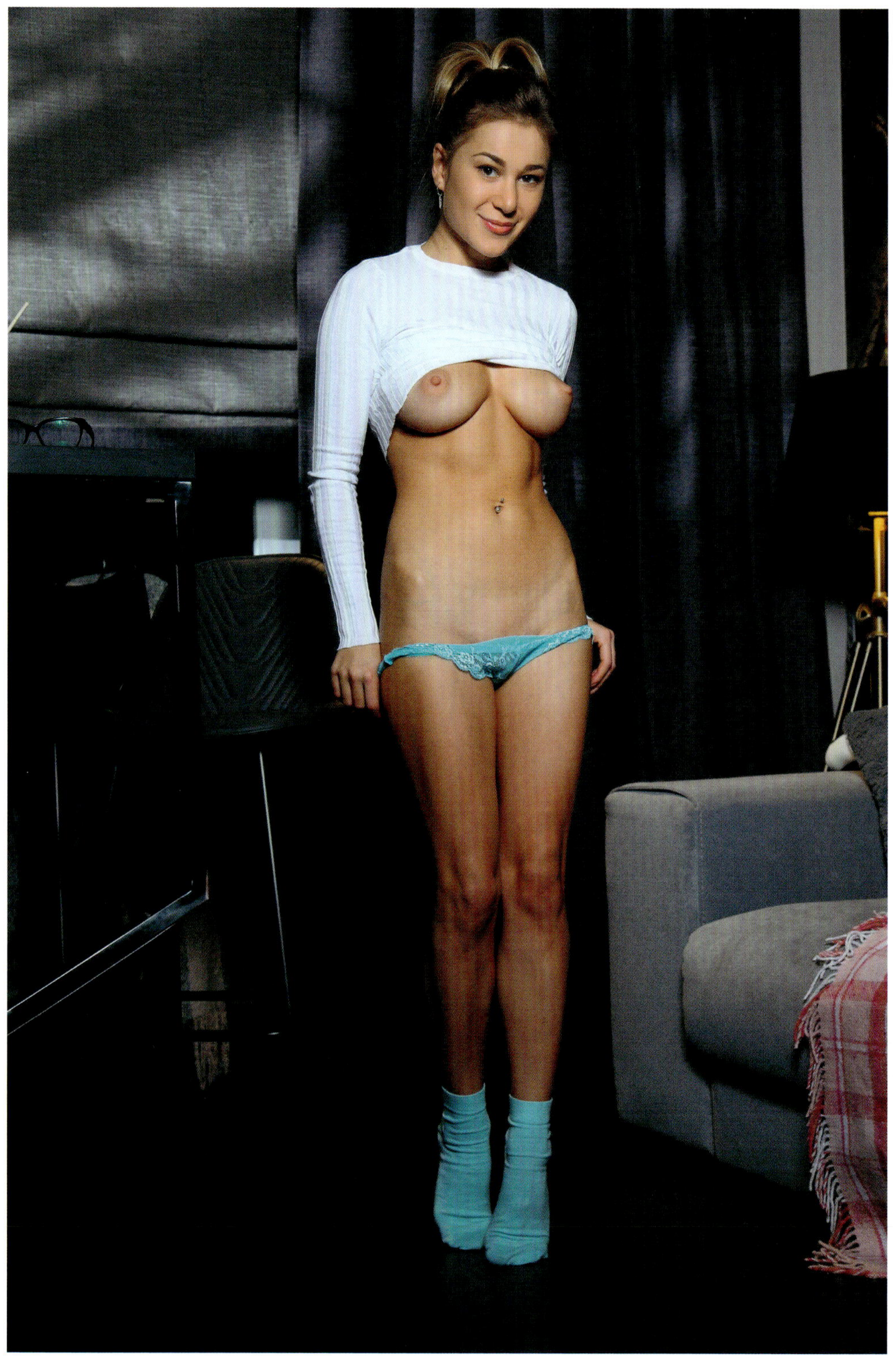

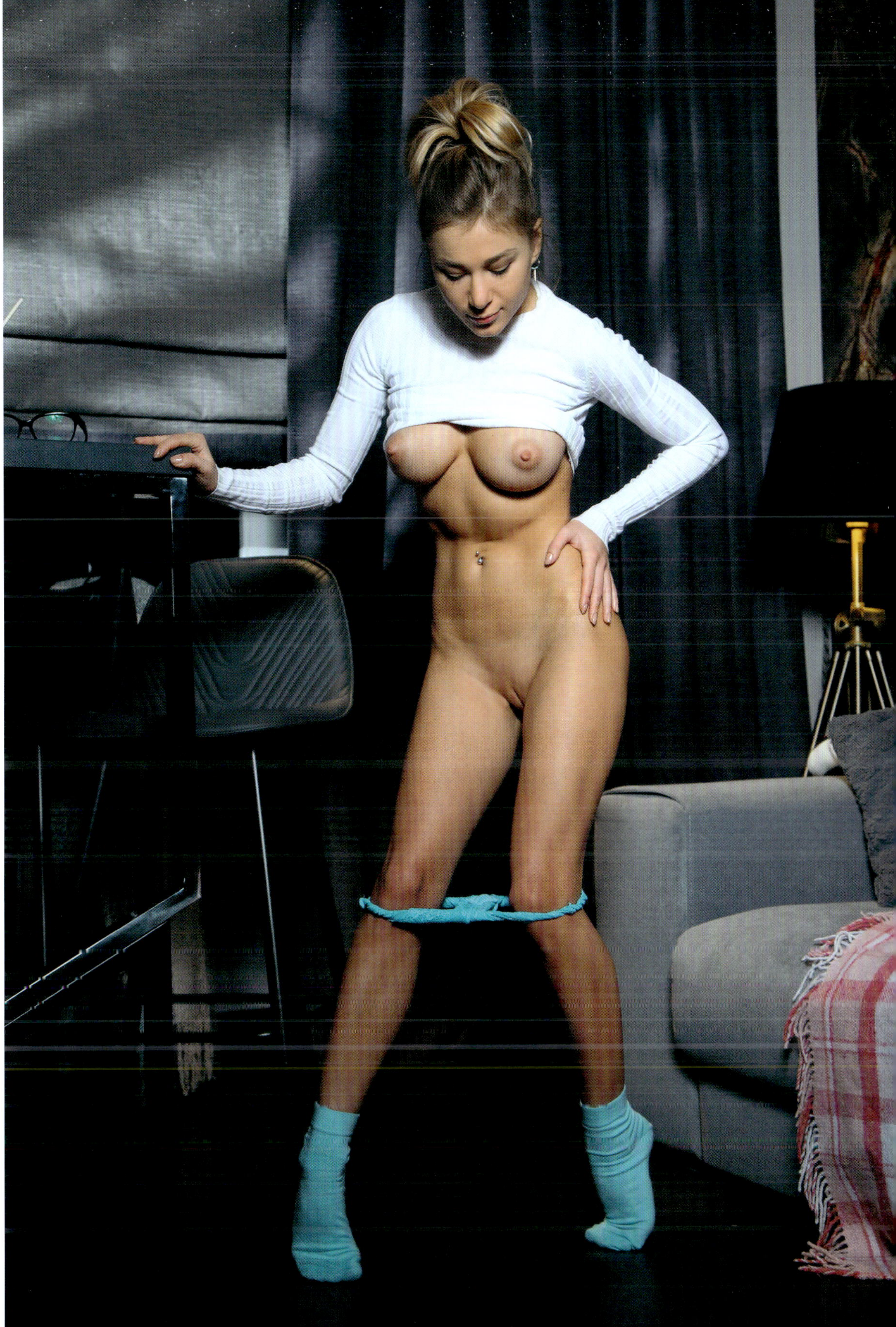

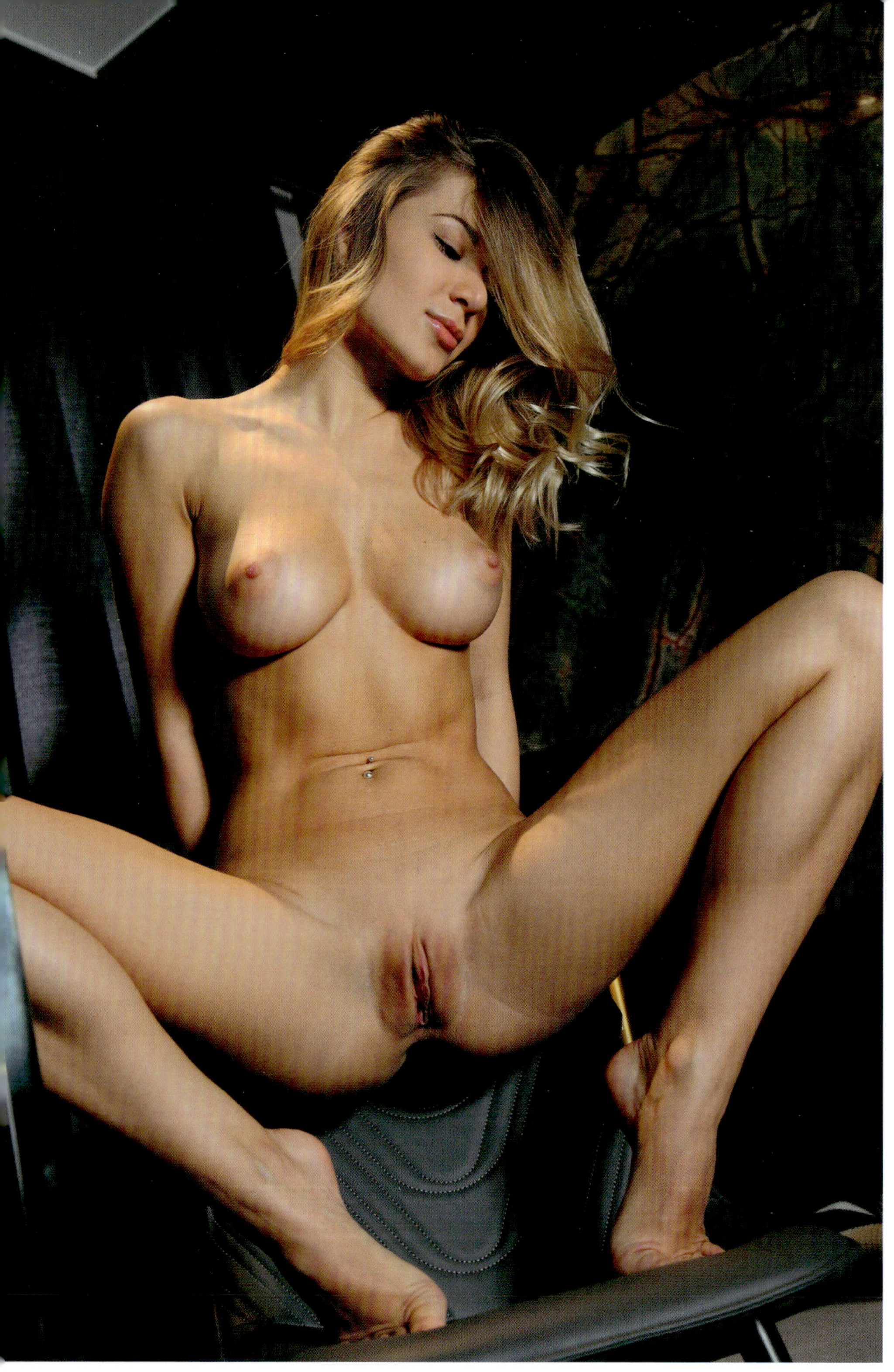

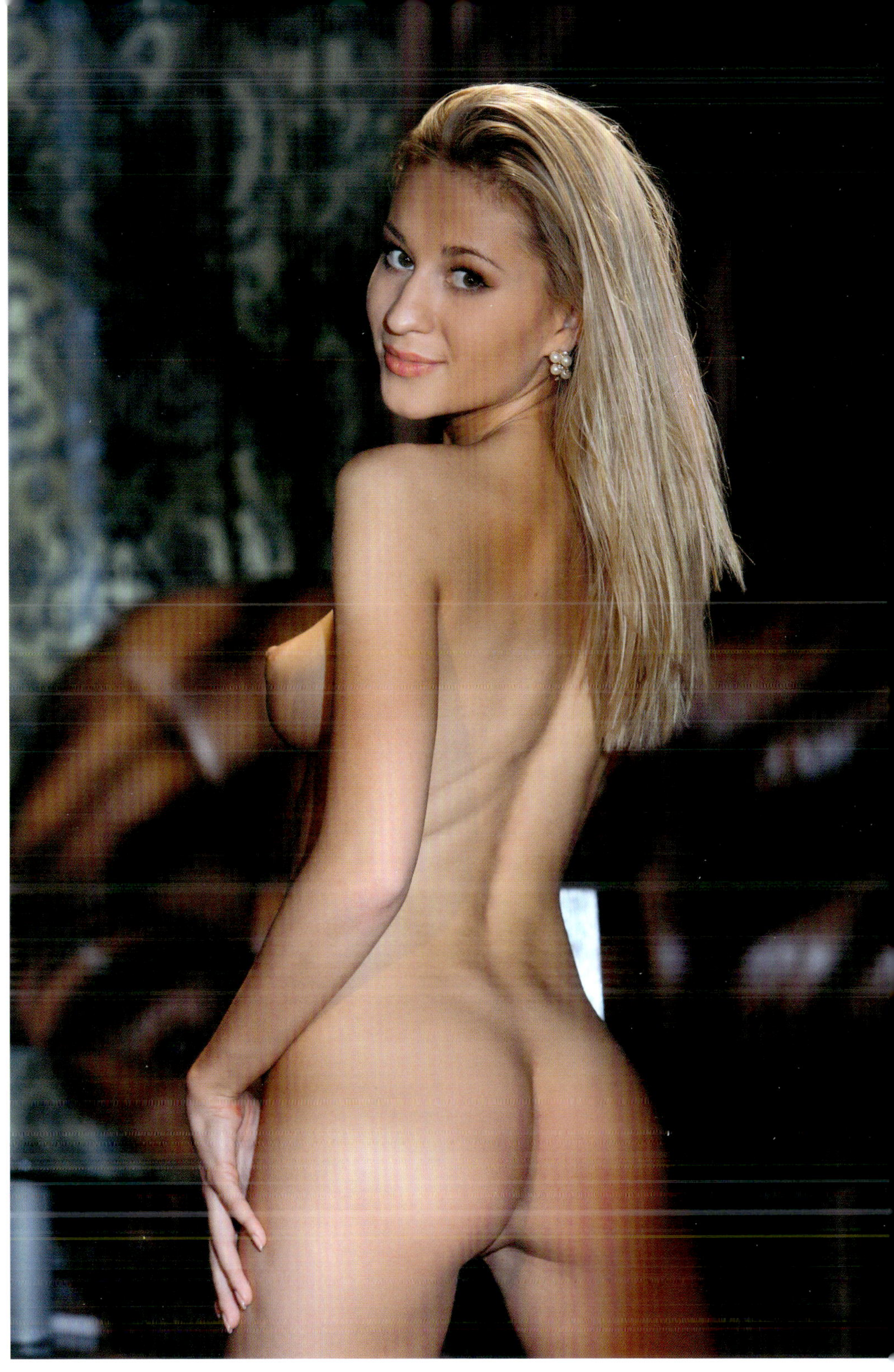

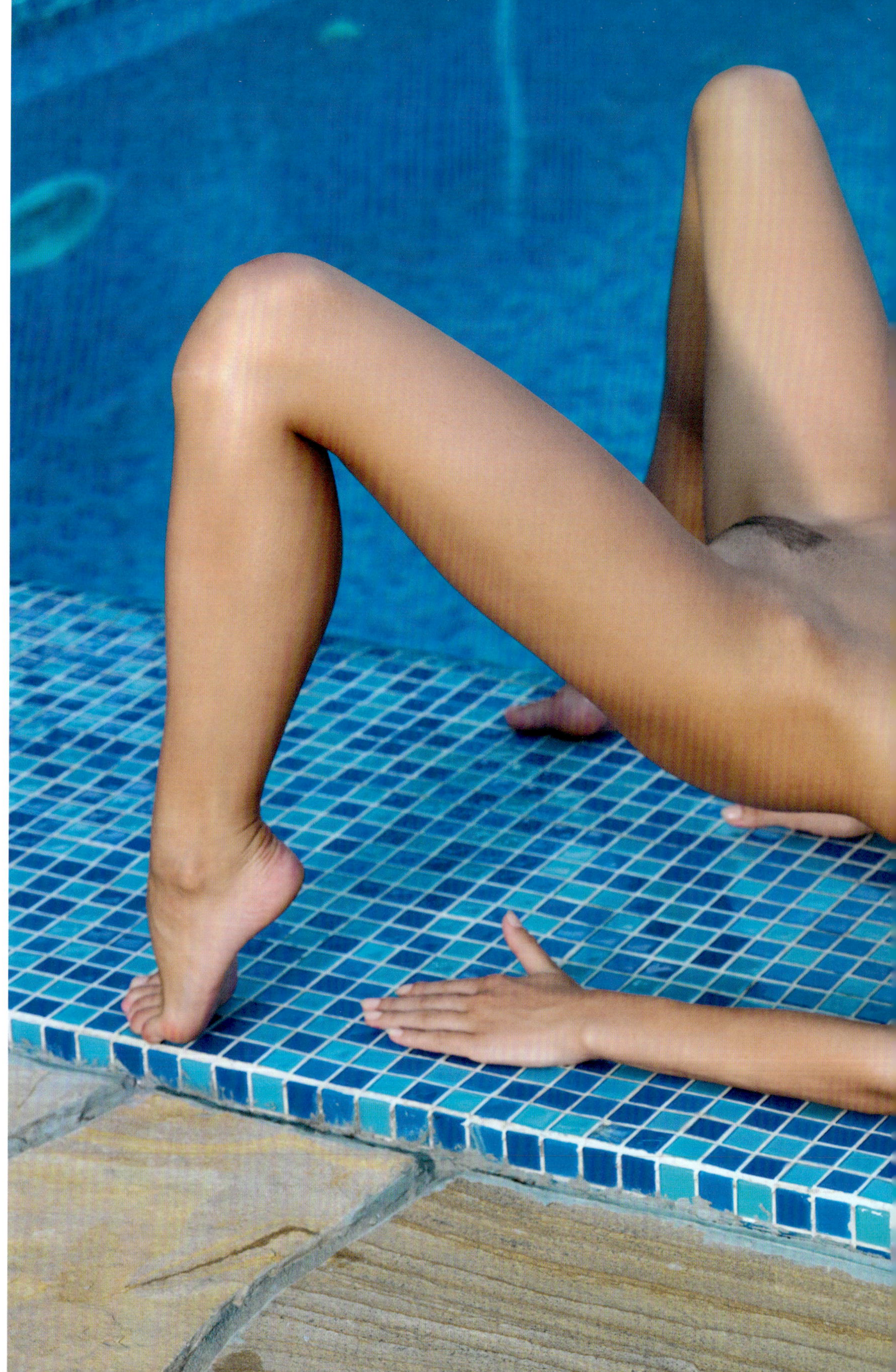

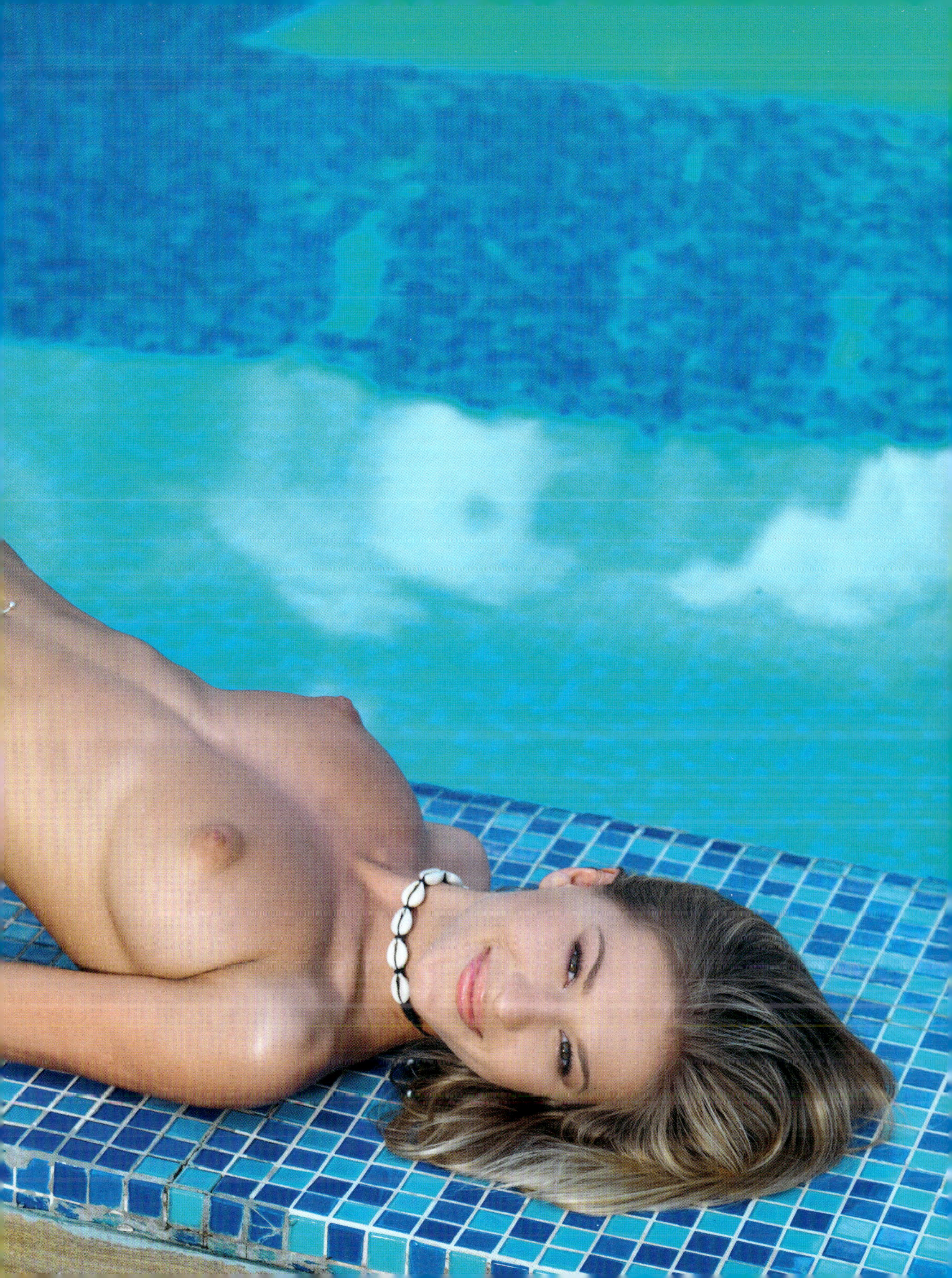

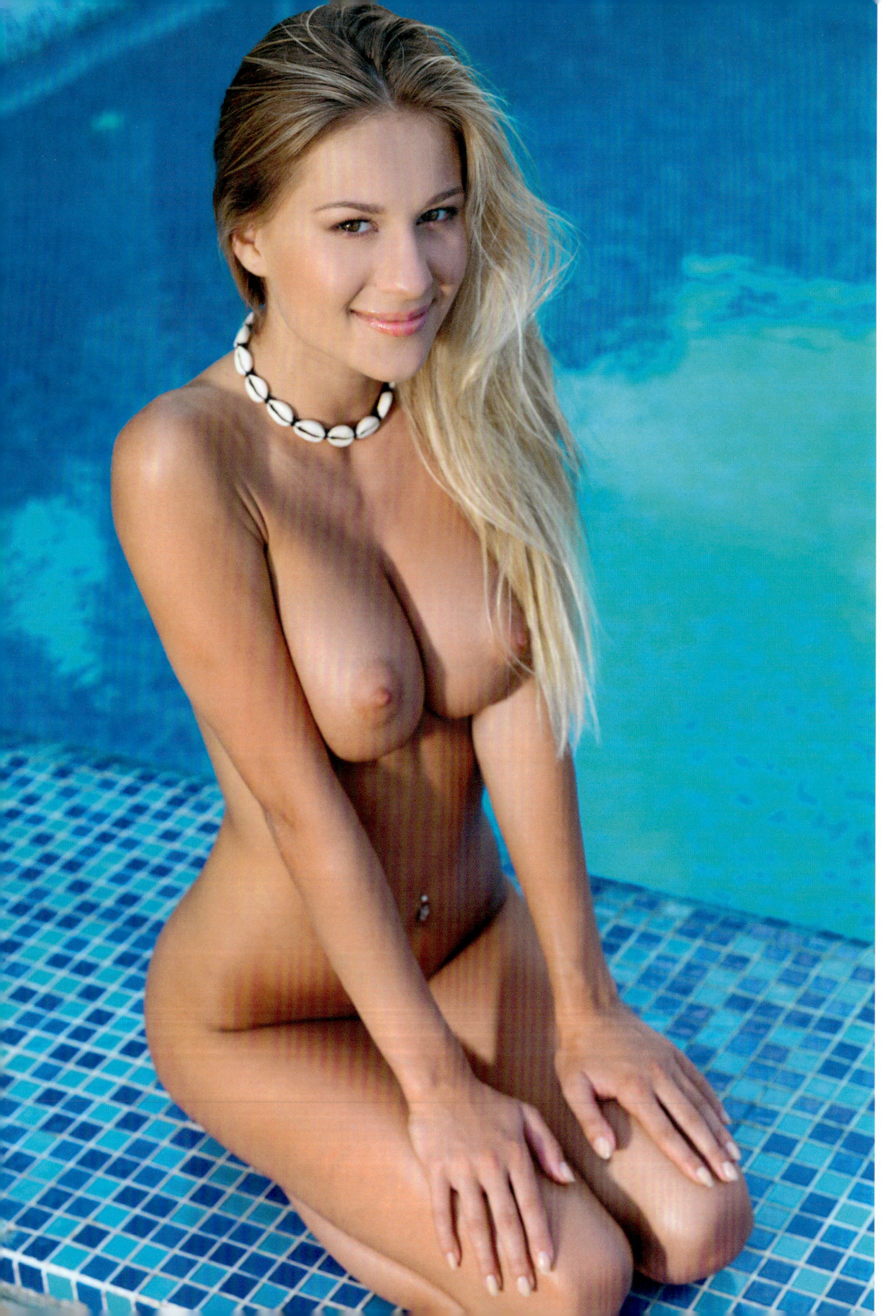

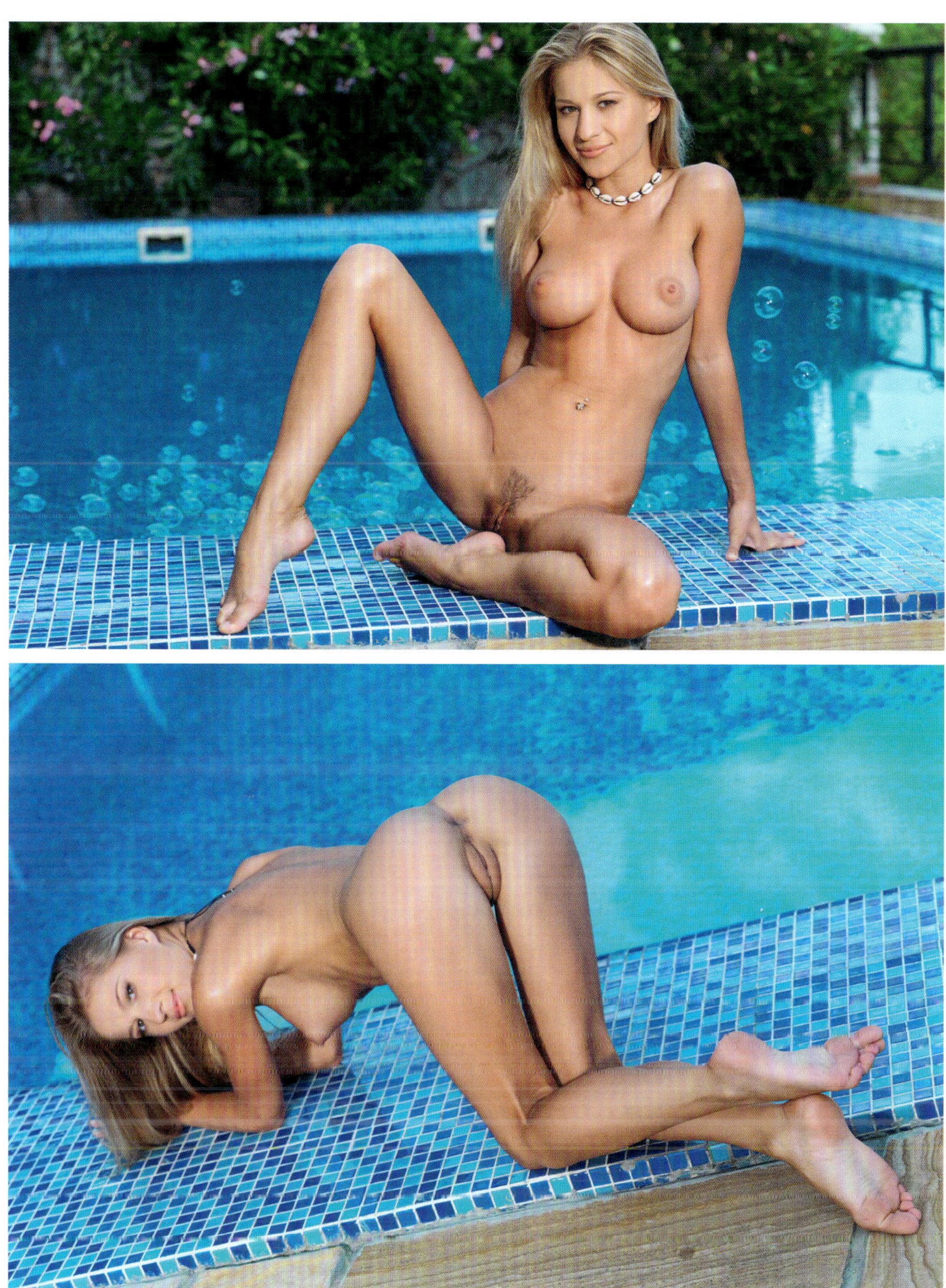

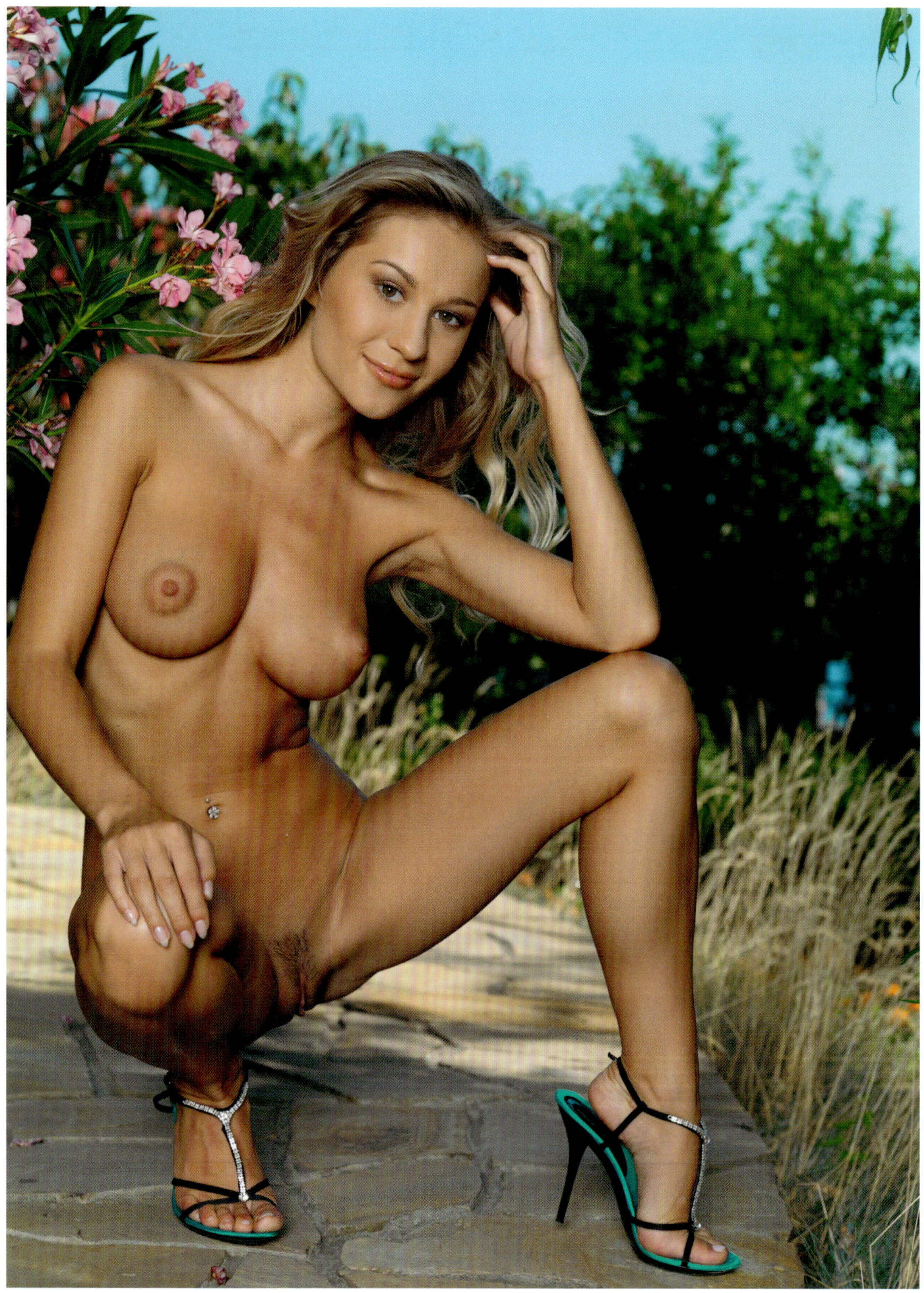

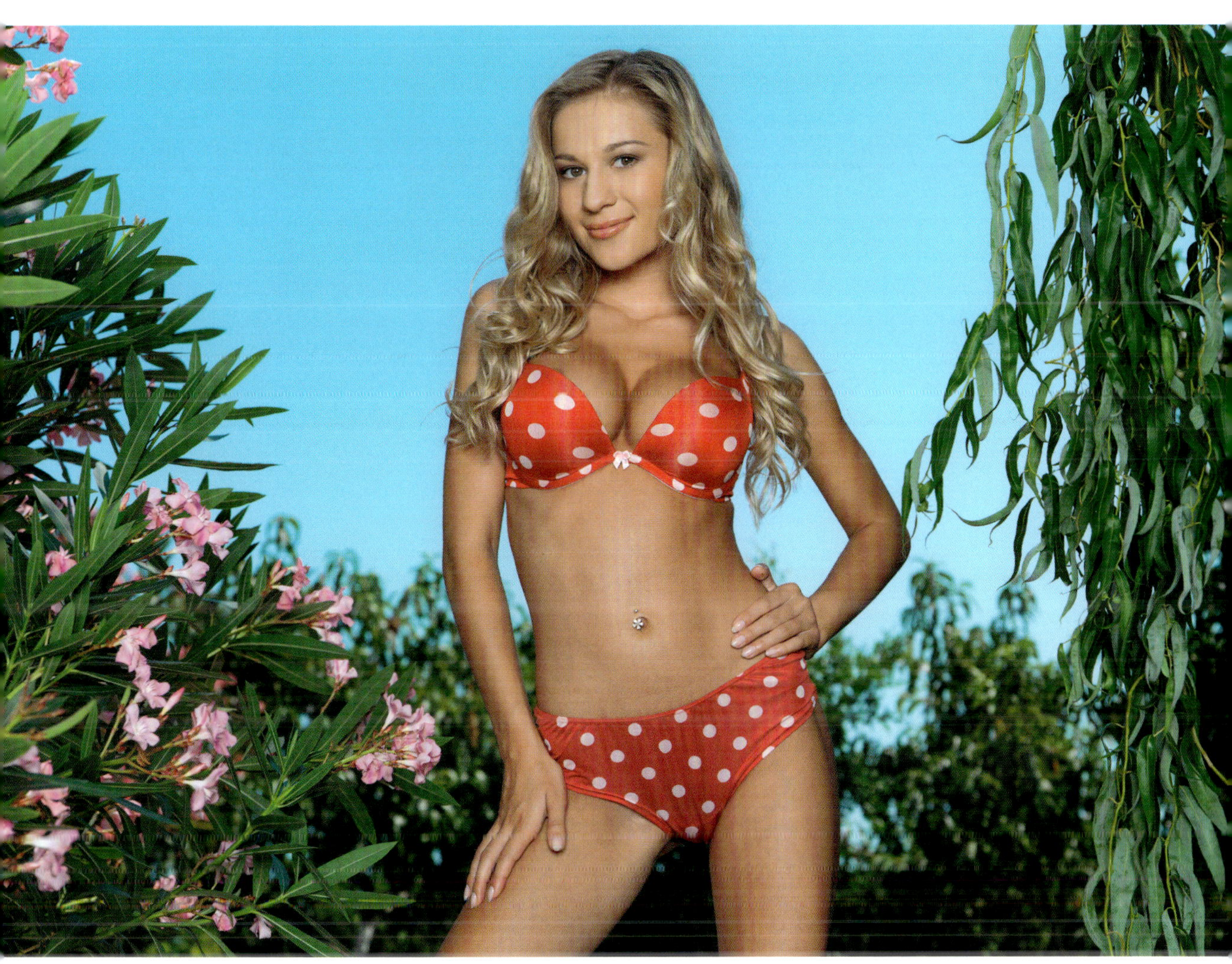

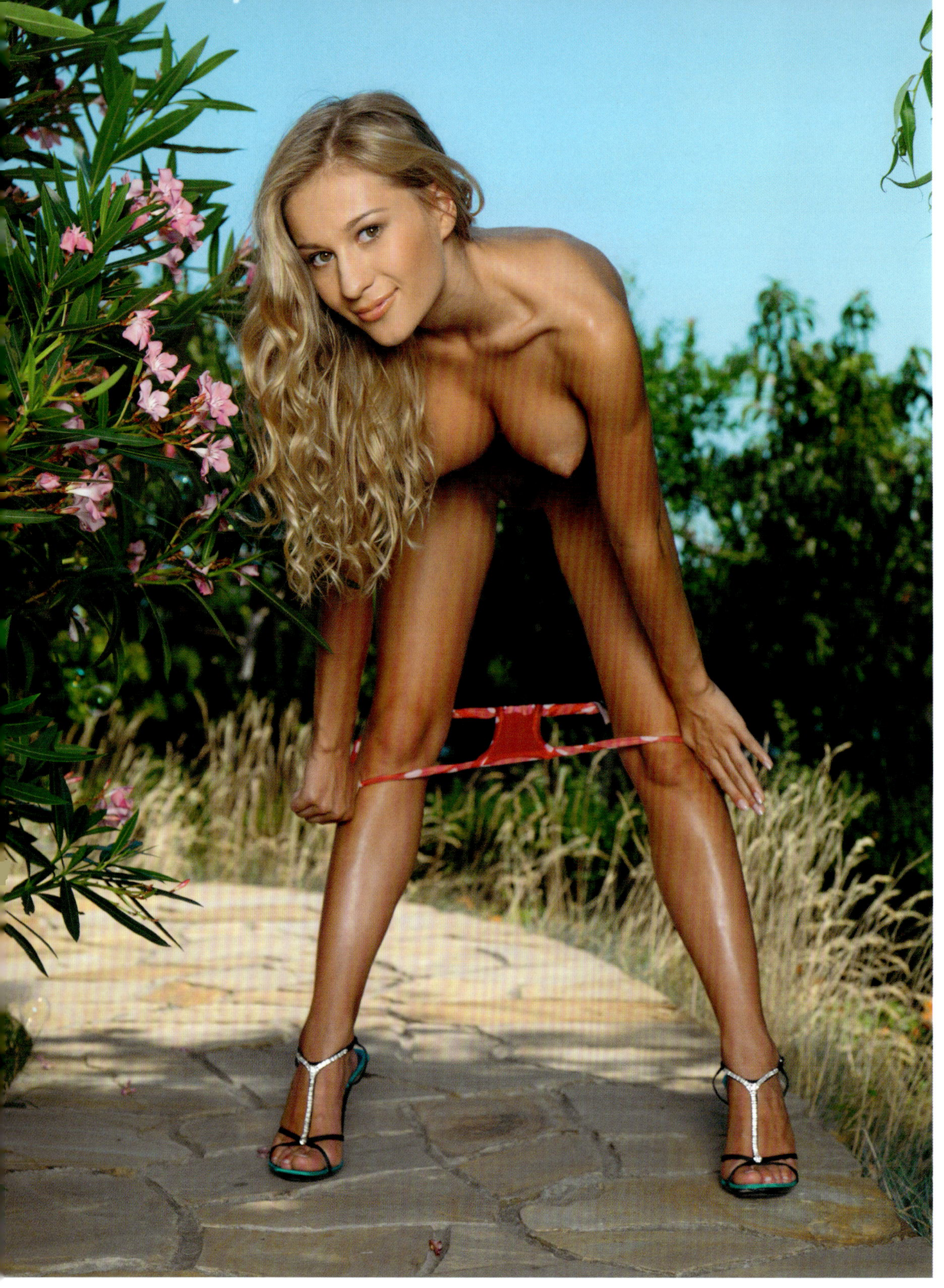

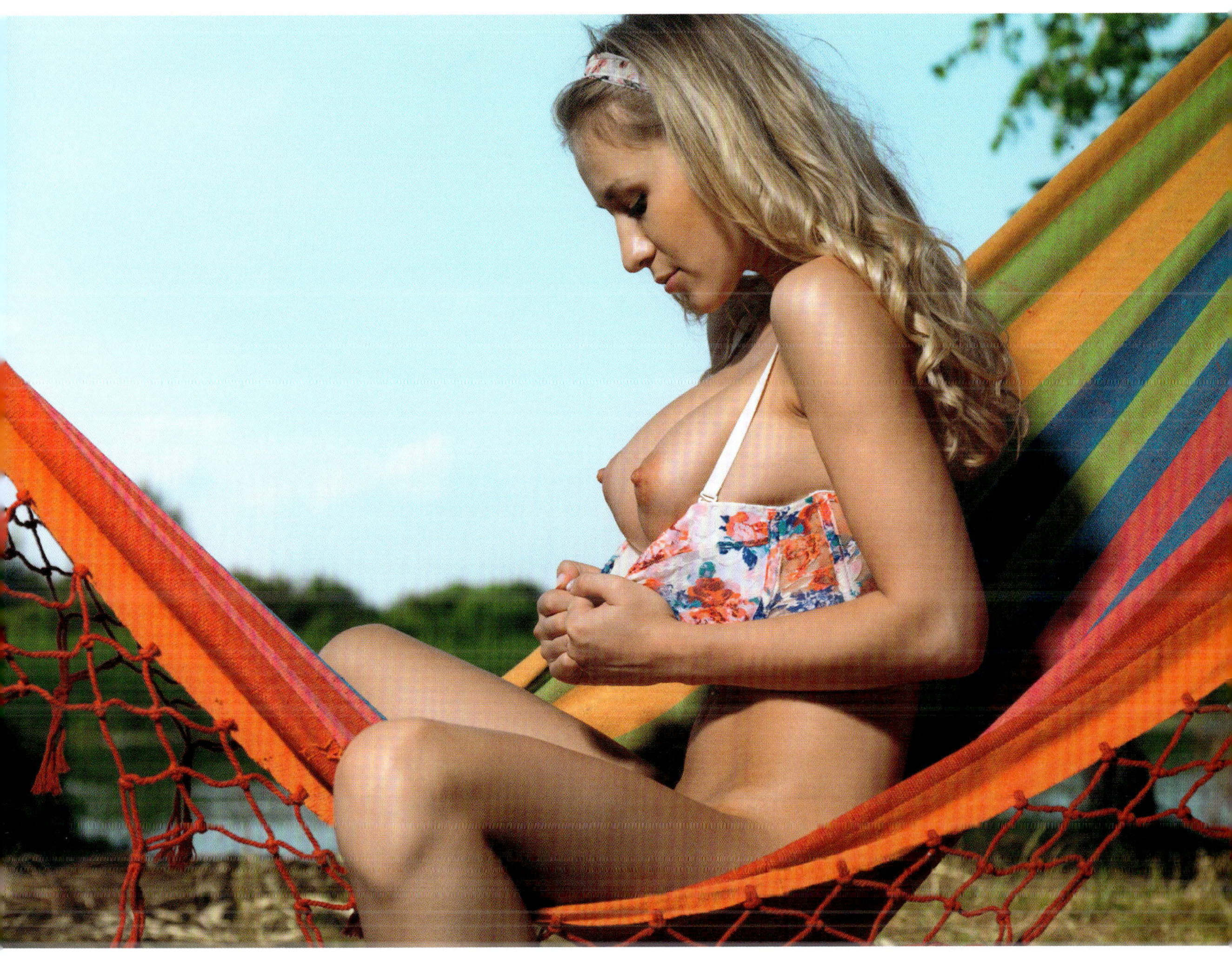

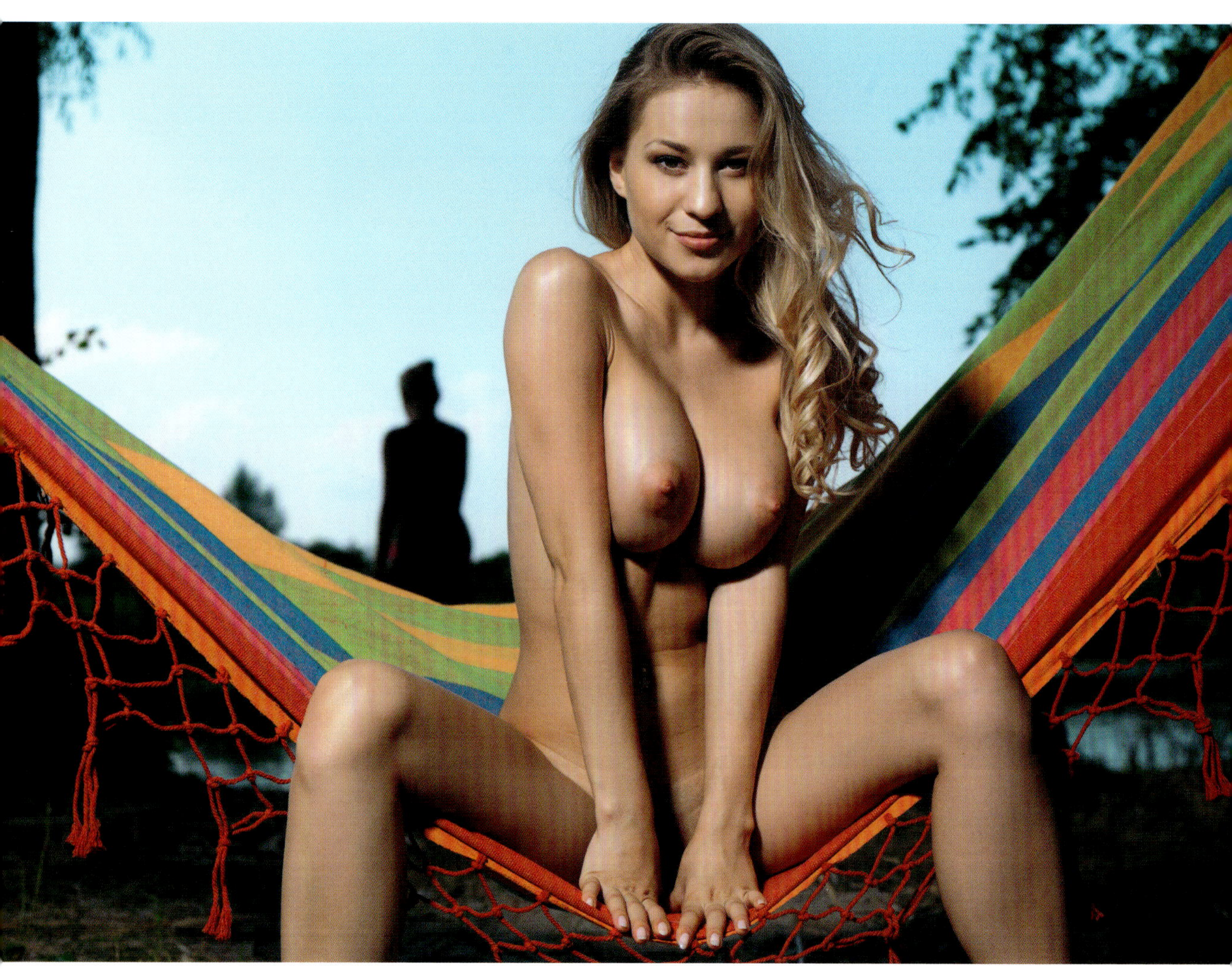

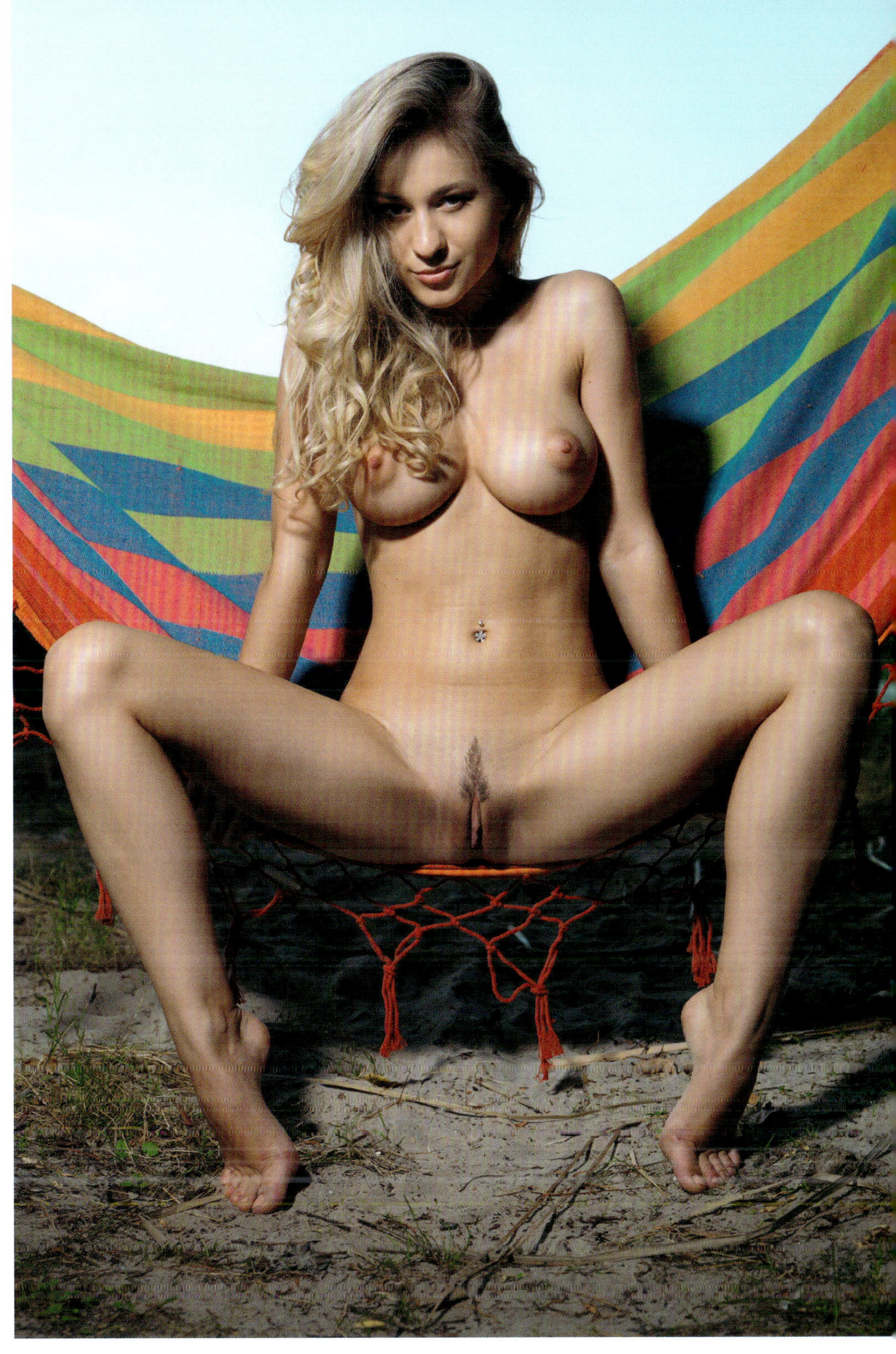

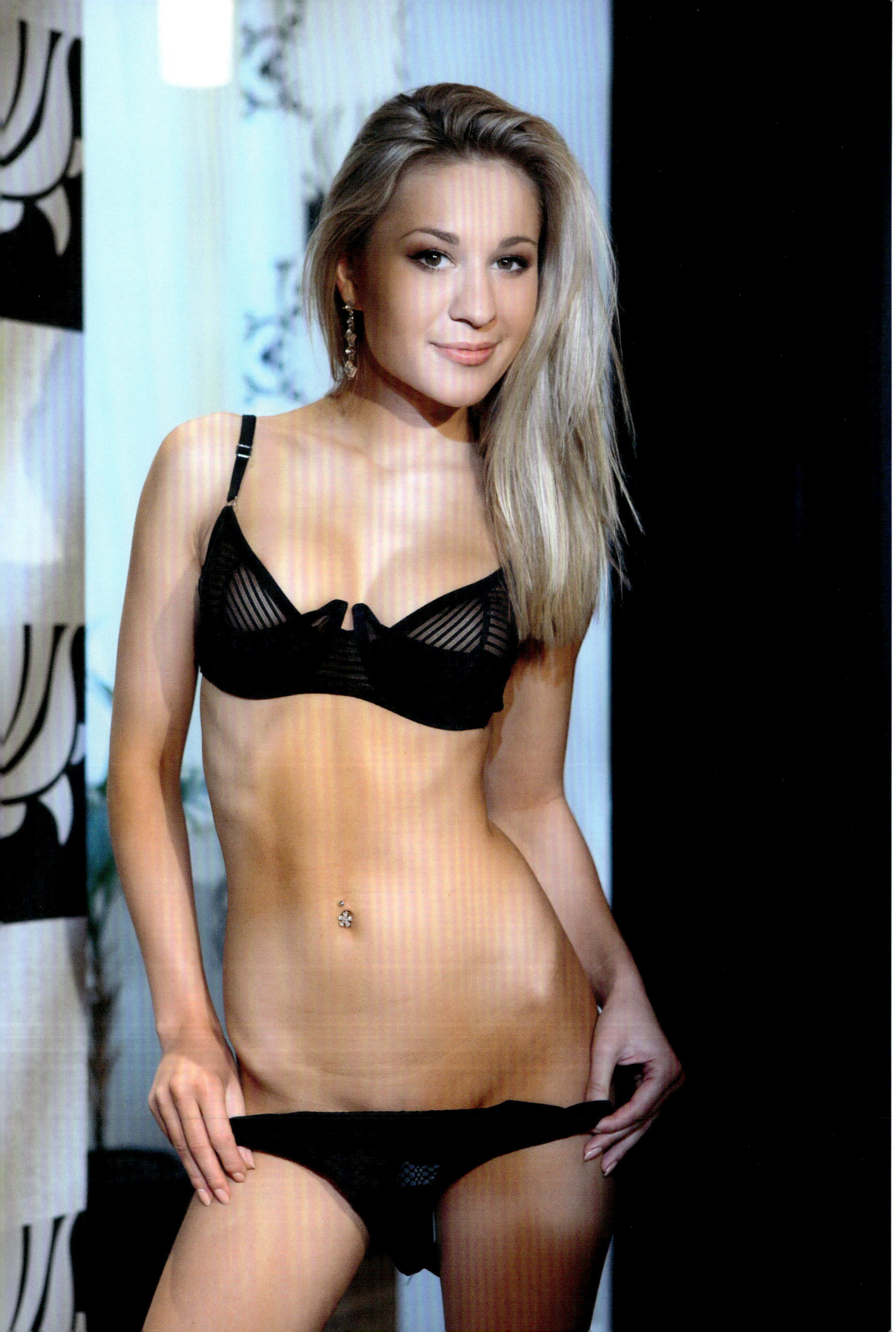

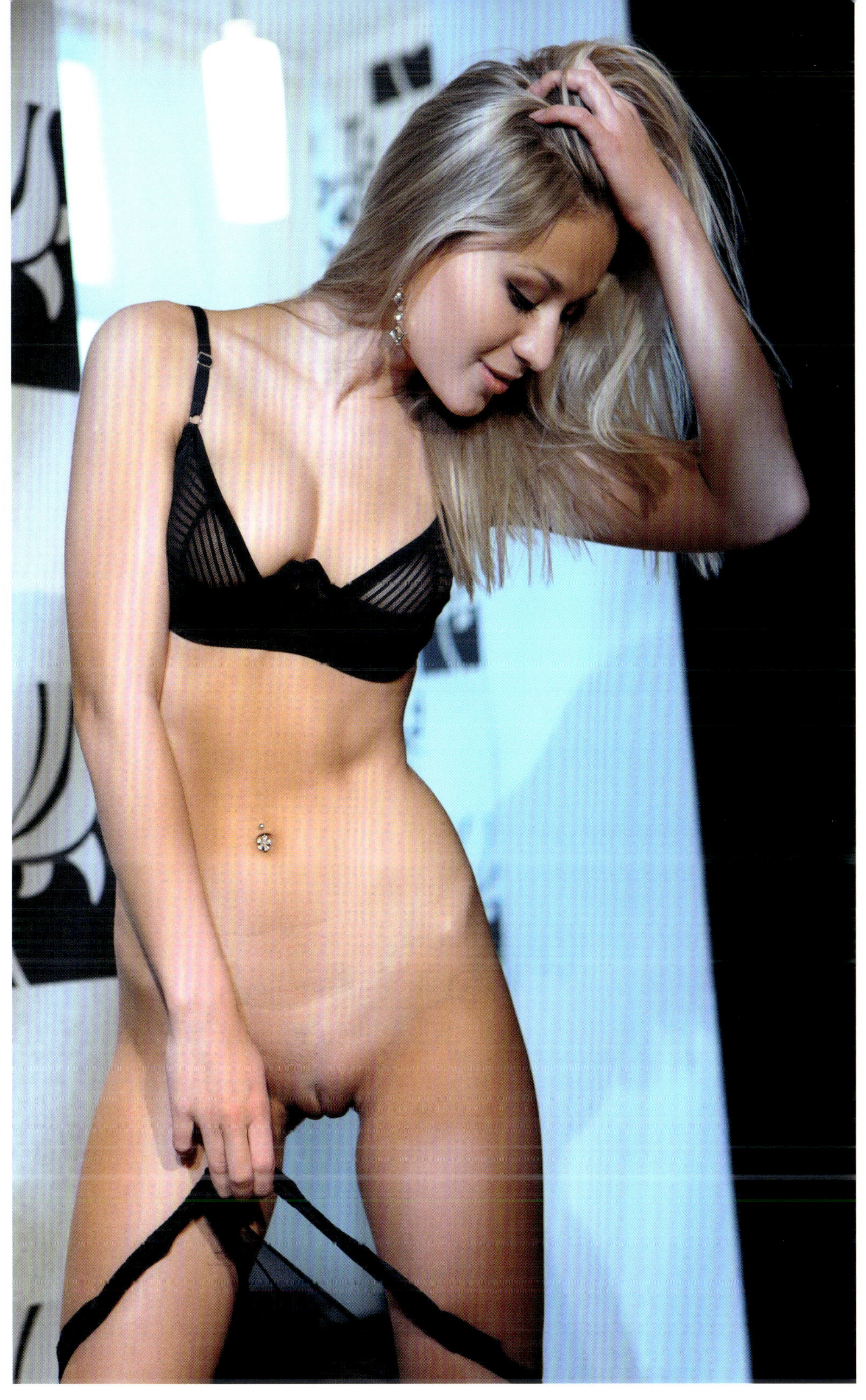

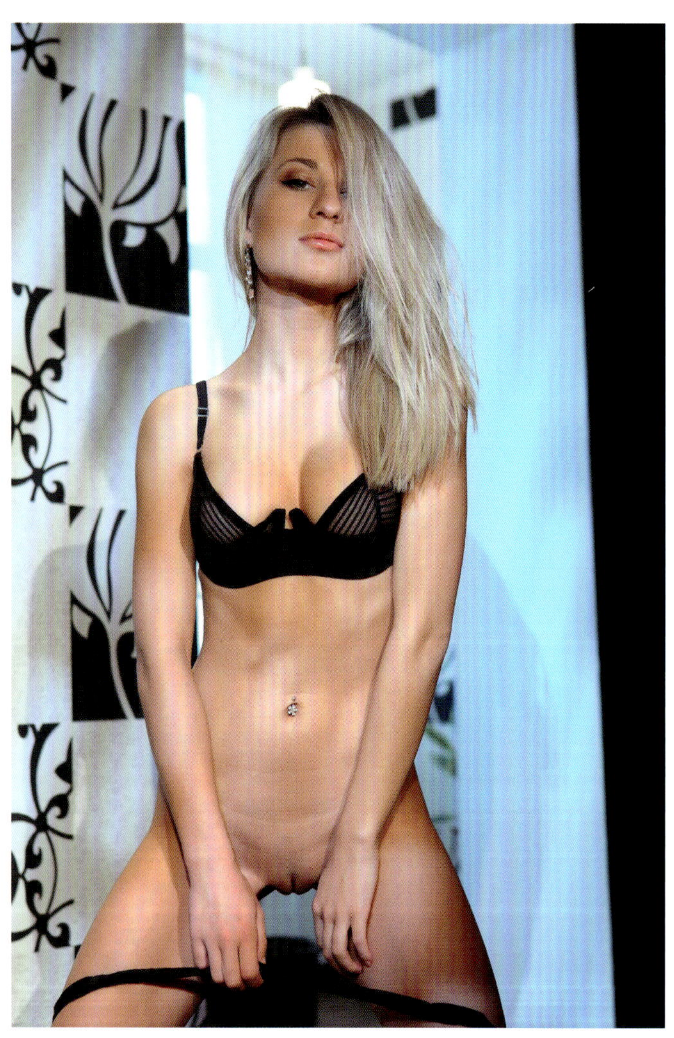

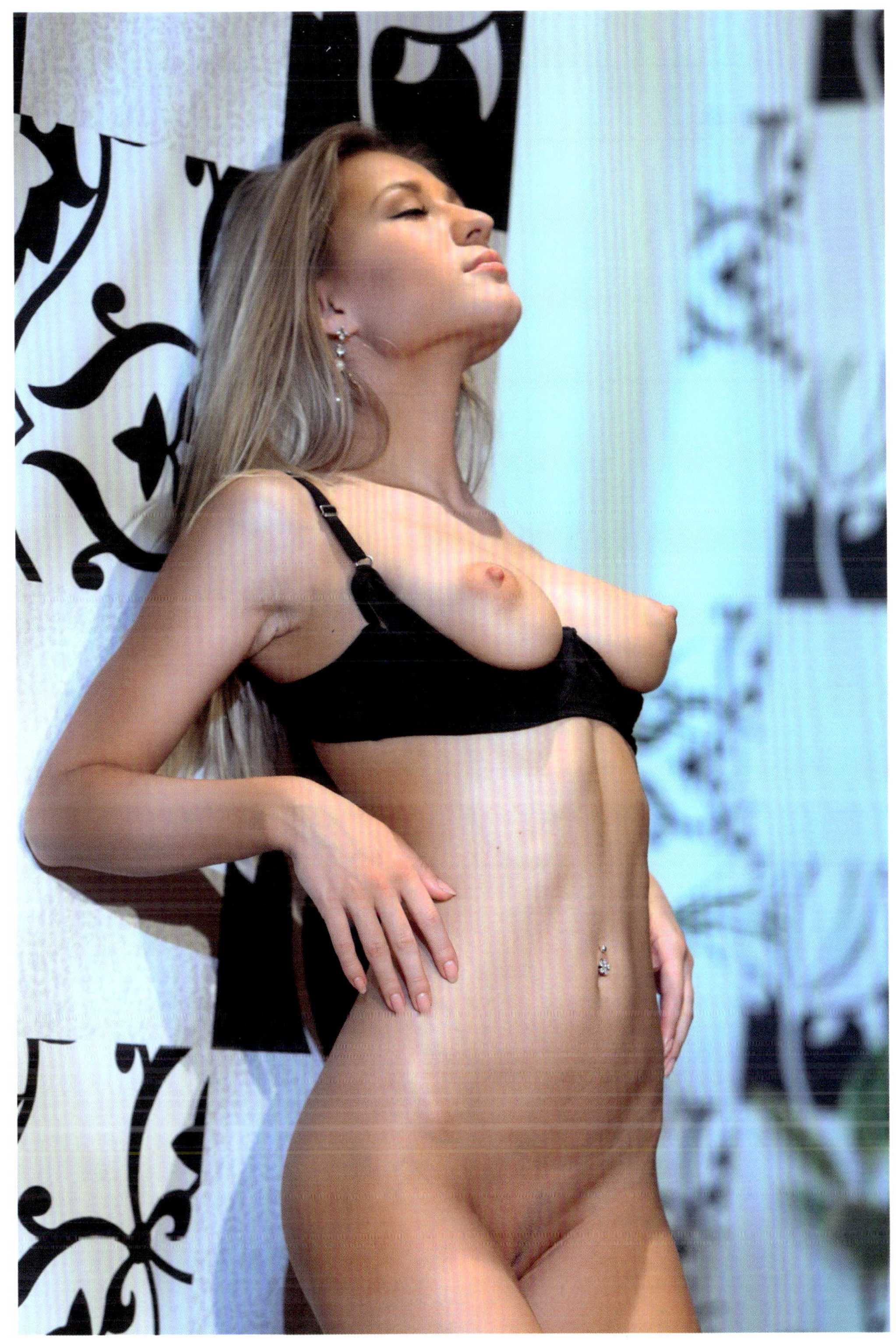

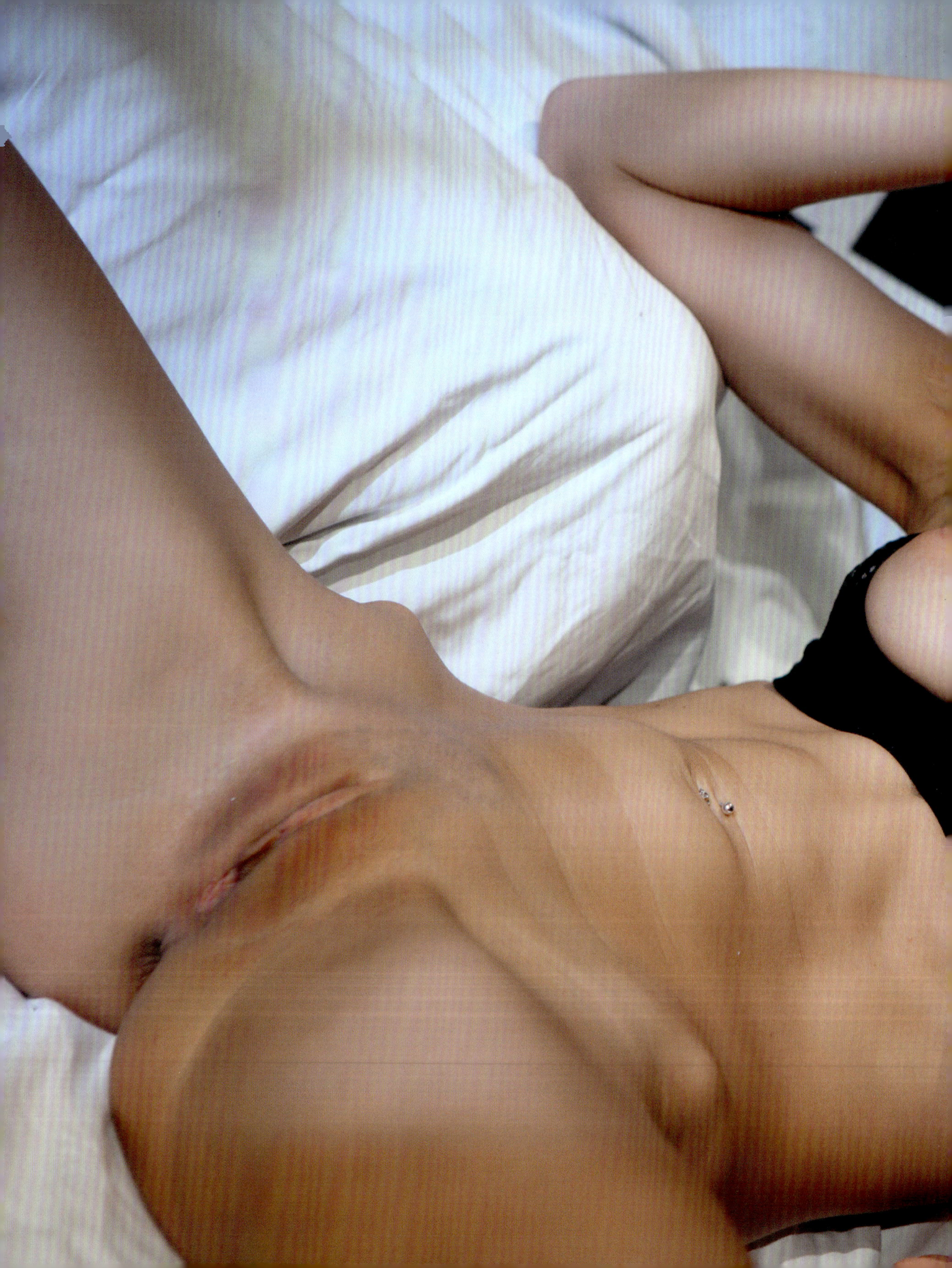

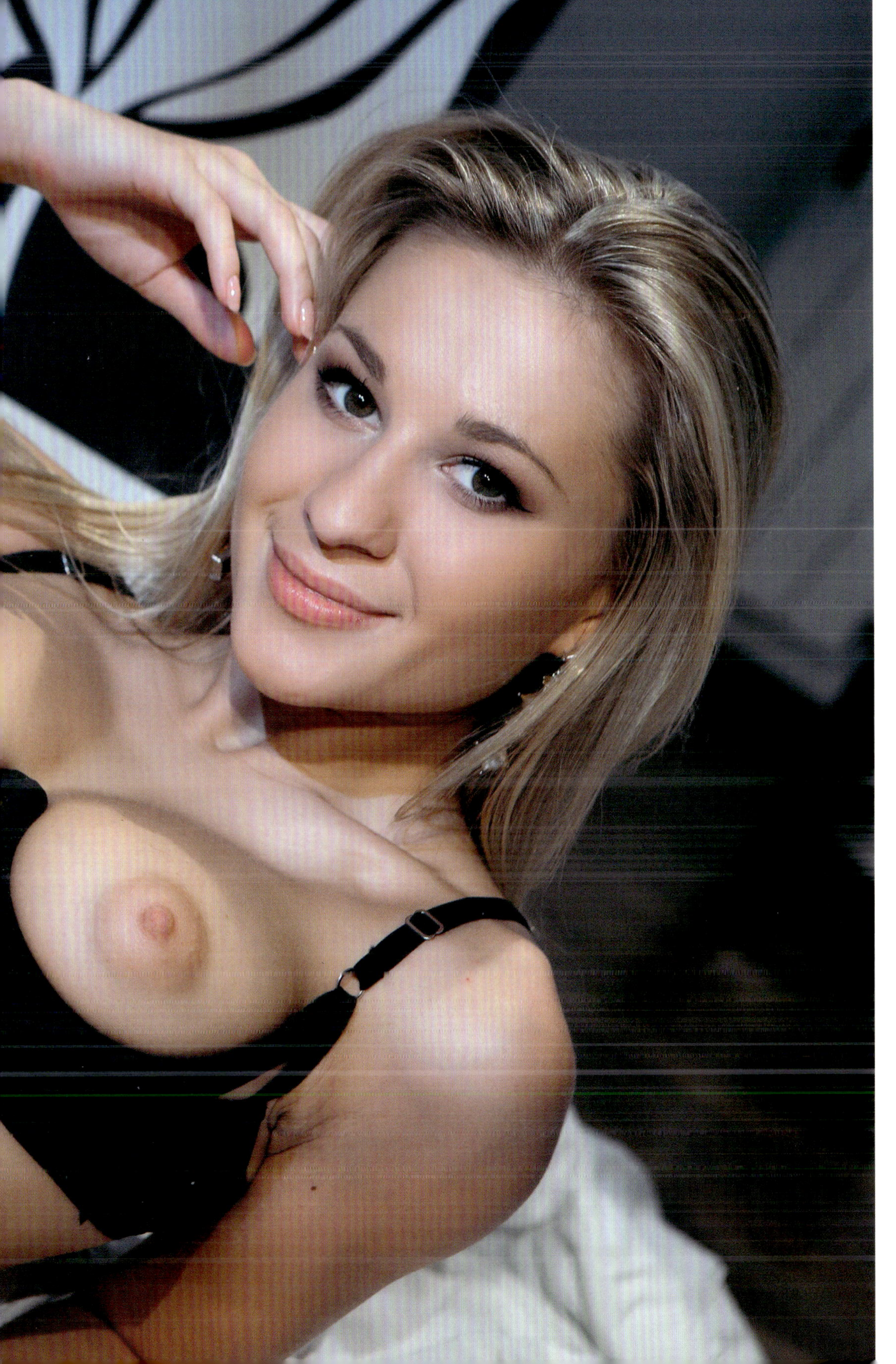

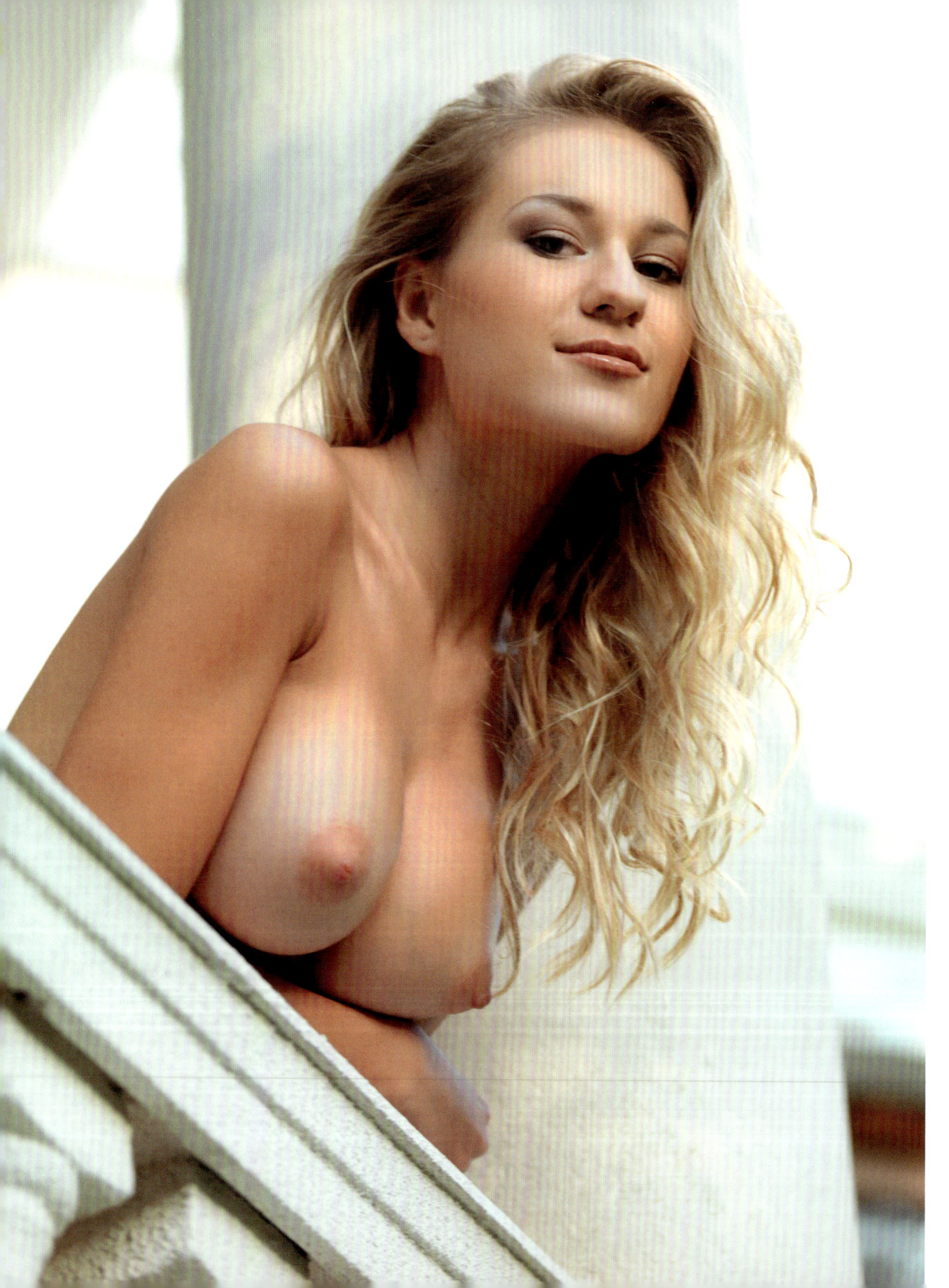

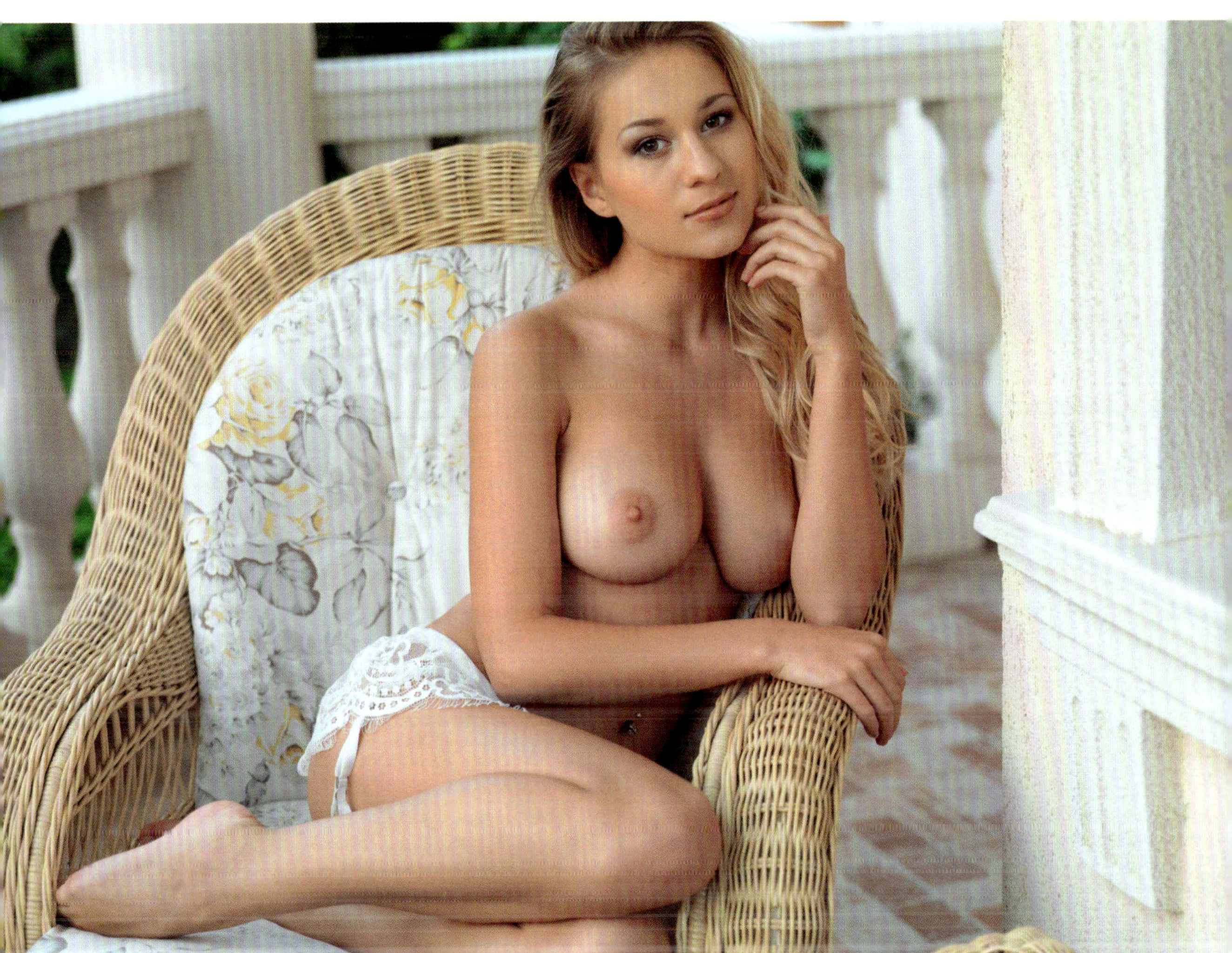

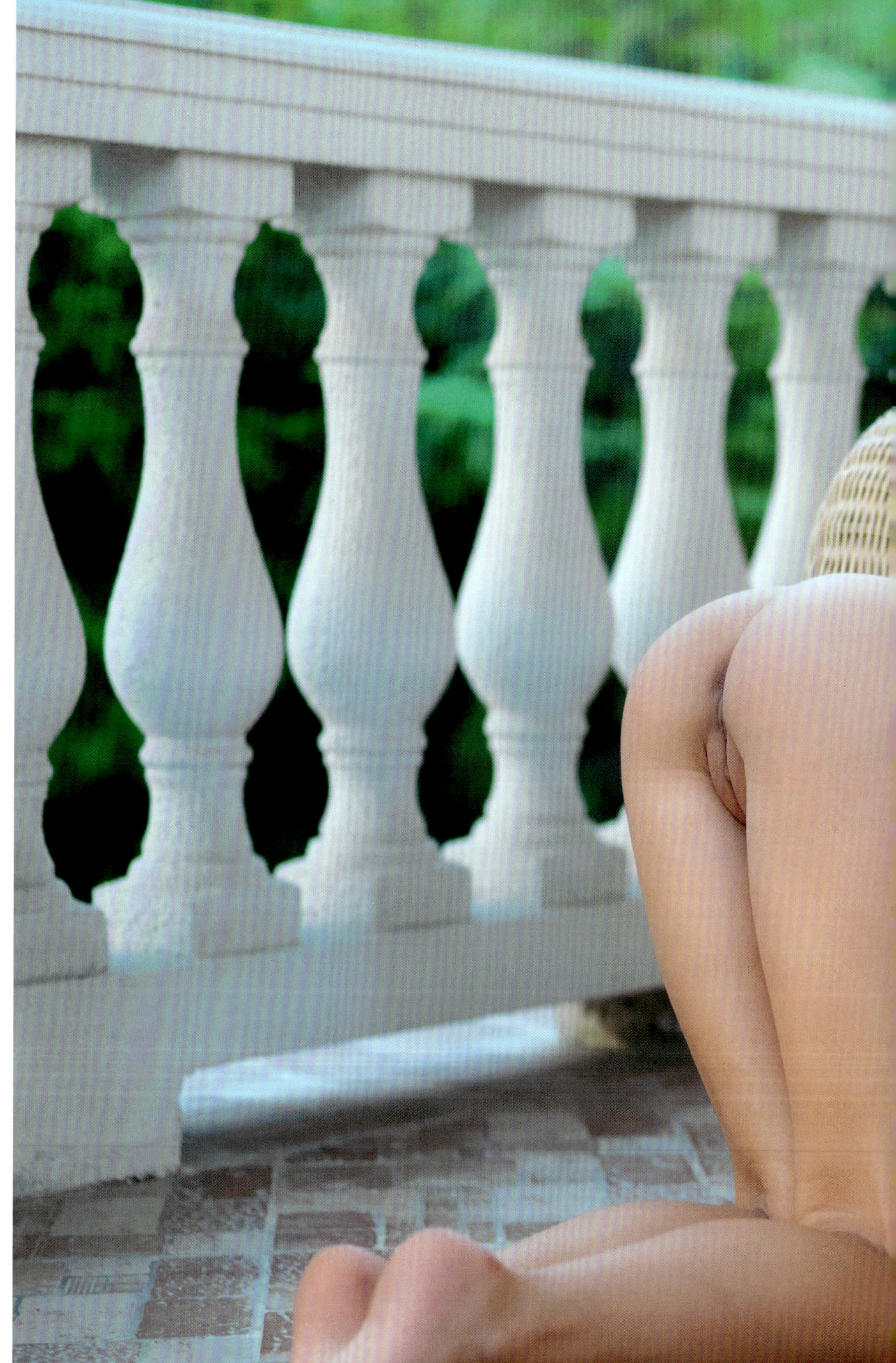

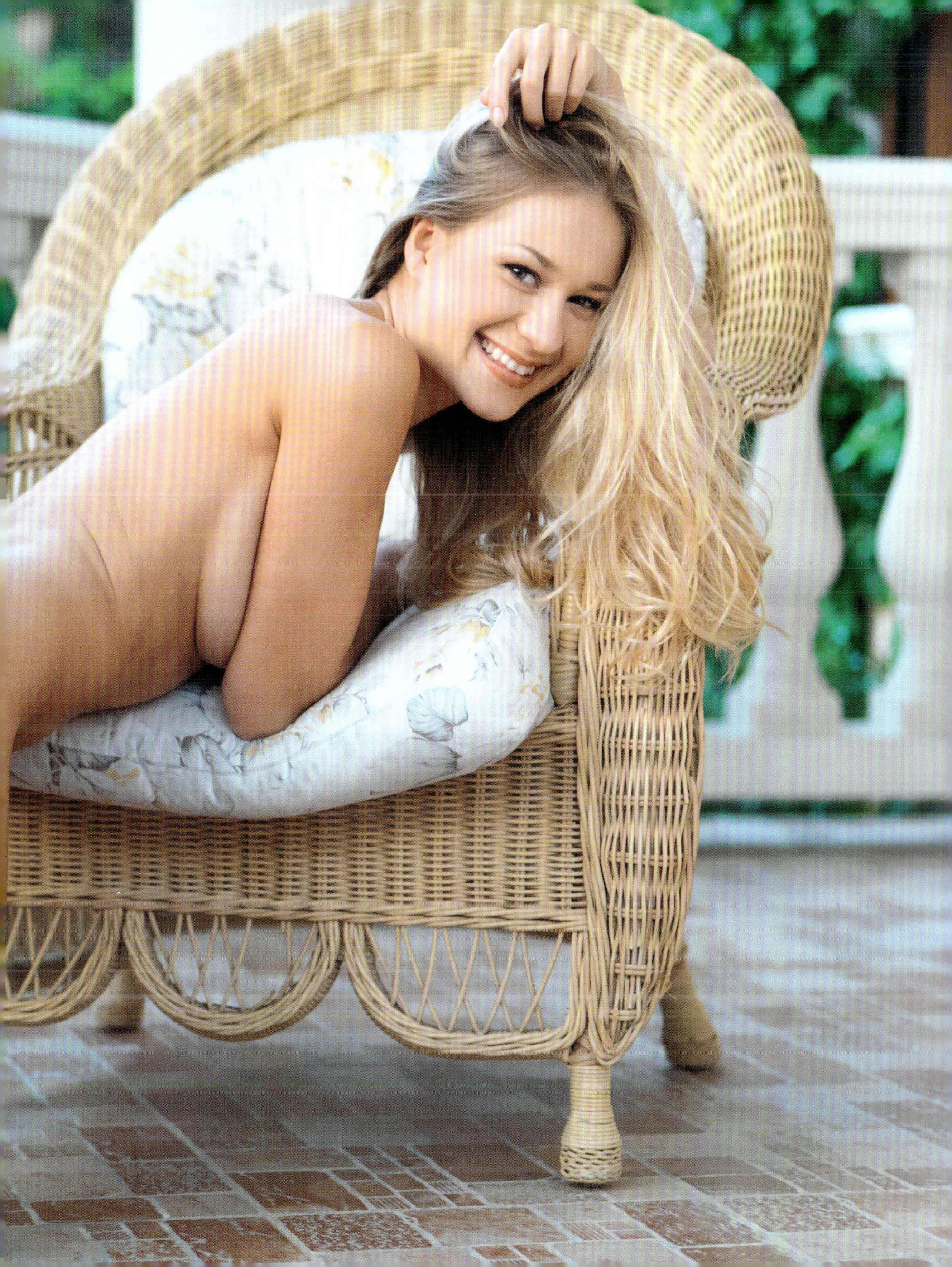

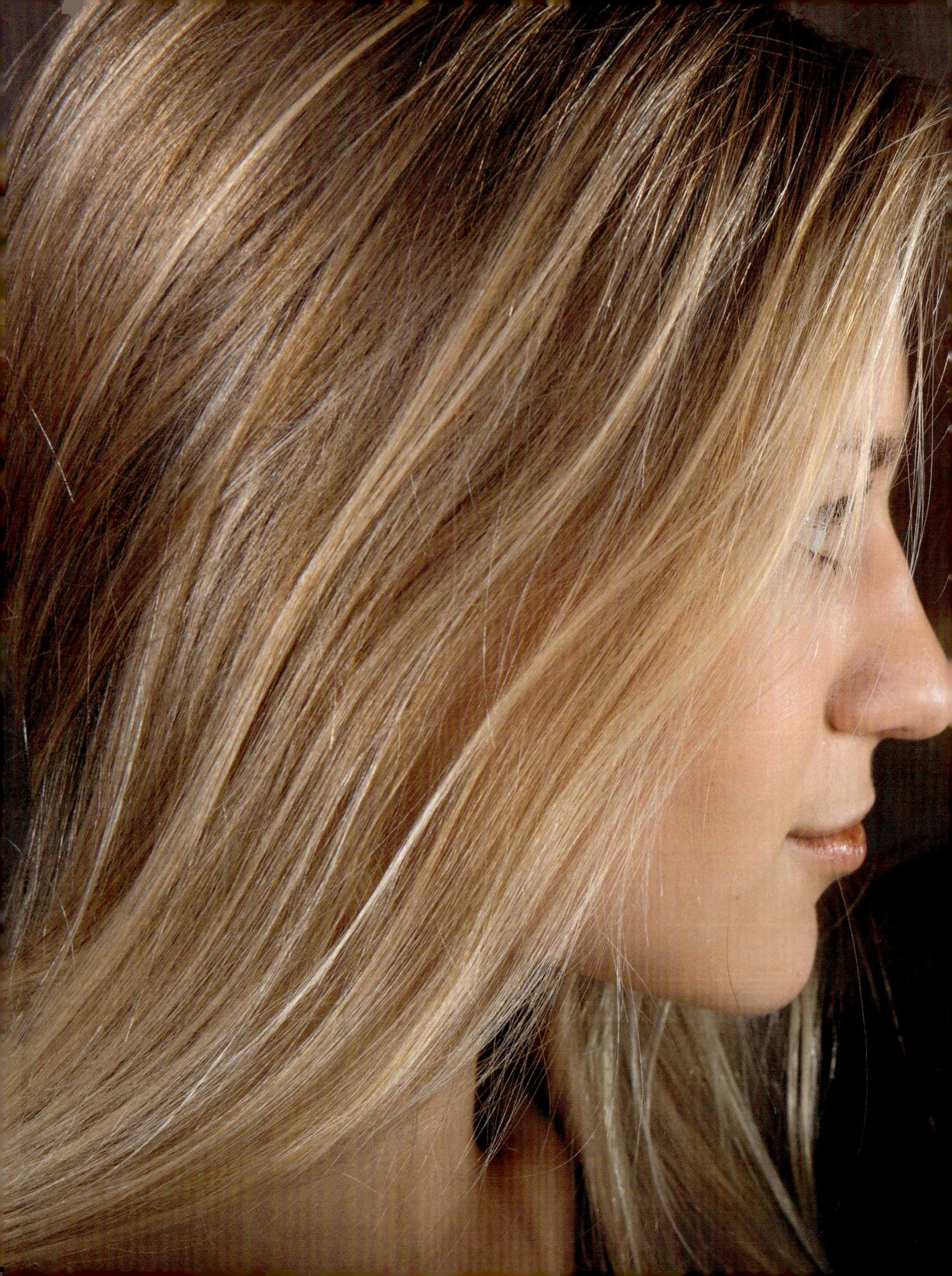

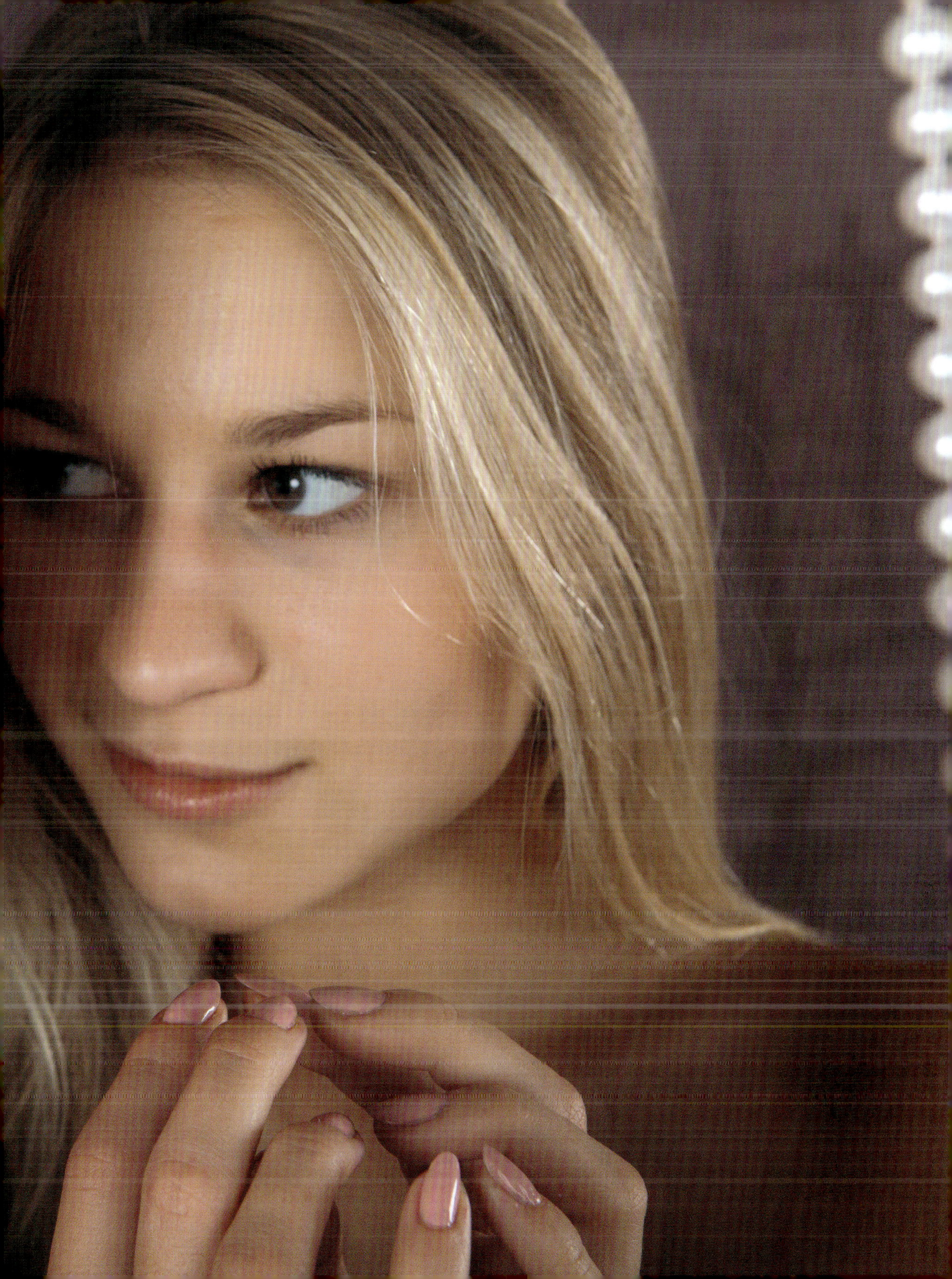

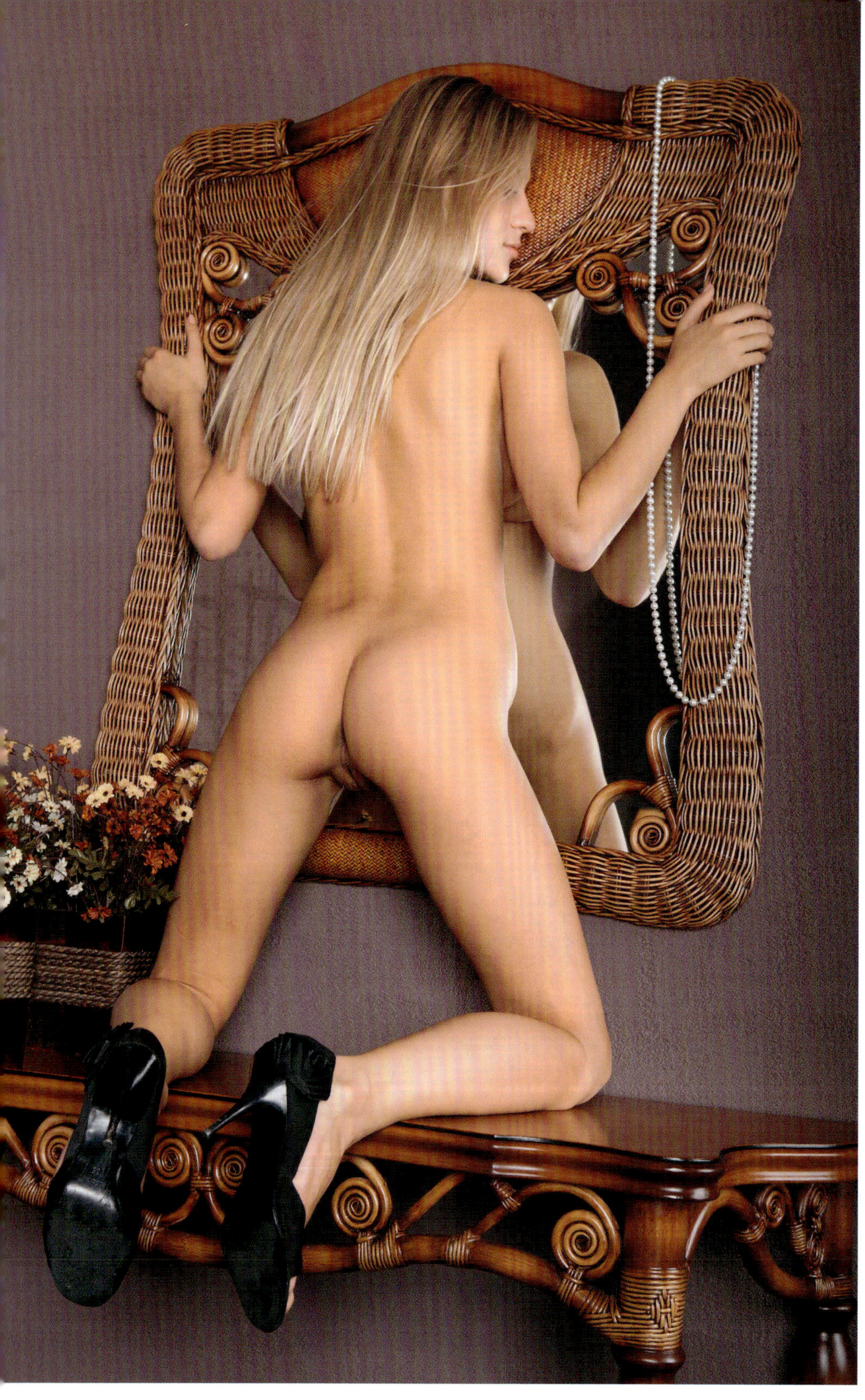

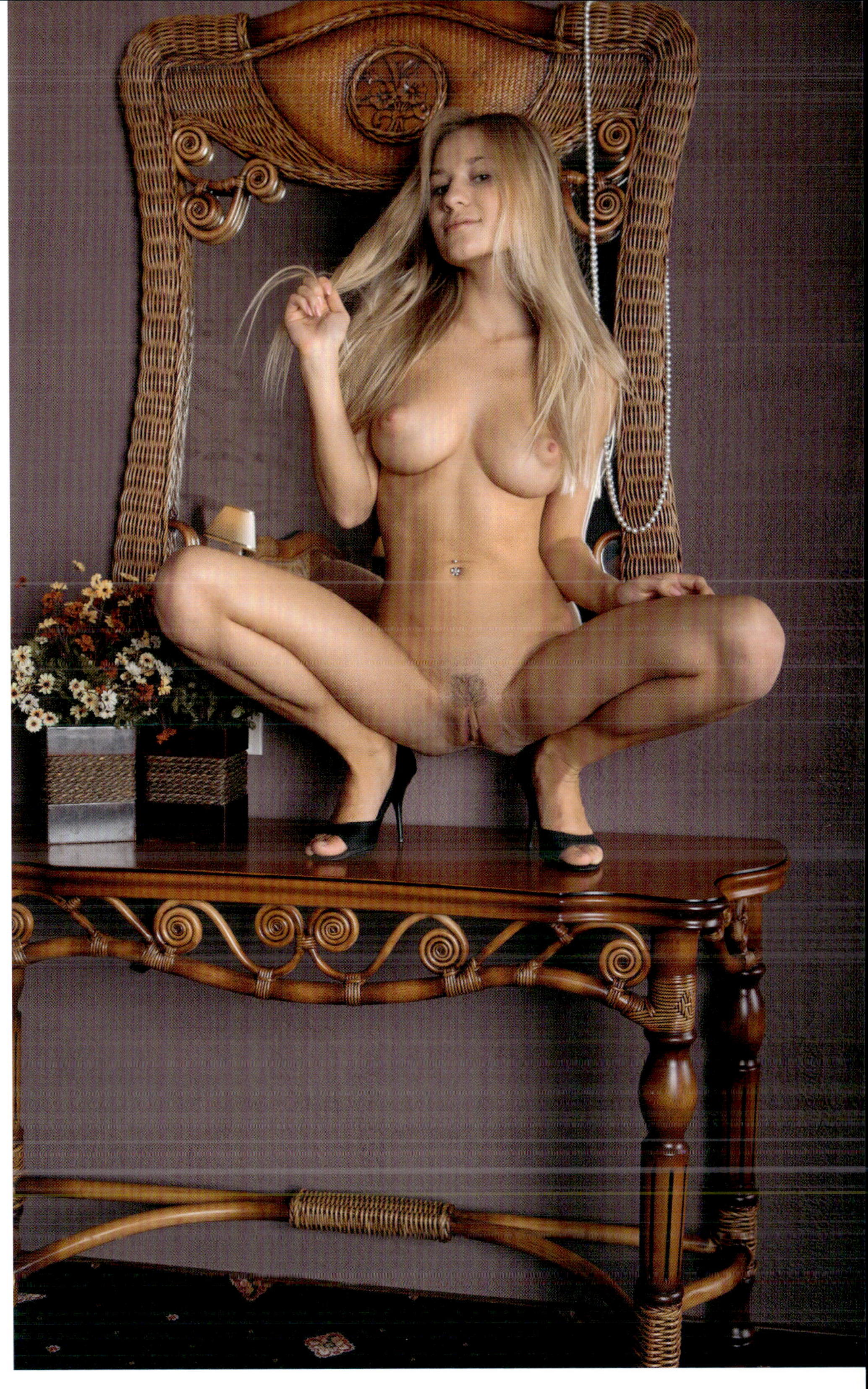

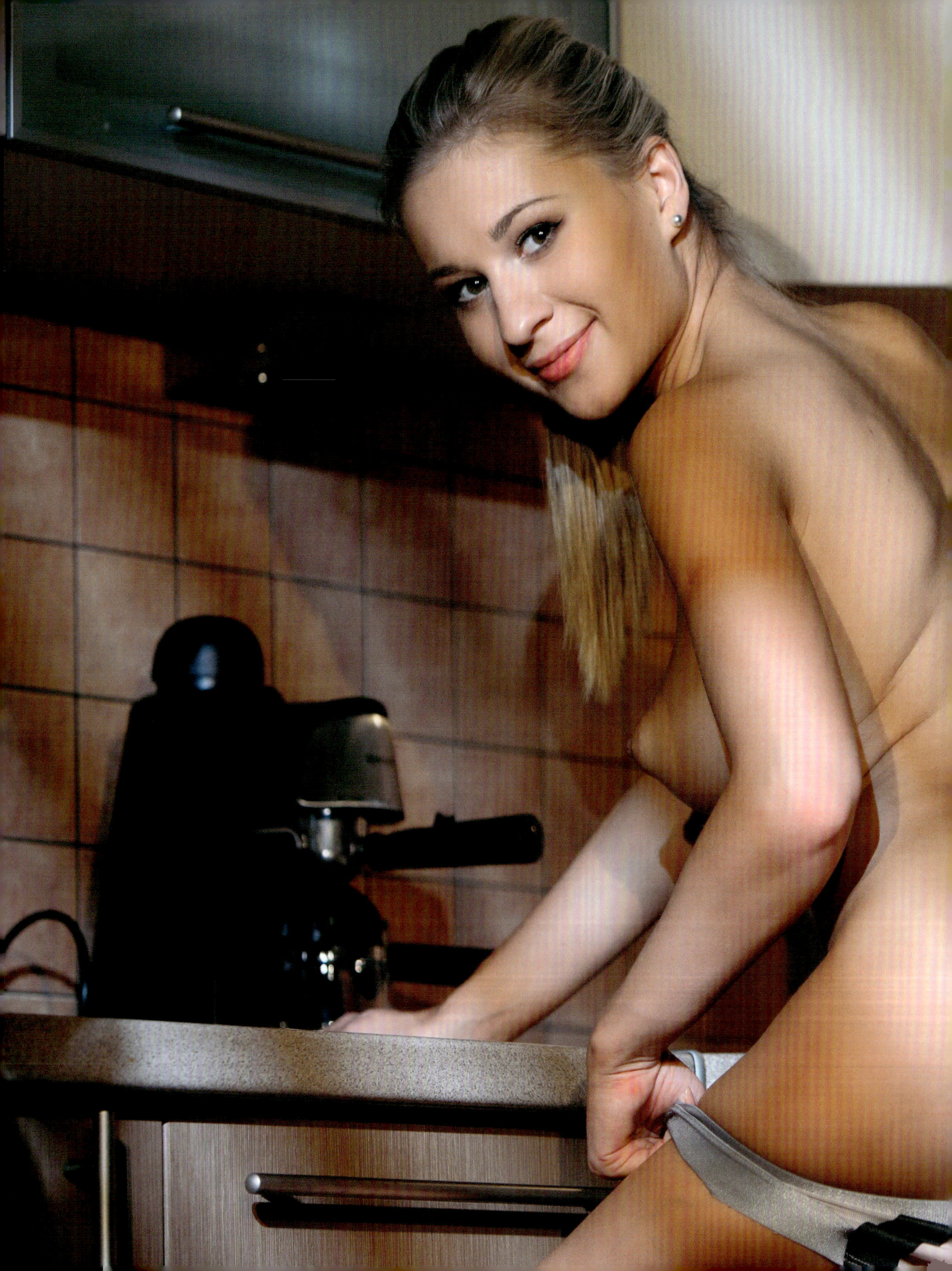

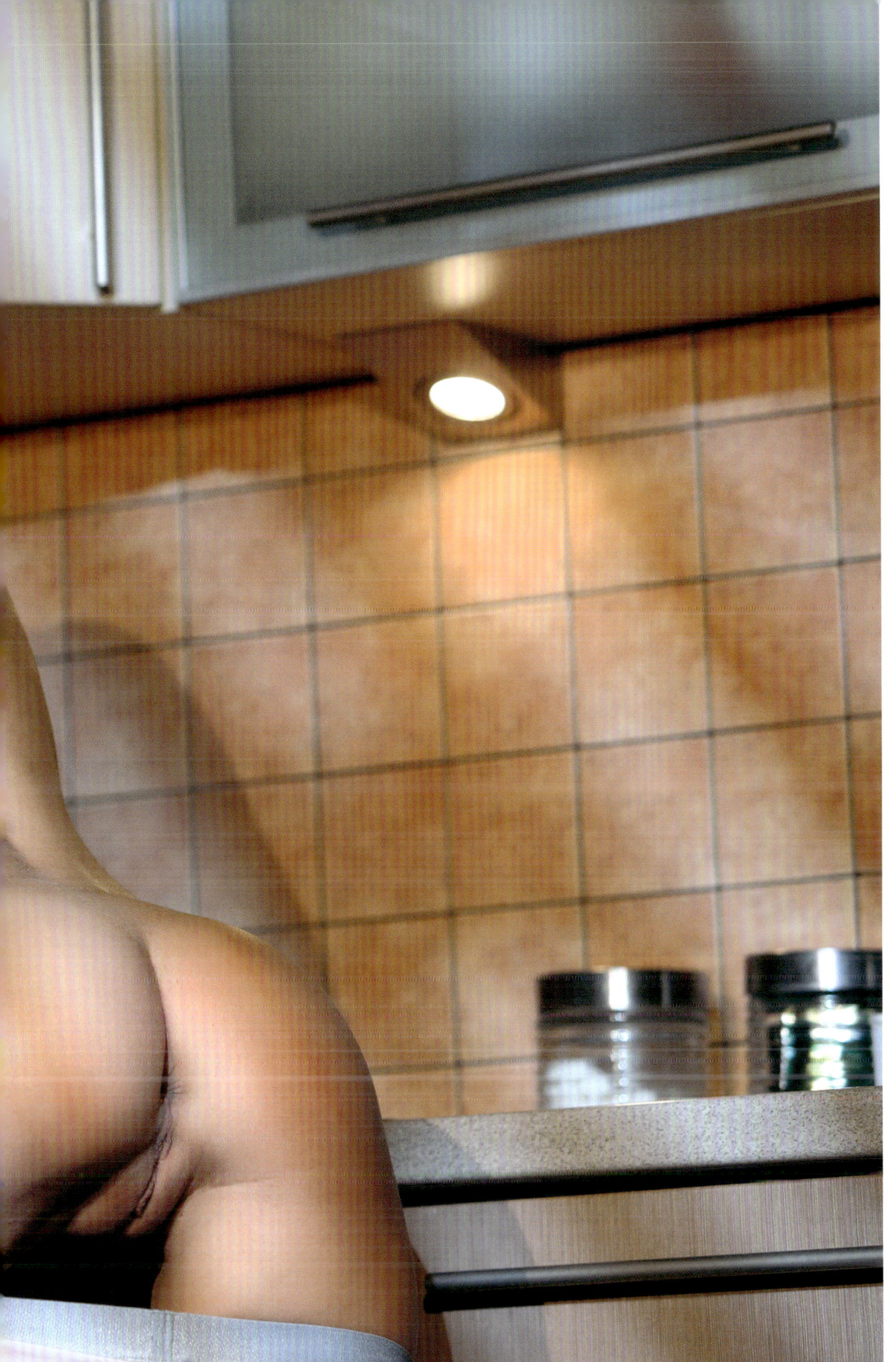

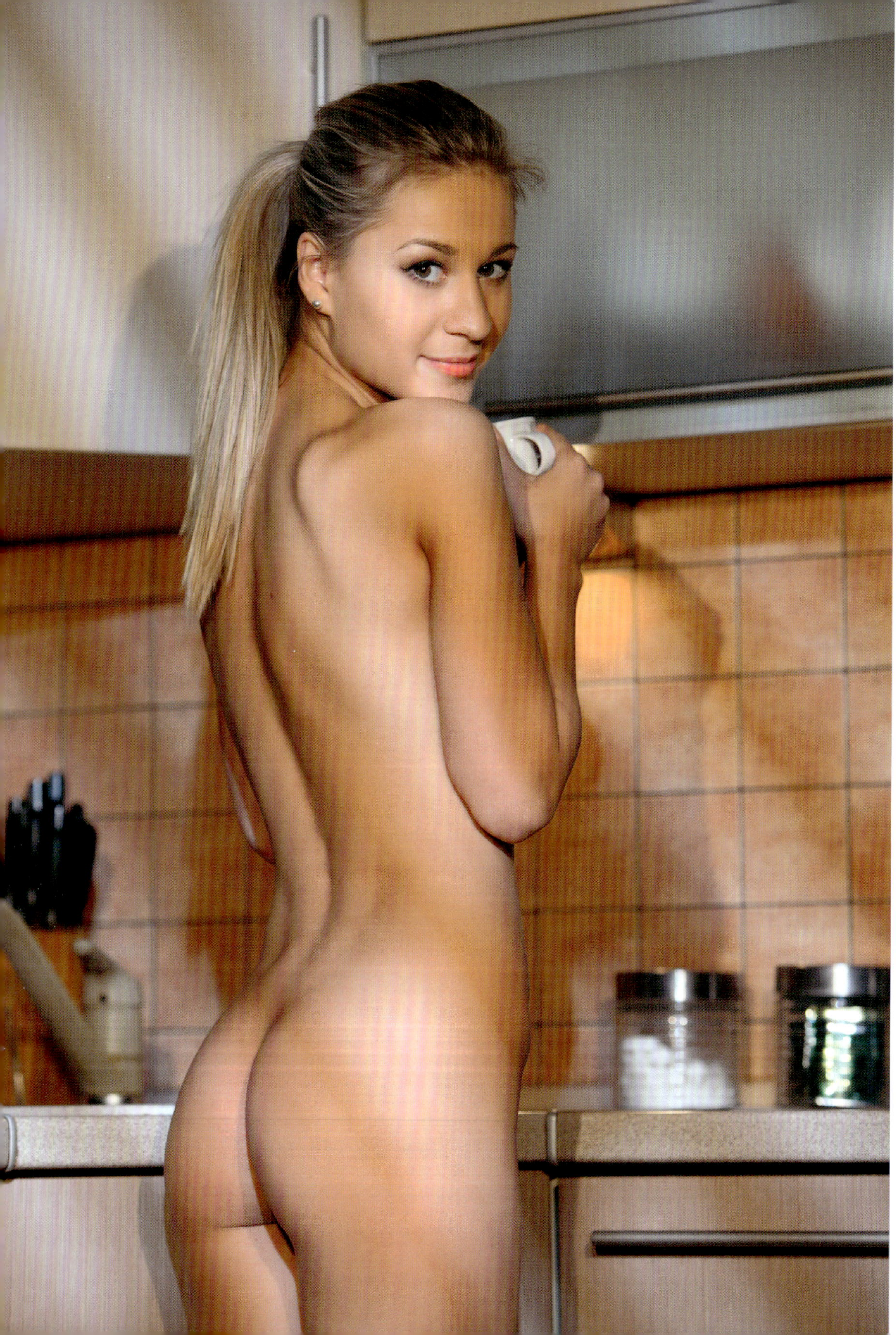

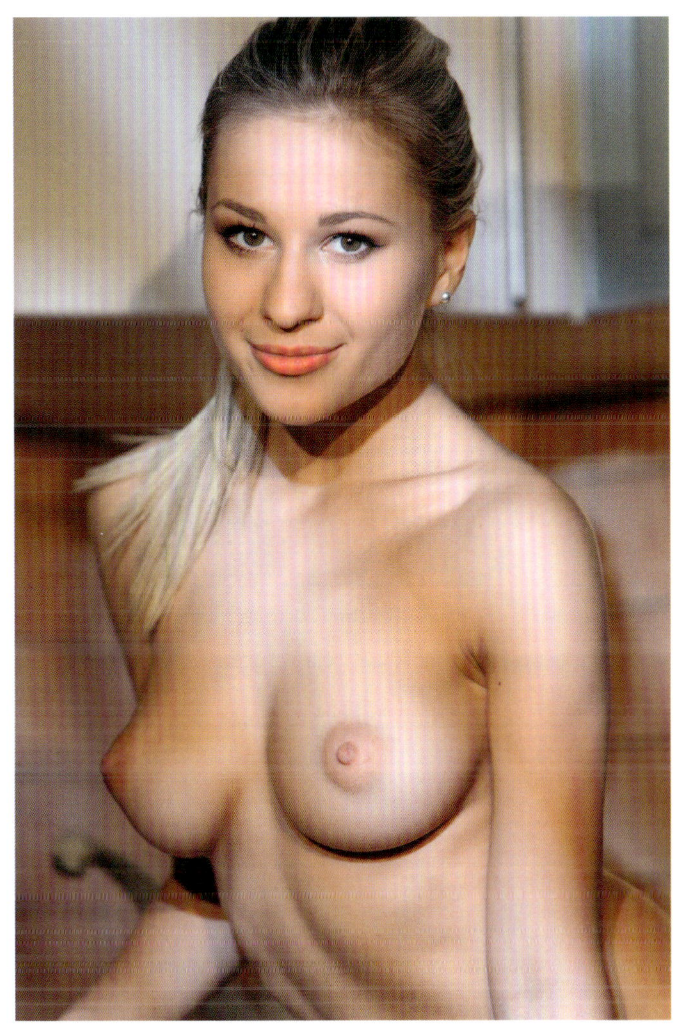

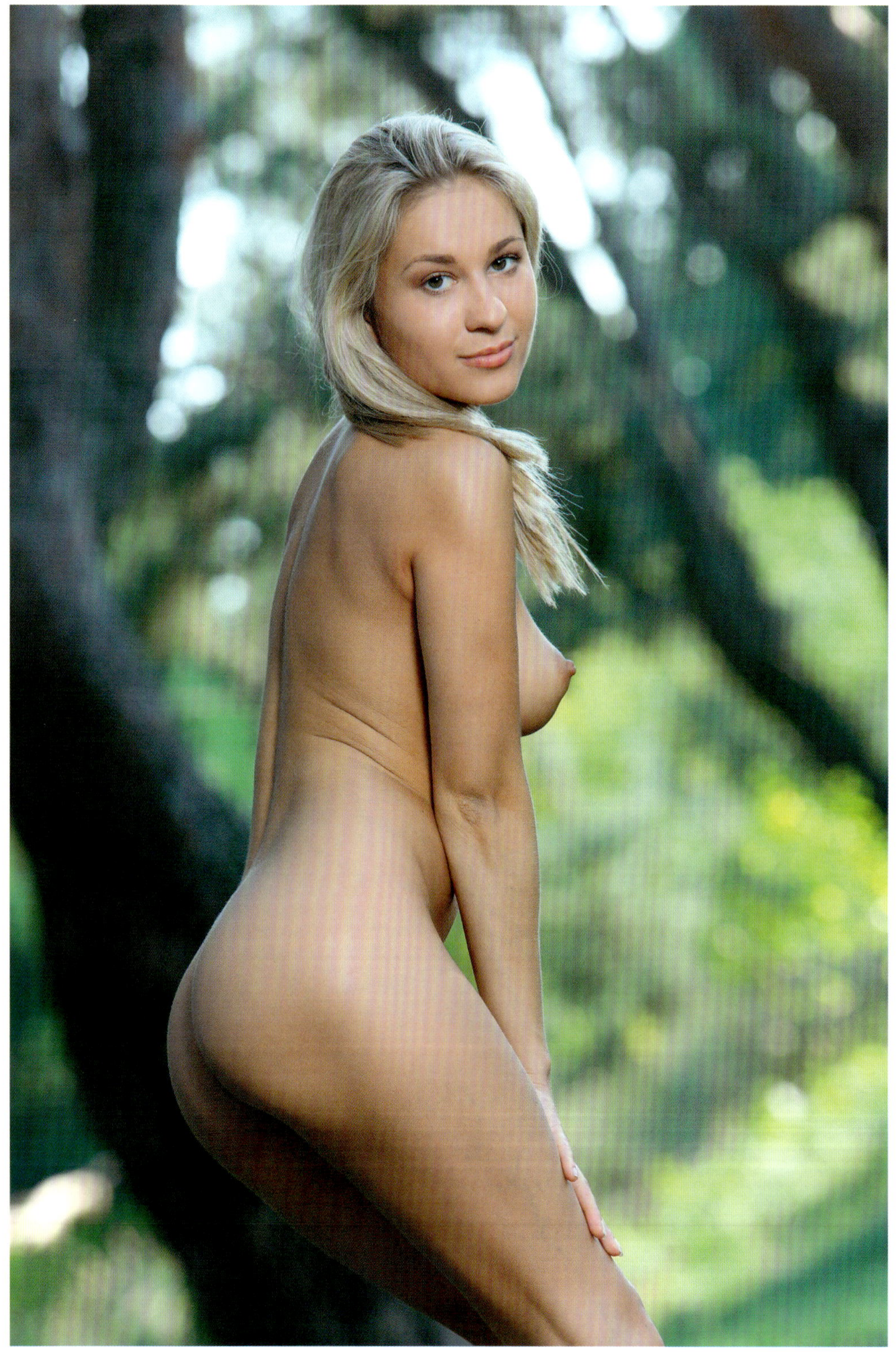

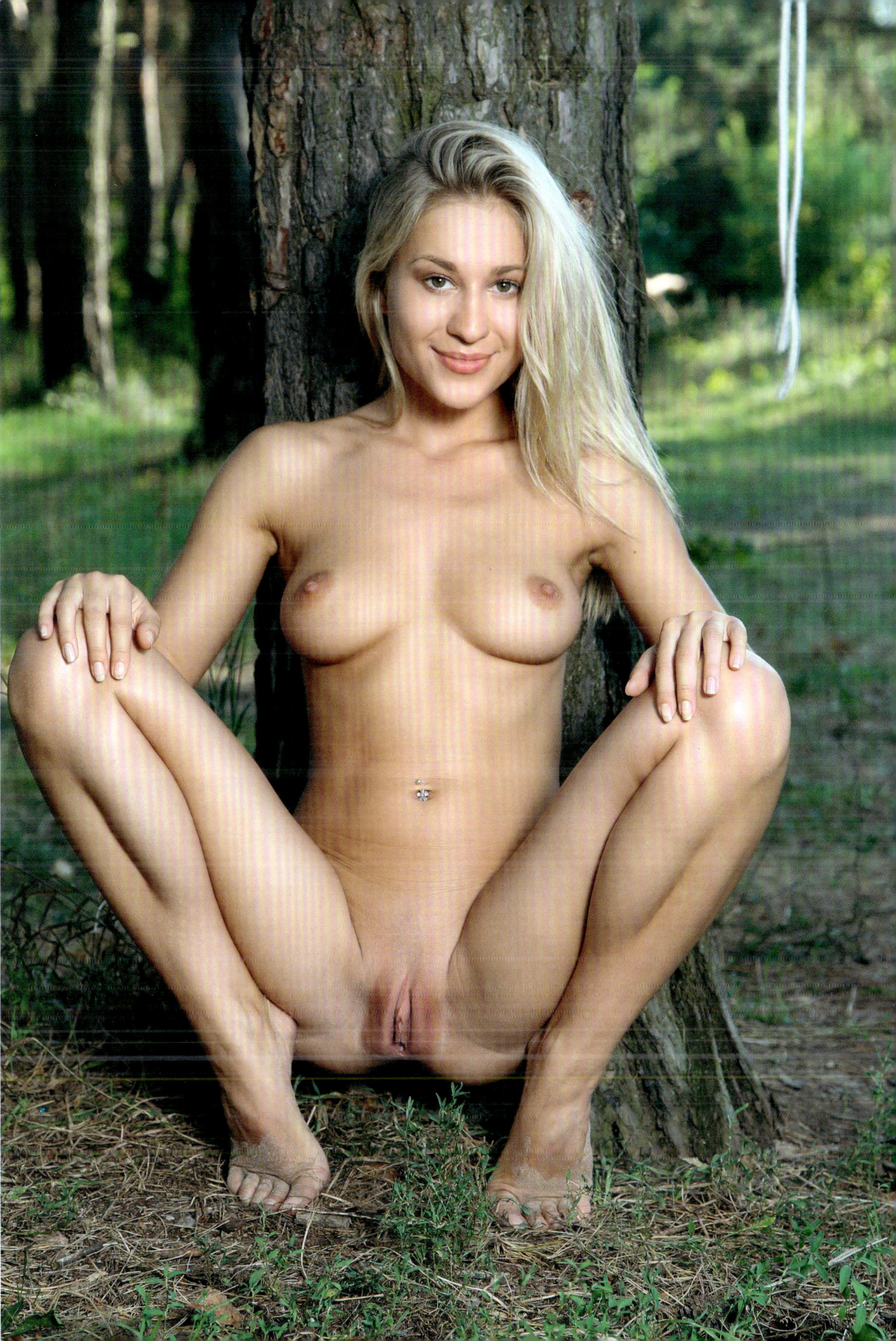

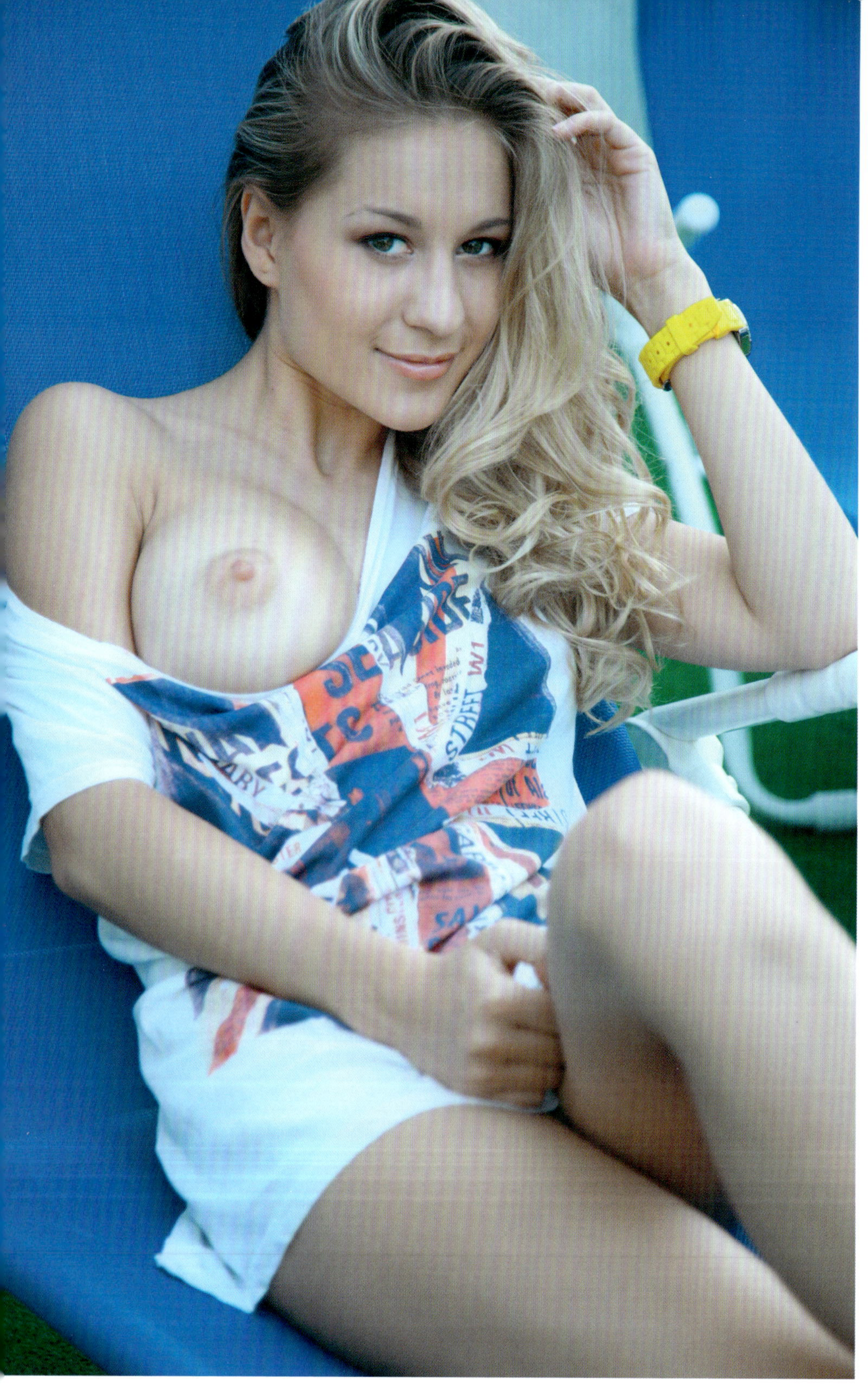
STREET W1

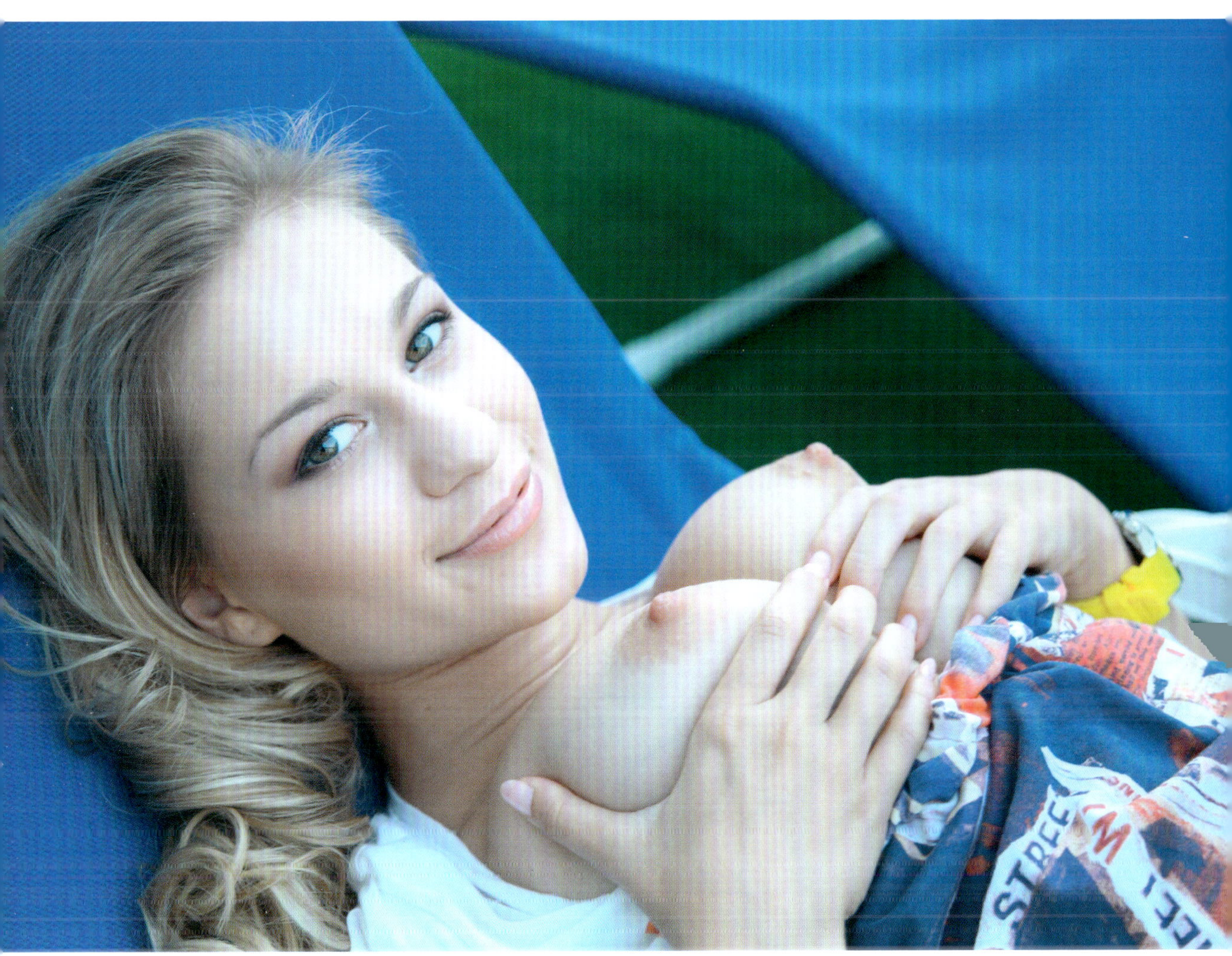

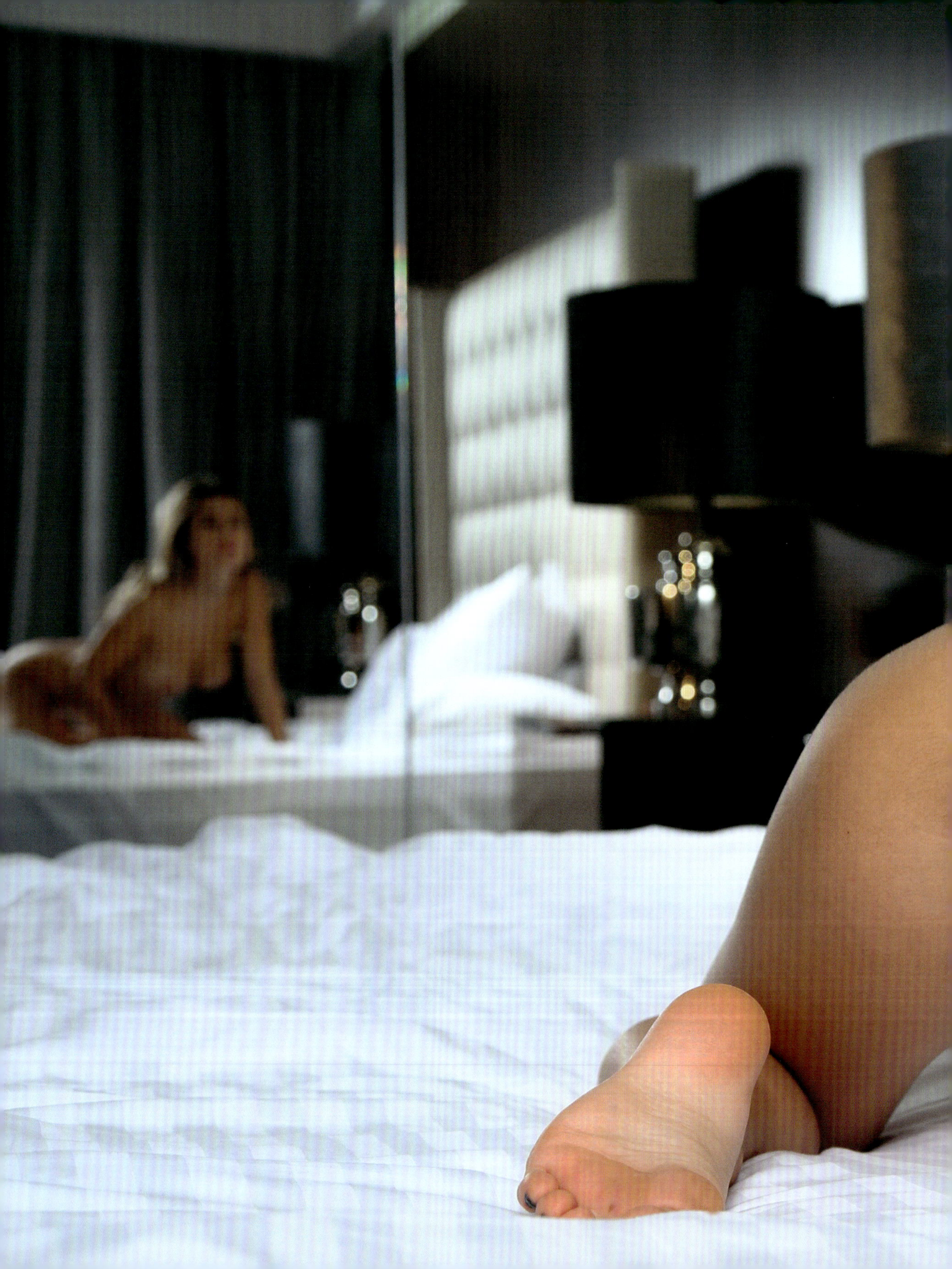

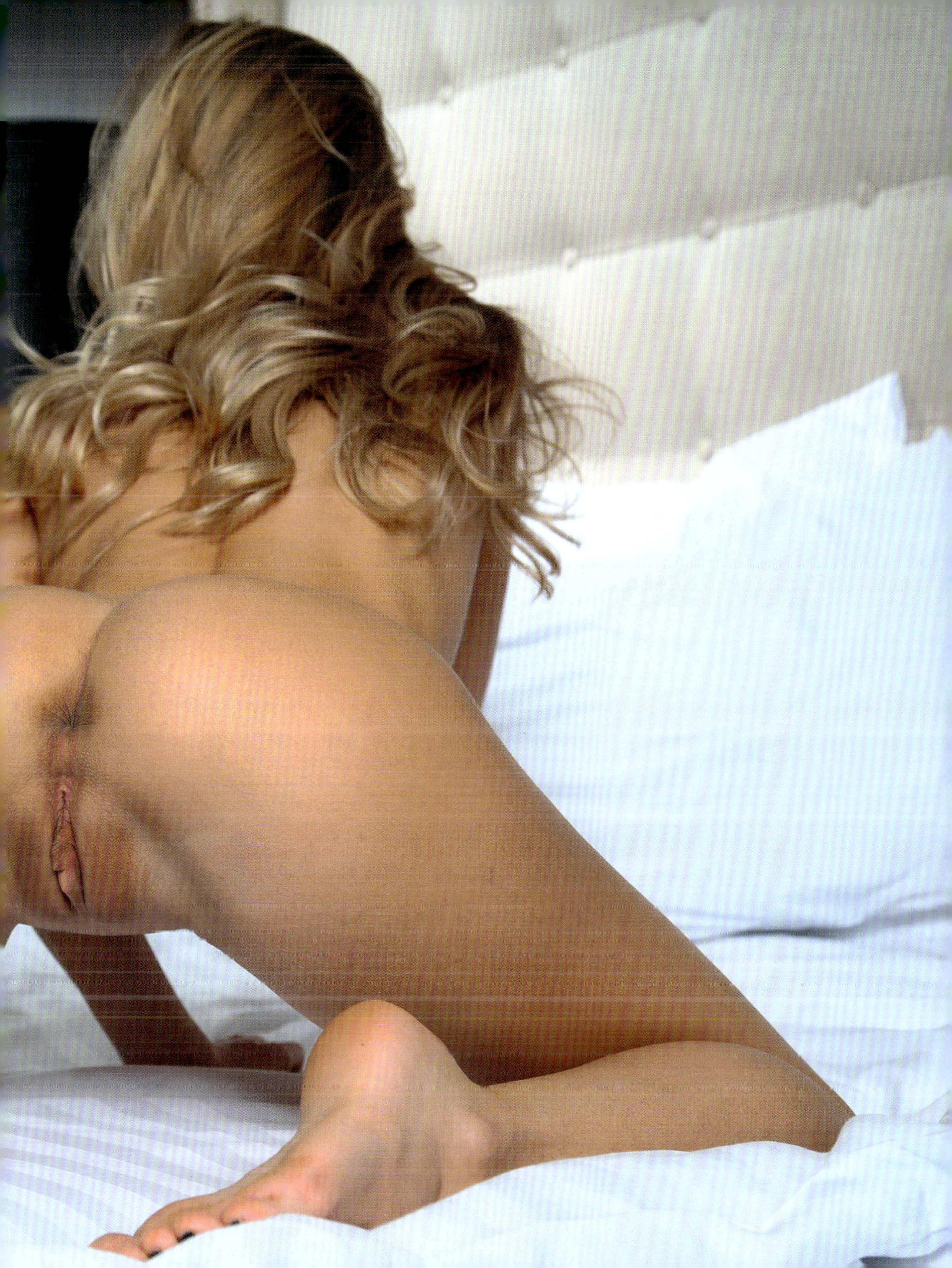

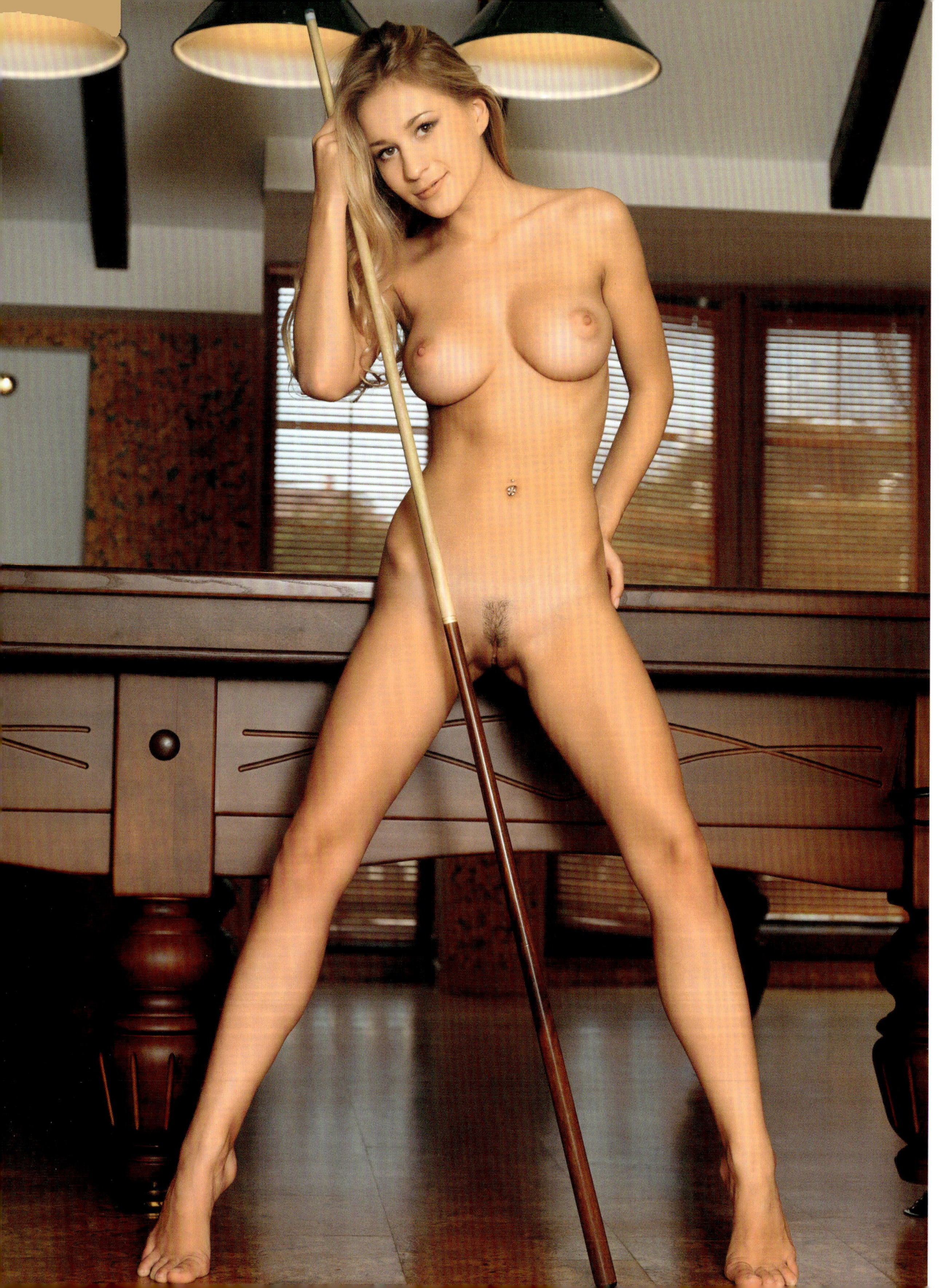

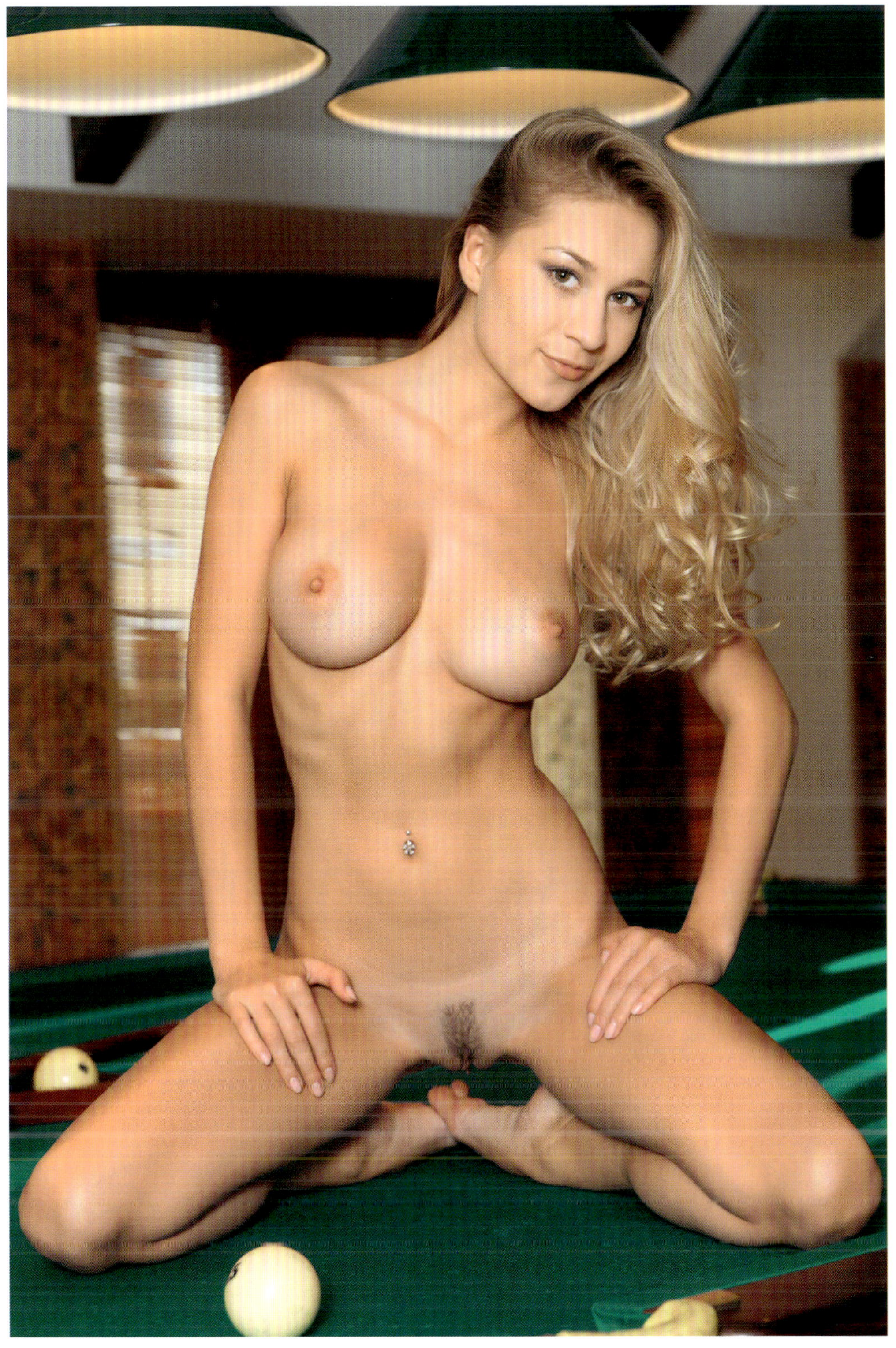

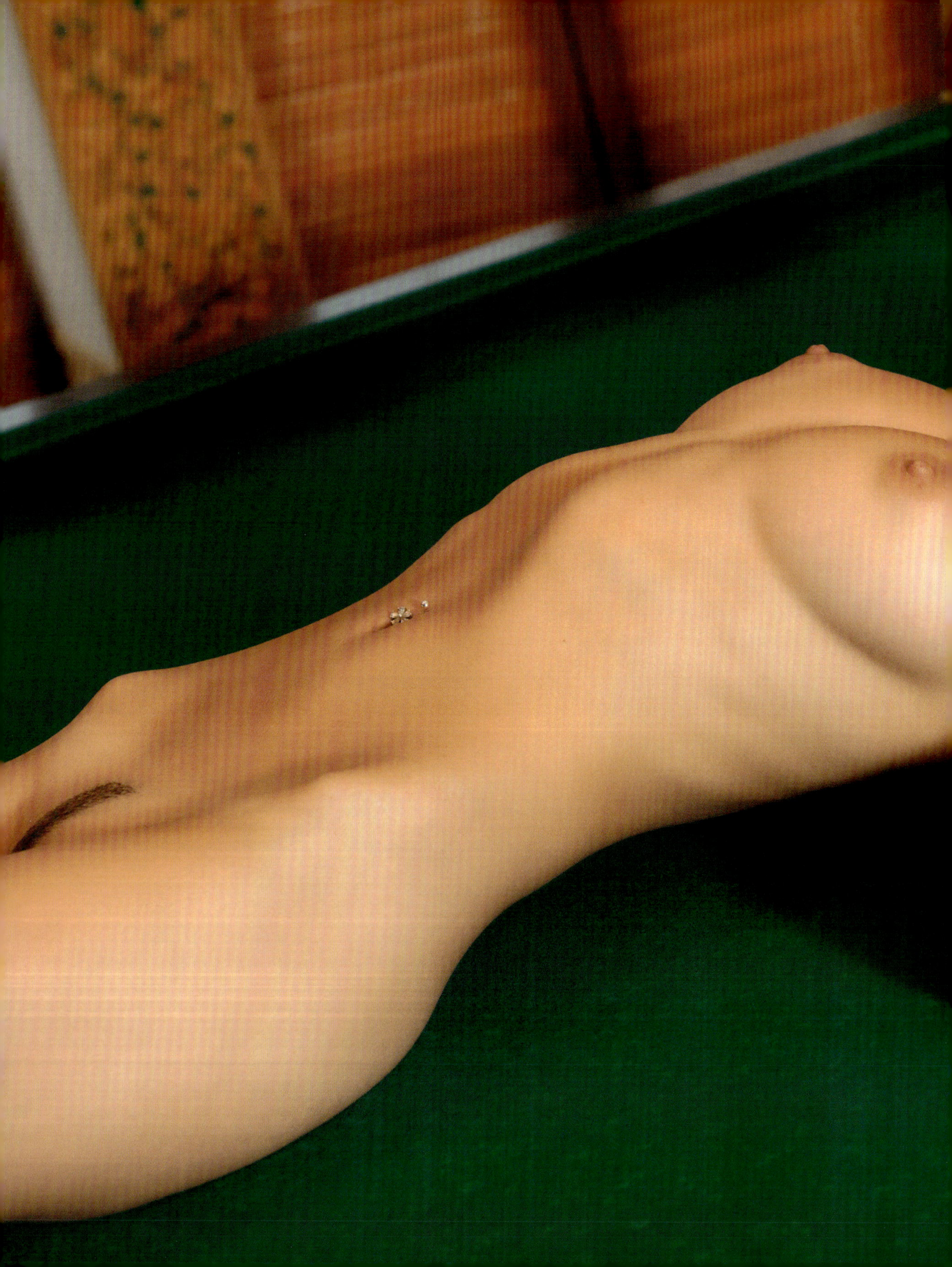

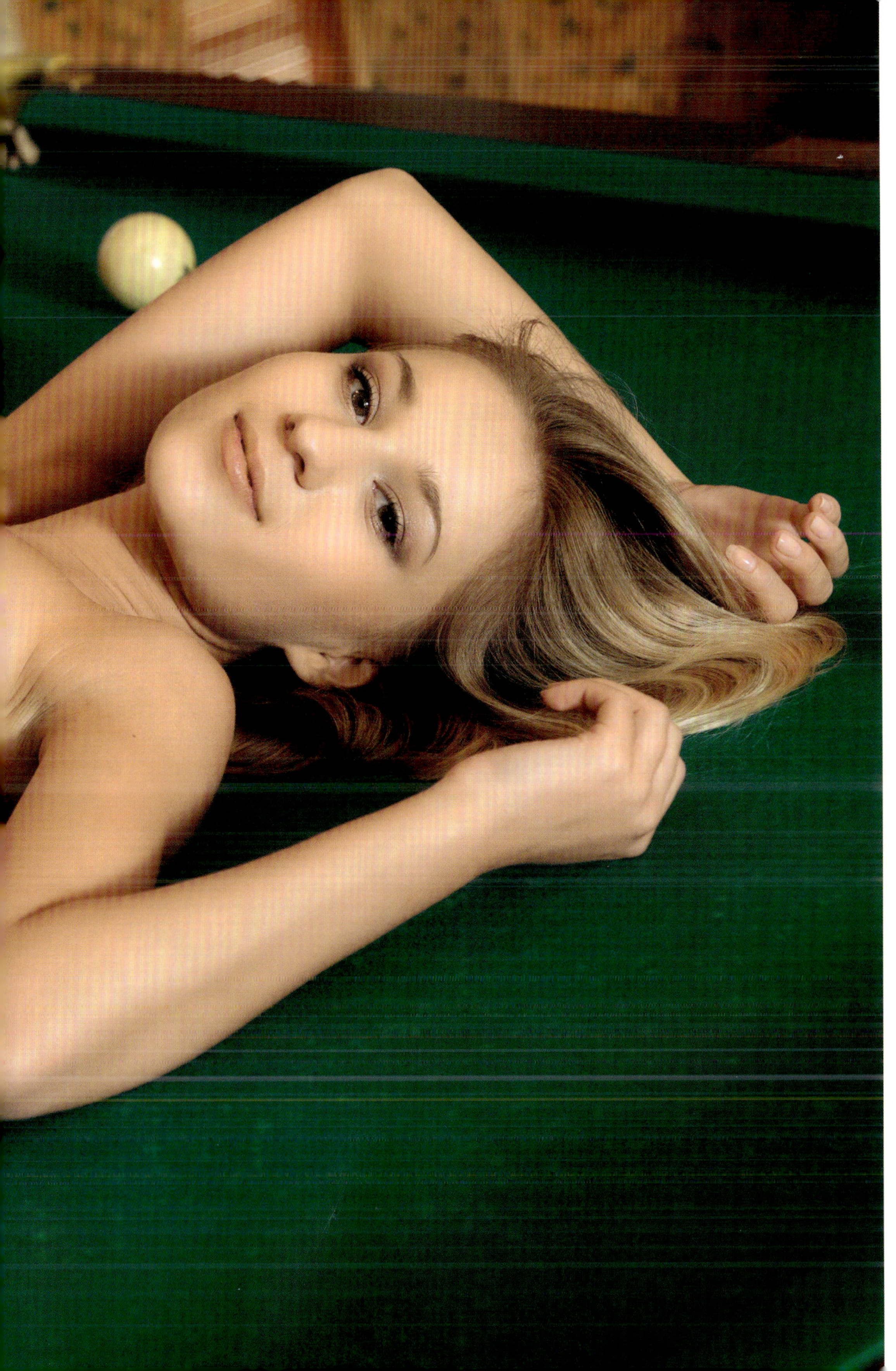

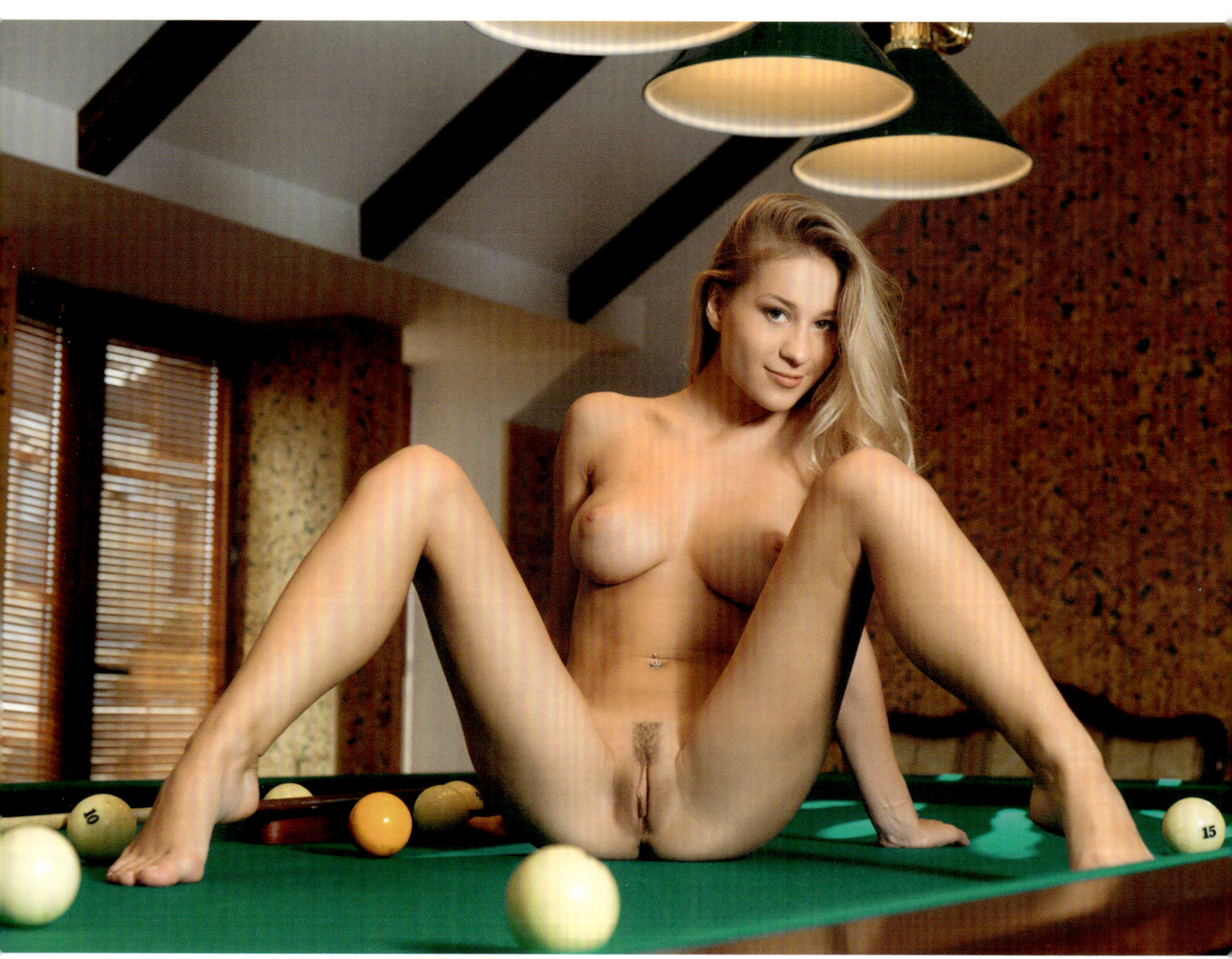
10
15

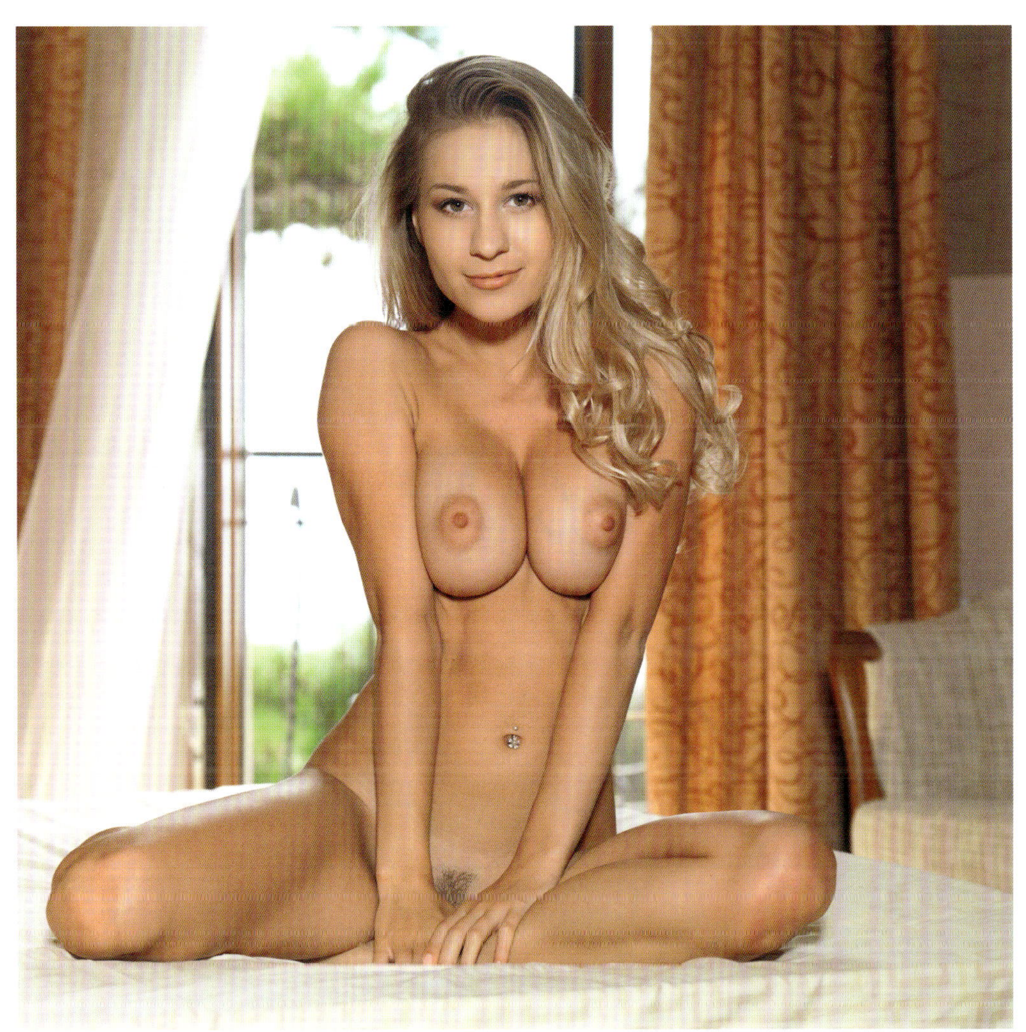

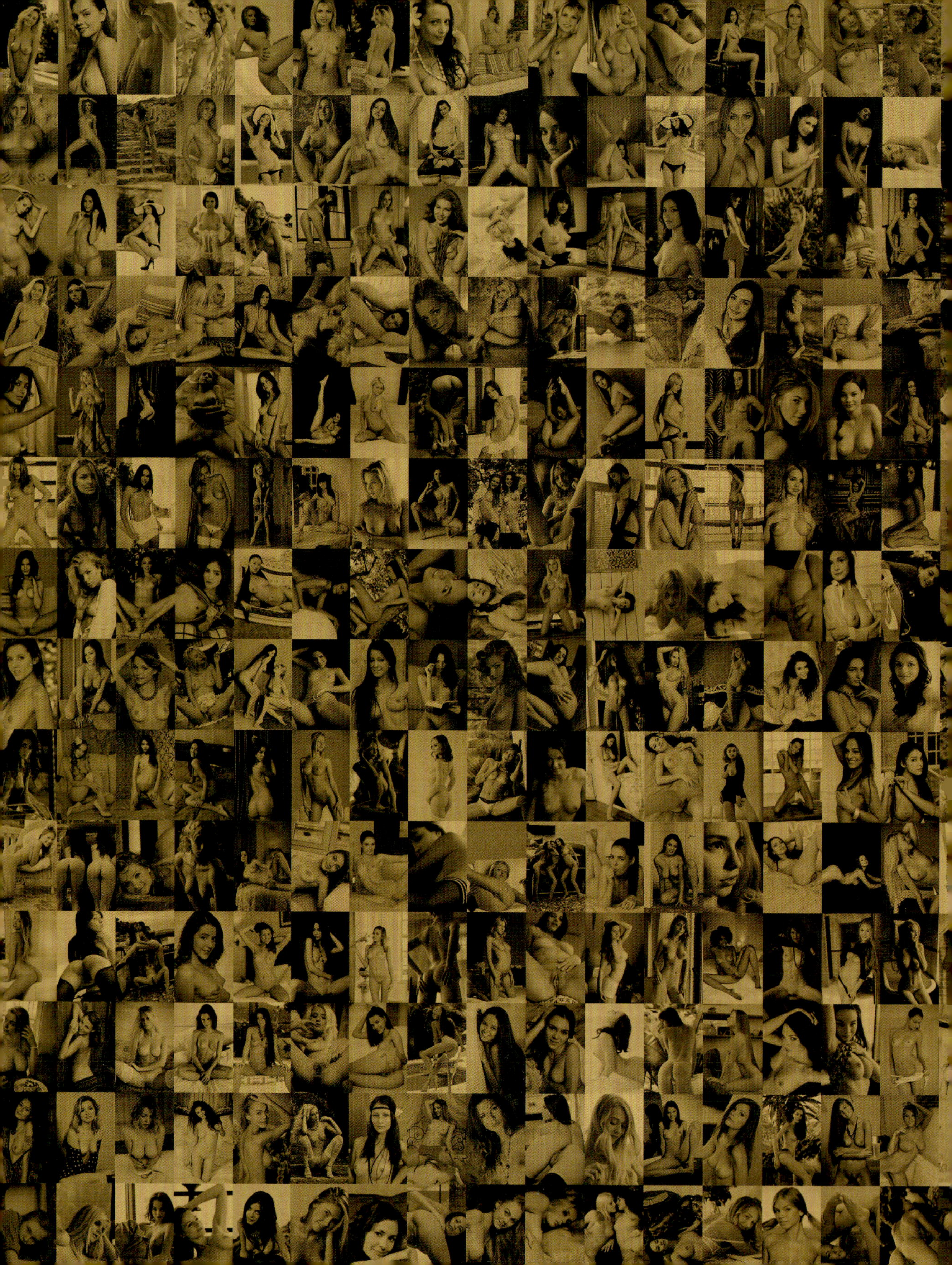